NON-PROFIT ORGANIZATIONS

Real Issues for Public Administrators

American Society for Public Administration
Series in Public Administration and Public Policy

NON-PROFIT ORGANIZATIONS

Real Issues for Public Administrators

Nicolas A. Valcik
Teodoro J. Benavides
Kimberly Scruton

Routledge
Taylor & Francis Group
New York London

First published 2015 by CRC Press

Published 2019 by Routledge
711 Third Avenue, New York, NY, 10017
2 Park Square, Milton Park, Abingdon, Oxon OX14 4RN

International Standard Book Number-13: 978-1-4665-7232-4 (Hardback)

Visit the Taylor & Francis Web site at
http://www.taylorandfrancis.com

Nicolas Valcik dedicates this book to James E. Valcik.

Teodoro Benavides dedicates this book to his grandfather Teodoro J. Benavides.

Kimberly Scruton dedicates this book to Dennis,
Kiden, and Kolby Scruton, with love.

Contents

SECTION II PUBLIC RELATIONS ISSUES

SECTION IV CRIMINAL OR UNETHICAL ACTS IN NON-PROFIT ORGANIZATIONS

Foreword

Nicolas Valcik, Teodoro Benavides and Kimberly Scruton's book, *Non-Profit Organizations: Real Issues for Public Administrators*, provides readers with an informative overview of how non-profit organizations should establish operating practices and policies to ensure public trust.

Historically, non-profit organizations have performed duties and services in support of various causes throughout the world. In our time, non-profit organizations have become a critical part of our society and are involved in various and diverse ways to improve people's lives. This book provides an excellent understanding of how non-profit organizations must also accept responsibility for managing their people and resources in a manner that serves the general public, donors, government officials, and recipients of services.

This book authored by Valcik, Benavides, and Scruton provides readers with a pragmatic and informative overview of how non-profit organizations can benefit from clarity of purpose and mission, transparency, and accountability. Those seeking to gain an understanding of how non-profit organizations should address internal controls and manage public relation issues will also benefit greatly from the thought-provoking questions and case studies of real events, which add to the intrigue and insightfulness of this work.

Even seasoned professionals who are involved in non-profit organizations as part of a management team, governance structure, or as a volunteer will benefit and learn from how other non-profits have managed difficult fiscal and public relations issues. However, it is a must read for anyone recently appointed to a leadership role with a non-profit organization, someone who is considering a career in this type of organization, or someone who is considering serving on a non-profit organization board.

The book also provides some practical training for individuals who serve as directors on boards of non-profit organizations. Readers who browse the pages can discover how a public relations crisis is quickly defined not by what you know but by what you don't know. Clearly, board of director members and the organization's leadership team will benefit from board members who ask that additional question during a crisis to discover and gain a better understanding of the problem.

The book's format lends itself to leisurely browsing of case studies that involve scandal, misuse of funds and questionable expenses, poor judgment, and nepotism, all which could result in significant negative publicity for a non-profit if not appropriately managed by the leadership team and the governing board.

Non-profit organizations rely primarily on donations, government, foundations, and commercial activities. As such, the authors provide excellent examples of where a board's fiduciary duties were not executed in a manner that created transparency in the organization, for both donors and the general public. These examples provide an exceptional training tool for organizations to enhance performance and create a culture of continuous improvement.

This book explores the important and various roles that governing boards should perform to ensure that non-profit organizations don't find themselves in difficult political situations with donors, the general public, and other constituents. Foremost, the authors stress the importance of appointing board members who have skills and expertise that will serve the organization's mission, policy development, and managerial decision making.

Over the past years, I have served in various administrative positions at West Virginia University, with my latest assignment being that of vice president for administration and finance. During my tenure, I have faced many challenges that might have been prevented or at least easier to respond to if I had the benefit of reading this book.

Narvel G. Weese, Jr.
Vice President for Administration and Finance
West Virginia University

Preface

Non-profit organizations rely heavily on the personnel who are employed, elected, or volunteer to work for the organization. The National Center for Charitable Statistics (NCCS) reported 25.4 percent of Americans over the age of 16 had volunteered for a non-profit organization between 2009 and 2013 (NCCS, 2013). However, many people who join or work for non-profit organizations lack a very basic understanding of how such organizations operate. In many cases, a non-profit organization is a small group operated entirely by elected board members who have little or no previous experience with non-profit organizations.

Graduates from undergraduate programs in public administration or business more often than not have no formal training in non-profit organizations. Usually such training for managing non-profit organizations is offered only at the graduate level, and even then is offered only as electives or as part of a "certificate" or track in the overall program. In 2012, only 30 percent of the US population had a bachelor's degree and only 10.9 percent held any type of graduate degree (Perez-Pena, 2012). The number of graduates in the United States who hold a master's degree in public administration (or related field) or a master's degree in business who have any training in managing a non-profit organization is extremely low, given the number of non-profit organizations that exist and are in need of professional management over their revenues, expenditures, and assets.

In the United States alone, there were 1,409,430 tax-exempt organizations registered in 2013 with the Internal Revenue Service (IRS). These public charities had combined revenues of more than $1.59 trillion (2011), $1.49 trillion (2011) in total expenditures, and $2.87 trillion in assets (2011) (NCCS, 2013). The amounts of revenue, expenditures, and assets are even larger for non-profit organizations overall when considering the NCCS number is only for public charities and only for those non-profit organizations that generate enough revenue to file taxes with the IRS. The magnitude of revenues, expenditures, and assets moving through non-profit organizations' financial structures is alarming when considering the lack of trained personnel available to manage these types of financial streams. Without properly trained personnel to manage financial assets and personnel effectively, the financial liabilities and risks to a non-profit are increased dramatically. Considering most non-profit organizations are small in size, this factor reduces the probability that the organization has a trained person with the requisite experience or skills to successfully manage the non-profit's assets.

This book was developed primarily for non-profit organization graduate students and members of non-profit organizations, as well as practitioners who may not have previous real-world experience working in the non-profit environment. The case studies were selected from a wide range of actual situations to provide readers with a perspective that enables them to consider their own decisions if faced with similar challenges. We selected case studies that ranged from unethical behavior to poor operational decisions to illegal activities. Many of the case studies address more than one issue that threatened the organization's finances and its credibility to their stakeholders and the public. This book will allow readers to review difficult and complex case studies in order to create a checklist of issues to be aware of when working in a non-profit environment. It is the authors' hope that this book will create a "safe" environment for administrators to "live" through the case study without suffering the consequences of lost resources or assets to their organization in reality.

Acknowledgments

I thank everyone who has helped me with this book. I also thank the three reviewers we had for this project, Melissa Watkins, Donielle Maust, and Ruth Riggs. Their feedback was invaluable to us. My coauthors Teodoro Benavides and Kimberly Scruton, did great work on this book. Both authors had different perspectives and insights, which proved to be indispensable when working on a book of such complexity detailing the challenges public administrators must face. I thank my supervisor Liz Reynolds at West Virginia University, as well as my coworkers and colleagues who provided support and encouragement while I was working on this project. The employees in my department who work diligently for West Virginia University while making everything look easy deserve a special thanks. I acknowledge Andrea Stigdon for providing the book with a great cover design and performing the tedious duty of proofing and editing the raw manuscript before the book was submitted to the publisher. Most of all, I thank my friends, family, and wife, Kristi, for their love and support of all of my endeavors.

Nicolas A. Valcik

I thank my mother Maria M. Benavides, and my father Manuel T. Benavides, who encouraged me to attend college and to become the first one in our family to earn a college degree. My mentor, Dr. N. Joseph Cayer, who inspired me to seek a career in public service is owed a debt of gratitude as well. Most of all I thank my wife, Aretha, who is always on my side and has been the inspiration to continue my new career and passion, which is teaching.

Teodoro J. Benavides

I am very grateful for the opportunity to benefit from the expertise and knowledge of my coauthors, Nicolas Valcik and Teodoro Benavides. Their distinct perspectives resulted in this outstanding work. Nicolas's leadership and support were instrumental in our successful collaboration and completion of this project. I extend my sincere appreciation to the project's reviewers, Melissa Watkins, Donielle Maust, and Ruth Riggs. Their evaluation and comments assisted in shaping this work. I acknowledge and thank Andrea Stigdon for her contributions to the editing and artwork of this book. I am filled with gratitude to the administration, faculty, and staff of Methodist University, and specifically my colleagues and students in the Reeves School of Business, whose passion for education and desire for excellence direct my efforts. Most importantly, I thank my husband Denny, my sons, Kiden and Kolby, and my family, who provide me with their constant support, love, and encouragement that inspire me each day.

Kimberly E. Scruton

About the Authors

Nicolas A. Valcik

Nicolas A. Valcik currently works as the director for institutional research and as a research associate professor in the Eberly School of Arts and Science — Public Administration Department at West Virginia University. Nicolas was formerly an associate director of strategic planning and analysis for the University of Texas at Dallas and served as a clinical assistant professor for public affairs for the University of Texas at Dallas. Nicolas earned a doctorate in public affairs, a master's degree in public affairs in 1996, a bachelor's degree in interdisciplinary studies in 1994, all from the University of Texas at Dallas, and an associate's degree in political science from Collin County Community College in 1994.

Prior to 1997, Nicolas worked for a number of municipalities, across different departments, as well as for Nortel. In 2013 Nicolas authored *Hazardous Materials Compliance for Public Research Organizations: A Case Study,* and in 2012 he coauthored with Paul E. Tracy *Case Studies in Disaster Response and Emergency Management*; both books were published by Taylor & Francis. In 2011, Nicolas coauthored with Ted Benavides *Practical Human Resources Management for Public*

Managers: A Case Study Approach, published by Taylor & Francis. Prior to 2011, Nicolas authored *Regulating the Use of Biological Hazardous Materials in Universities: Complying with the New Federal Guidelines*, which was published by Mellen Press in 2006. Nicolas has served as editor for three volumes of *New Directions for Institutional Research* (Volumes 135, 140, 146 and coedited 156) in addition to writing numerous articles and book chapters on institutional research topics and homeland security issues. Nicolas specializes in several areas as both a researcher and a practitioner: higher education, information technology, human resources, homeland security, organizational behavior, and emergency management.

Teodoro J. Benavides

Ted Benavides currently serves as a faculty member for the University of Texas at Dallas (UTD) in the School of Economic, Political, and Policy Sciences' public affairs program. He also served as a senior vice president for the Waters Consulting Group, which does executive search, compensation studies, and organizational analysis for public sector organizations, from June 2006 to August 2008.

Ted served from 1998 to 2004 as city manager of Dallas, Texas. He was responsible for administering all programs and services for the city's 1.2 million people and overseeing an annual $1.9 billion municipal budget and directing a workforce of 12,000 employees.

From 1996 to 1998, Ted was city manager of the City of Denton, and from 1990 to 1996, he served as one of five assistant city managers in Dallas. Previously, he held a number of other positions with the City of Dallas, including director of the Budget and Research Department, assistant director of the Health and Human

Services Department, assistant director of capital budget programs, capital budget administrator, and budget analyst. He joined the City of Dallas in March 1978.

Ted earned a bachelor's degree in education, political science, and history from Texas A&I University (now Texas A&M University–Kingsville) and a master's degree in public administration from Southern Methodist University. He also is a graduate of both Leadership Dallas and the Executive Institute of the Texas Municipal League at the LBJ School of Public Affairs in Austin and is a fellow of the National Academy of Public Administration. Ted serves as the president of the North Texas Chapter of the American Society for Public Administration and is on the Academic Relations Committee of the National Forum for Black Public Administrators.

Kimberly E. Scruton

Kimberly E. Scruton is currently the dean of the Reeves School of Business at Methodist University in Fayetteville, North Carolina, and an assistant professor of management. In previous roles, Scruton served as the head men's and women's tennis coach, assistant athletic communications and marketing director, interim athletic director, and associate vice president for development at Shenandoah University. Scruton earned her undergraduate degree from West Liberty University, her graduate degree from Central Michigan University, and her doctorate from Shenandoah University. In 2013, Scruton authored *Dissatisfaction and Attrition among Female Faculty in American Universities: An Analysis of the National Study of Postsecondary Faculty*, which was published by Mellen Press. Prior to her career in higher education, she worked as a marketing director and manager in sport and retail industries. In her research, Scruton focuses on topics including management, leadership, motivation, gender studies, non-profit and for-profit organizational dynamics, organizational culture, organizational behavior, job satisfaction, decision making, higher education, cooperative and intentional learning communities, intercollegiate cross-gendered coaching, and athlete perceptions.

INTRODUCTION

I

Chapter 1

Basic Concepts and Issues of Non-Profit Organizations

What Is a Non-Profit Organization?

A non-profit organization is characterized by how it uses its revenue. Such an organization does not make a profit to benefit stakeholders or an individual that owns (or administers) the organization. The organization uses any revenue that is generated to support the organization's mission, vision, and goals in perpetuity. There are a wide array of non-profit organizations attempting to fulfill different scopes of mission and vision to their targeted service group. For example, an organization that is tasked with feeding the homeless is very different in its function and mission from a group of Civil War re-enactors attempting to educate the population on a segment of American history. However, both groups work toward achieving their missions without the organizations making a profit.

Every country has different guidelines for what is considered to be a non-profit organization. In the United States, an organization is considered to be tax exempt (a non-profit organization) if the entity has obtained 501(c) status from the federal Internal Revenue Service (IRS) designating the organization as a non-profit organization. Administrators should also be aware that in the United States, state laws can potentially define what a non-profit organization is more broadly than federal statute. In other parts of the world, the standards could be very different on what a non-profit organization is by definition. Table 1.1 provides a summary of the various types of tax exemption by the Internal Revenue Service in the United States.

Table 1.1 Non-Profit Organizations in the United States 501(c) Status

Type of Tax Exemption	*Description of Non-Profit Organization*	*Example(s) of Organizations with the Specific Tax Status or Managing a Tax Status Fund*
501(c)(2)	Title-holding corporations for single-parent corporations	Thompson & Thompson
501(c)(3)	Charitable organizations that cannot be involved in political activities	Association of Institutional Research, Livestrong
501(c)(4)	Civic leagues and social welfare organizations	NAACP
501(c)(5)	Labor unions, agricultural and horticultural organizations	Teamsters
501(c)(6)	Business leagues, etc.	American Library Association
501(c)(7	Social and recreation clubs	Fairview Country Club
501(c)(8) and 501(c)(10)	Fraternal beneficiary societies and domestic fraternal societies	Beni Hassan Shrine Temple #64
501(c)(4), 501(c)(9), and 501(c)(17)	Employee associations	Draper Corp. 501(c)(9) employee benefit trust agreement
501(c)(12)	Local benevolent life insurance associations, mutual irrigation and telephone companies, and like organizations	Utility Cooperative
501(c)(13)	Cemetery associations	Woodward Hill Cemetery
501(c)(14)	Credit unions and other mutual financial organizations	Texans Credit Union

Table 1.1 (*Continued*) Non-Profit Organizations in the United States 501(c) Status

Type of Tax Exemption	*Description of Non-Profit Organization*	*Example(s) of Organizations with the Specific Tax Status or Managing a Tax Status Fund*
501(c)(19)	Veterans' organizations	Military Marksmanship Association
501(c)(20)	Group legal services plan organizations	Camp Ruach Hachaim
501(c)(21)	Black lung benefit trusts	National Black Lung Association
501(c)(25)	Title-holding corporations or trusts for multiple-parent corporations	Valwood, Inc.
501(c)(26)	State-sponsored, high-risk health coverage organizations	North Carolina Health Insurance Risk Pool, Inc.
501(c)(27)	Qualified state-sponsored workers' compensation organizations	American Association of State Compensation Insurance Funds

Source: IRS, 2012.

Each 501(c) status has certain restrictions and requirements for the different types of organizations. Unlike a private industry or business organization, a non-profit organization focuses on generating enough revenue to be self-sustaining. Therefore, the costs passed onto their clients (or customers) should be greatly reduced from what a for-profit entity would require to be competitive in the marketplace, because a for-profit entity needs to generate enough revenue to meet costs and earn a profit.

Unlike for-profit organizations, tax-exempt organizations in the United States are required to produce guidelines and operating procedures to obtain tax-free status with the governmental taxing agency. Any organization that fails to adhere to taxing agency guidelines may jeopardize the organization's tax-exempt status and risk subjecting all of its revenue to taxation deductions to the extent the organization qualifies for 501(c)(3) status and jeopardizing its donors' charity income tax. Non-profit organizations typically rely on governmental and private grants, donations, and small fees for goods and services to pay for payroll, facilities maintenance, and general overhead (i.e., utilities, vehicles, fuel).

History of Non-Profit Organizations in the United States

The history of non-profit organizations in the United States dates back to the Revolutionary War. The American peace/resistance movement began around the time of the revolution in 1776, and is considered to be the first non-profit organization formed in the United States. Later, a pattern was established where there would be a surge in the number of non-profit organizations formed after wars. This is true for the Second World War, after which professionals in the health and religious domains formed organizations to assist families that had lost the fathers and sons in the war. They also rehabilitated the veterans that had been traumatized by the war. The other moment when there was a notable surge in the number of non-profit organizations formed was during the Vietnam War. As the war raged on, American citizens formed many non-profit organizations that opposed the war. Many demonstrations took place in America. The war brought to light the difficulties that people in the developing countries are faced with. This led to the formation of numerous non-profit organizations in United States, whose focus was to improve the living conditions of the people in Africa and Asia through better health and education.

Although charitable organizations have been in existence for centuries, the formalization of non-profit organizations did not take effect until the 1970s. Of the currently classified non-profit organizations in the United States today, it is estimated that more than 90 percent have been created since 1950. The number of non-profit organizations was at its peak in 1970s, as Americans sought to help numerous causes, including helping developing countries out of their health and education problems. The initial source of funds for the non-profit organizations was primarily donations from individuals, governments, and foundations. This has changed of late, and the non-profit organizations have turned to commercial activities that are run by professionals. The proceeds from these ventures are never distributed, as per the requirements for exemption, but used to achieve the purpose of the organization.

Recorded Policies and Procedures

Non-profit organizations should maintain a set of bylaws, policies, or procedures that their organization uses as a guideline for proper management of the organization and to qualify for IRS 501(c)(3) status (United States). This written documentation should address what the organization can legally do according to the bylaws, the makeup of the board in the form of elected or appointed officials, and what the qualifications are for an elected board member, since they are legally responsible for the organization. In addition, the articles of incorporation define paid members who are hired by the organization to perform administrative duties, as well as define the scope of their job responsibilities. Secondly, if the non-profit organization has a membership component to the organization or an executive board, the written documentation should define who is a member of the organization and the positions that comprise the executive board.

If the organization uses voting to address such issues as changes in the bylaws or to the organization's leadership, the organization must define what constitutes the minimum number of members needed to hold a vote (a quorum) and composition of the membership (i.e., membership categories). The written documentation should define the mechanisms that are available for the members to cast their votes (i.e., online, mail, email, etc.), as well as which officer (or administrator) is responsible for counting the vote. The voting process is critical for many non-profit organizations, and the membership (if applicable) uses the voting process to direct the organization's actions. If the voting process is flawed or undefined, then this can cause considerable friction in the non-profit organization and can expose the organization to litigation.

If the non-profit organization has an elected executive board, the written documentation should define the duties of the executive positions as well as the qualifications to run and hold office for each officer. If other officers are appointed by the executive board, the bylaws should state what positions can be appointed, by which executive, and for how long the appointee can hold the position. Some of the items that should be considered when formulating qualifications for executive board members are education requirement, procedural requirement (i.e., nominated by a board member), residency requirement, experience level, years of service with the organization, or if the officer has to have an active membership with an additional organization (i.e., national organization in addition to a regional organization affiliation).

The bylaws should also address the issue of succession for each position, as well as contingency plans when officers resign or are voted out of their positions by the non-profit organization's membership. The bylaws will need to include language in the governing document for how each officer is elected, the term limits, term restrictions (if, for example, the person that is elected can only serve once), and how the officer can be voted out of office, as well as what the representation of the organization must be for a quorum and a vote to count.

Proper Documentation for 501(c)(3) Status

The 501(c)(3) status is usually referred to as the non-profit status. Organizations that have this status are exempt from federal taxation. Nongovernmental organizations fall under this category of tax-exempt organizations. For the non-profit status to be approved, the organization must be organized either as a corporation, a limited liability company, an unincorporated association, or a trust. The organizing document must have a purpose clause that limits the activities of the organization to a single purpose. The organizing document is also required to have a dissolution clause that distributes the assets of the non-profit organization to the federal or state government upon the dissolution of the organization. The document should specify whether the organization is a public charity or a private foundation. A public charity tends to have a more favorable tax exemption. The founders of the non-profit organization will need to complete Internal Revenue Service Form 1023. This form provides the organization recognition as a tax-exempt organization.

Controls over Financing

Control systems are important in ensuring that the accounting records of an organization are reliable. They reduce the possibility of the management or staff reporting a random error and also assist in ensuring ethical accounting practices. The authenticity of the financial reports is assured. In addition, the faith of the stakeholders in the organization is enhanced. In order to safeguard the assets of non-profit organizations and increase accountability to the stakeholders (donors), it is suggested that such an organization adopt an internal control system (ICS) to manage its financial health. The process of the preparation of the financial statement is required to be devoid of faults so as to make the final statements authentic.

The Dodd-Frank Act, which amends the Sarbanes-Oxley Act, requires that all companies provide management reports on the effectiveness of the companies' control over their finances. In addition, the larger companies are required to have the effectiveness of their control measures assessed by external auditors. Most non-profit organizations do not qualify as large companies and are, therefore, not subject to assessment by external auditors. Annual reports on the assessment of the control of finances are expected from the management and board of directors.

Transparency in the handling of finances by the non-profit organizations is paramount to gain the trust of donors whose contributions they are dependent on. There is increased pressure and requirements to create a controlled environment within the organization in order to provide effective internal financial controls. To foster an adequate financial control environment, business integrity, culture, ethical business practices, and leadership philosophy are essential. Use of generally accepted accounting principles (GAAP) is one of the ways of creating a controlled environment in an organization. The procedures and policies that aid in the implementation of the management directives constitute the internal control measures. The goal of these policies and procedures is to ensure that the non-profit organization achieves its objectives.

The management is able to determine whether other components of internal control are working effectively through continuous and separate evaluations. If any anomalies in the internal controls are realized, then the management is able to identify and work diligently to provide corrective measures. The controls have the overall objective of avoiding or minimizing financial loss within the organization. With this in mind, it is imperative that the controls are wide ranging. Long-term arrangement for the supervision of the employees, protection of the organization's assets, and financial reviews have to be put in place. The possible financial management controls include monitoring of income and expenditure; budgetary controls; having the internal audit regulate the finances of the organization and update reviews; and providing clear and consistent expectations to employees. The measures taken to safeguard the assets of the non-profit organization are referred to as the physical controls. It is critical to monitor employees through proper supervision, which can significantly reduce the possibility of an error or fraud occurring. The accounting of the firm's finances should be done by qualified, licensed professionals.

Financing

The amount of funding required by a non-profit organization differs among the various organizations. This will be determined mostly by the size and goals of the non-profit organization. The bigger the scope and operations of the non-profit organization, the larger the amount of funding is required to assist it in running its activities. There are several sources of funds for non-profit organizations. These include grants from international organizations, corporations, and national governments; sale of goods and services produced by the organization; private donations; and membership dues. Some non-profit organizations are heavily reliant on the funding from the resident government. It is understood, however, that the goals of the non-profit organizations might coincide with those of the government, justifying the government's donations to these organizations. Some non-profit organizations have different missions and will behave differently and do not accept or rely on grants from governments and intergovernmental organizations so as not to compromise their nature or purpose.

Much of the funds generated by the non-profit organizations needs to be spent in provision of services to the clients and meeting their material needs, if that is the case. The overhead costs of the non-profit organizations are expected to be lower than is often seen in for-profit organizations. The overhead costs are the banking and bookkeeping costs, salaries, and office expenses. Ideally, most non-profit organizations are required to have the overhead costs consuming less than 20 percent of the funds generated. There are some extreme cases where the overhead costs are not allowed to go beyond 5 percent to 7 percent. The World Bank was allowed to have the overhead costs to be as high as 37 percent. The drawback with high overhead costs is that the funds for programs may be reduced, and the organization may be criticized for benefiting its staff more than the population that it intends to serve. Lowering the overhead to extreme levels may, on the other hand, result in the operation of the organization being impaired. This, therefore, is a delicate balance to maintain. The desire to lower the wage costs is what drives many non-profit organizations to require staffs that consist of volunteers.

Mission

The mission statement of an organization briefly describes the organization's purpose, its present state, and provides the answers as to why an organization exists, what it does, whom it desires to serve, and how it will go about accomplishing this. Non-profit organizations are concerned with the provision of the core needs to the people or cause that they serve. The founders of these organizations are therefore often driven by compassion to initiate these types of ventures. This compassion should be reflected in the mission statement. The difference that the non-profit organization hopes to bring to society, and the specific activities and programs carried out by the organization, should be mentioned in the mission statement. It should be constructed and worded in a form that communicates an explicit idea of what the non-profit organization desires to be and accomplish. The mission statement should influence the culture, type of decisions, and type of donors that the organization attracts. The mission statement guides the non-profit organization and ensures that it remains true to the initial premise under which it was formed. It is important to have a clearly written and defined mission and vision for any organization.

Vision

The vision statement of a non-profit organization provides an explanation of what it aspires to be and to achieve in the future. It is an outline into the optimal desired future state of the organization. The vision statement assists in the formulations and development of the strategic planning process for the non-profit organization. The vision is generally created for the owners of the organization, board of directors, and staff as a guide toward the anticipated future of the non-profit organization.

There are several benefits to having well-written vision and mission statements. Through the mission, an organization explains its purpose for existing (current state), and through its vision, it identifies where it is planning to go (future state). This allows for increased alignment of processes and resources, including human and financial.

Organizational Framework

The organizational framework of the non-profit organization provides details on how the responsibilities of the organization are structured and shared among the employees. It provides an outline of the decision-making processes and flow of work responsibilities and communication involved in the operations of the organization. The organizational structure is used to present a pictorial demonstration of the hierarchical system, plus the different levels of responsibility in the non-profit organization. It is oftentimes included in the literature, websites, and other promotional materials of the initiative in order to give information to the potential donors and other stakeholders on how the activities are carried out and coordinated by the non-profit organization.

Most donors and funding agencies are usually interested in knowing how the non-profit organization operates before deciding whether to make contributions. This structure reveals the apparent wage burden that the organization is likely to have, plus the level of efficiency it is likely to have. These are factors that determine whether the donors will commit their funds to a particular non-profit organization or seek an alternative organization. It is also helpful to the new employees, as it assists them during the orientation period in the organization. This organization structure is also important to the management of the non-profit organization, as it makes it possible to identify the overstaffed and understaffed departments. The recruiting of new employees or interdepartmental transfers then takes place accordingly. It is advisable to include the community members of the board of directors of a non-profit organization, and further explain the role they play in the decision-making of the organization. The organization structure chart can be used to demonstrate this, and it might put the organization in a better position to receive the funds required.

Membership and Client Documentation

Membership rosters and client lists are valuable tools for a non-profit organization. A membership list records historically who was involved with the organization. Newer members of the organization can use this historic list to contact previous members for mentorship or provide clarity as to why certain policies were enacted or organizational decisions were made. Membership rosters are also important for the collection of dues and the distribution of volunteering duties according to the membership's skills and experiences. A client list is useful for determining who is using the organization's goods or services and which goods and services are in highest demand. In this way, the organization can focus its efforts on providing what is needed most and avoid wasting time and resources.

Recruitment/Marketing Drives

Because non-profit organizations depend so much on their members and clients for their existence, it can become essential for these organizations to engage in activities that will recruit more members or encourage more clients to use their services. Recruiting efforts will replenish membership whenever older members leave the organization or can expand the membership so that the organization can expand its mission. Recruitment and retention efforts can also prevent decreases in revenue received from member dues, donations, and the sale of goods and services. Declines in membership will constrain what the organization can accomplish, which can lead to eventual dissolution of the organization.

For organizations that exist to provide goods and services to specific clients, marketing aimed at notifying potential clients of the goods and services that are available can help the organization achieve its mission. To do this, an organization will need to be able to publicly market its goods and services through different media outlets and will need to determine what type of return on investment is acceptable to consider the marketing effort to be sustainable. The organization may want to conduct smaller pilot programs to see what is viable from a marketing perspective.

Donors

For many non-profit organizations, donors are critical for their survival. The administrators or the executive board must be able to obtain funding from donors if the organization's primary mission is to serve clients. For non-profit organizations that rely on membership fees or the sale of goods or services, having donors is not their main revenue stream and will not be as critical for their sustainment of operations.

Infrastructure Needs

While many individuals understand and are familiar with large non-profit organizations such as the American Red Cross or United Way, which require massive infrastructure resources, there are many smaller non-profit organizations that require significantly fewer resources than their bigger counterparts. An administrator of a non-profit organization should assess what the organization needs in terms of resources for facilities or information technology requirements. These two categories can be very costly and will need to be budgeted on a yearly basis. Infrastructure costs include, but are not limited to, rent, utilities, licensing fees, and information technology. For organizations that require no facilities or information technology resources, overhead costs may include maintaining a bank account open, attorney fees, or insurance premiums. Many organizations, for example, may be small and spread out over a large geographic area that would not have physical facilities, but may have a website and web-hosted application that is critical to the sustainment of the organization.

Size of a Non-Profit Organization

The size of an organization may lend itself to be more or less stable, dependent upon the mix and commitment of the members. For a non-profit organization that has paid, full-time administrators, the organization can potentially be much more stable in operation and consistency than a non-profit organization that consists only of volunteers and an executive board that rotates roles and leadership assignments on a regular basis. In addition to a larger membership, there will be, in theory, more individuals that will want to actively participate with the organization and bring in valuable skills and experience that can benefit the organization tremendously.

Volunteers

Non-profit organizations traditionally rely heavily on volunteers to carry out the bulk of the organization's mission to its members and targeted people that the organization serves. If a non-profit organization is large enough, the executive board should seriously consider purchasing liability insurance to protect the organization from unforeseen events (i.e., accidents, canceled conferences due to weather, etc.). Additionally, the organization may want to consider a training program for volunteers (which may very well include elected board members), as well as confidentiality agreements for volunteers where organizational data is confidential.

Appointed Positions

The appointed staff members in most non-profit organizations include those in management by virtue of having specific skills that are required for the roles they play in the organization. The highest governing body in a non-profit organization is the one that is often tasked to make such appointments. Positions that require the appointment include the positions of the program manager, the accounts officer, and the administrative officer. It is then the prerogative of the program manager to identify the people that work under him or her as the project coordinators, followed by the field officers. The appointed management team is tabled to the members of the board, which is the highest decision-making body for most non-profit organizations, for approval.

Financial Reserves

The financial reserves are defined as the total surplus of funds that have accumulated in the non-profit organization throughout its period of existence. It is calculated by taking the sum of all the surpluses in funds amassed each year, less the deficits experienced. The records of the financial reserves are usually evidenced in the balance sheet. The reserves are considered as the net worth of the organization. They are the amount of resources that would be left over for distribution if the non-profit organization were to close down. The reserves are not always held in terms of cash and can be invested in assets such as vehicles, equipment, and buildings. The reserves serve the purpose of acting as a safety margin for the organization to pay off debts and financial emergencies such as unbudgeted expenditure. They grant the management of the non-profit organization much flexibility in the managing of resources without having to seek the permission of the donors first.

The reserves are useful in paying for unplanned for expenses such as sponsoring the maternity leaves of the staff members, replacement of worn out equipment, fees for representation and legal advice, for researching and developing the organization, provision of severance payments, and provision for general emergencies. Most non-profit organizations have challenges in building up reserves. This is because most of the funds are received from donors, and these funds are usually restricted. If there is any surplus of the donor funds, the management is required, as per the agreement with the donor, to carry forward the surplus amount for the next financial period. The organization, therefore, has to focus on generating the needed financial reserves from unrestricted funds. Once the stakeholders' conditions are met, then the non-profit organization can retain the surpluses for future work. Generation of reserves should be a part of the financing strategy of the non-profit organization.

A non-profit organization should have a reserves policy that should be made public. The rationale behind the policy must be explained and justified. Financial reserves can be created by the non-profit organization using a number of methods. The methods of generating reserves include maximizing the unrestricted income, maximizing the potential of the restricted income from donors, maximizing the project income, and minimizing the expenditure that is controllable.

Conference Planning

The need for constant familiarization with the problems facing the society that is served by a non-profit organization requires it to regularly hold forums with the target group and the media. These forums are usually in the form of press conferences, roundtables, seminars, debates, and other similar types of events. Indeed, a non-profit organization's activity level is measured by the number of events it plans and attends annually. Close cooperation with the people served by the organization is very important, as the aim of the non-profit organization is to improve the living conditions of the targeted population. The success of these endeavors requires the non-profit organization to have excellent conference planning.

The non-profit organizations' events should be organized in such a way that they appeal to the targeted audience and draw as many participants as possible. This, therefore, might require the mode of planning and announcement of the upcoming events to be unique, hip, and appealing to the individuals needed to attend. It is at these events that the intentions of the organization are presented to the targeted audience and their feedback taken into consideration. Other underlying problems that the target group might face that are not addressed by the non-profit organization can also be identified and considered in the activities to be carried out by nongovernmental organizations.

Conference planning requires the members of the non-profit organizations to have event planning and management skills. The regional non-profit organization is expected to organize various types of events once a month. The events organized should be planned for at least 30 days in advance. The majority of the events planned by the non-profit organizations are 1-day events. Those that exceed that period usually last no more than 2 days. The time taken in planning and anticipating an event is often dependent on the type of event being planned, but is never less than 30 days. Events taking more than 1 day with international participants may take not less than 60 days of preparation. In choosing the location for the conferences, the capacity of the conference hall is the major determining factor, followed by the price and location of the facility. The accessibility of the conference venue, especially for people with disabilities, is also given consideration.

Controls over Personnel

In non-profit organizations, the members of staff should be aware of their responsibilities and the lines of authority in the organization. They should also be informed of the lines of reporting and the levels of responsibility within the organization. There should be no uncertainty in the non-profit organization in regard to whom is responsible for what and to whom to report. The failure of that leads to fraud and costly errors occurring in the organization. What makes it worse in such a situation is the fact that the accountable people cannot be pointed out. The members of the board, who are referred to as trustees, are responsible for the running of the non-profit organization and have the mandate to ensure that the organization is not abused by rogue management, associates, and employees. Their control systems are supposed to be constantly maintained and very rigorous in order to fulfill this mandate. This mandate of having control over the activities of the personnel is exhibited through the procedural controls and the reporting structure of the organization.

PUBLIC RELATIONS ISSUES

II

Chapter 2

Boy Scouts of America — Atheist Court Case — 1990

Phase I — Situation

You are an executive director of the Boy Scouts of America (BSA), an organization whose primary goal is the development of character and the training of young boys in the values and responsibilities of citizenship. The activities of the BSA are designed to instill leadership abilities and to foster values that will stay with the boys throughout their lives (Boy Scouts of America: About, 2014).

Robert Baden-Powell, the founder of Scouting and the first Chief Scout of the Boy Scouts Association, wrote in the first Scout Handbook in 1908, "No man is much good unless he believes in God and obeys His laws," essentially making spirituality and religion an integral part of Scouting (Mechling, 2001). By 1959, when the sixth edition of the Boy Scout Handbook was published, the interpretation was that the BSA was nondenominational. No theology or practice of any specific religious denomination was to be imposed, but rather boys from all faiths could join. However, the key was faith, which excluded atheists who did not have faith (a confidence, trust, and belief) in God (Mechling, 2001).

According to John Alexander, "Recognition of God as the ruling and leading power in the universe, and the grateful acknowledgement of His favors and blessings is necessary to the best type of citizenship and is a wholesome thing in the education of the growing boy ... the Boy Scouts of America, therefore, recognize the religious elements in the training of a boy, but it is absolutely non-sectarian in its attitude toward that religious training" (Mechling, 2001).

The BSA has historically interpreted atheism as being at odds with the Scout Oath and Scout Law, as it is the explicit denial of the existence of God. Atheists Mark and Elliott Welsh attempted to join the Boy Scouts: Mark as a Cub Scout and Elliott, his father, as an adult partner. They were denied membership, the Welshes felt, because they refused to recite the Scout Oath, as doing so would affirm their belief in God.

In a challenge to a historical interpretation, a lawsuit was filed in 1990 on behalf of the Welshes, alleging that they were denied membership based solely on their unwillingness to profess a belief in God. The lawsuit was filed pursuant to Title II of the Civil Rights Act of 1964, which prohibits places of public accommodation from discriminating on the basis of certain criteria, including religion (Welsh, 1990). Title II of the Civil Rights Act of 1964 specifically states that, "All persons shall be entitled to the full and equal enjoyment of the foods, services, facilities, privileges, advantages, and accommodations, as defined in the section, without discrimination or segregation on the grounds of race, color, religion, or national origin."

The Welshes contended that the BSA is a "place of public accommodation" because it is a place of "entertainment." The BSA contends it is neither a "place" nor an "accommodation," nor does it provide "entertainment."

Questions that should be asked by the administrator at this phase:

1. What is the best way to communicate the issues and merits of your case to members and corporate supporters?
2. Which of your ideals are being challenged, and to what extent?
3. Is your best strategy to emphasize and reaffirm your mission?
4. How has this case affected (or could potentially affect) your corporate partnerships and sponsorships?
5. What are some potential strategies you can use to mitigate any negative press?

Potential Issues for Public Relations

The Welsh case will surely result in opposition from atheists and others who fight against discrimination. That opposition may very well result in extended exposure through traditional media and social media. Through the media's zeal to increase readership or viewership, it is likely that the exposure will be slanted to create controversy and negative opinions of the BSA. Such attitudes in the court of public opinion have the potential to have a severe impact on corporate sponsorship, federal funding, and membership enrollment.

As a director of the BSA, you must decide how to handle this public relations issue. Do you simply ignore the negative exposure and opinions, rely on the final judgment of the court in the Welsh case, and trust that any negative publicity will eventually run its course? Should you mount a counter-campaign stressing the organization's core values? If so, how will you implement the strategy and plan the counter-campaign?

Phase II — First Issue

As a result of case law in *Welsh v. Boy Scouts of America*, it was ruled that the BSA has the right to include or exclude anyone it chooses from membership in its organization.

On June 12, 1991, the BSA issued a position statement reaffirming its position on "Duty to God," stating its commitment to "the moral, ethical, and spiritual development of our youth. Scouting is not a religion, but duty to God is a basic tenet of the Scout Oath and Law." The statement went on to say that Scouting is inclusive of all religions and doesn't impose its core beliefs on anyone, nor does it "define or interpret God. That is the role of the Scout's family and religious advisors" (Position, 1991).

On February 6, 2002, the national executive board of the BSA passed a resolution expressly excluding atheists from membership, because of their unwillingness "to accept the values and standards" of BSA. In an "organization whose very reason for existence is to instill and reinforce values in youth," the statement continued, "the BSA's values cannot be subject to local option choices but must be the same in every unit" (BSA National, 2002).

In addressing the leadership of the BSA, Bishop Gary E. Stevenson, presiding bishop of the Church of Jesus Christ of Latter-day Saints, commented on the duty to God as fundamental to Scouting by saying:

> I believe it constructive counsel for each of us to pray that divine direction manifest itself upon those who have the [great] responsibility to lead this organization properly. Boy Scouts of today face issues not faced by generations before them: declining morals, technology, addictive behavior and declining academic performance to name a few. I believe that the key to solving these issues lies in family and duty to God. If boys truly understood what their duty to God entails and lived it, they would grow safely into manhood. … Scouting must never overlook this core principle. (2013)

Questions that should be asked by the executive director at this phase:

1. How can you assess the damage this case has done to the BSA's image?
2. What is the image of the BSA that you want to project?
3. How could this case affect your fundraising efforts?
4. What criteria should you use to determine the best person or group to speak about your mission and image?

Potential Issues for Public Relations

Excluding atheists from membership in the BSA is a highly emotional topic. David Silverman, the current president of American Atheists, said, "Legally, the Scouts can practice bigotry, but morally, they shouldn't." Therein lies the most pressing public relations issue facing the BSA: how to defend itself against the public perception of the moral aspect of religious discrimination, which includes the discrimination against those who do not believe in God.

Phase III — Second Issue

It does not require any stretch of the imagination to recognize the merit of the arguments made by those who object to the BSA's position. As atheists, Mr. Welsh and his son consider their beliefs to hold the same value as those with religious affiliations.

The majority of Americans believes in a supreme being — God — and do not consider it bigotry to choose to associate with like-minded people. It is the BSA's belief that the degree of moral compass required from an individual to become a pillar of his community, and also an effective leader, originates first from the ability to affirm belief in a supreme being.

Whether or not to allow atheists to be members of the BSA may be an issue decided by details. BSA membership has declined since 1972 by 11 percent for Boy Scouts and 23 percent for Cub Scouts (BSA Traditional, 2013). The exact reasons for this decline are not specifically known; however, you must pay attention to this trend and research and investigate it to determine its relevant details and cause.

You, and all of your fellow BSA leaders, must take steps to reverse the trend if you want to stay viable as an organization. Without knowing the details associated with the cause of the decline in membership, there is no way to make adjustments to change the trend.

Societal changes in America have moved mountains and changed hearts, due in part to the belief that all of God's children are equal in his sight, and that the judgment about those who have different beliefs from the BSA's should come from God alone, not from any person or organization. If the BSA does not pay attention to all of the intricate details of people's perceptions, and become more aware of overall societal and religious changes in interpretation and acceptance, it may very well find itself a defunct organization.

Questions that should be asked by the executive director at this phase:

1. Should the BSA be more inclusive, allowing members with other beliefs — and nonbelievers — to join?
2. What steps are you taking to address the decline in your membership?
3. How can you determine if politics has played a role in the stance you've taken on atheists?

4. Should you consider re-evaluating your membership policies in light of the issue raised by the Welshes?

Potential Issues for Public Relations

You run the risk of a continuing decrease in existing memberships, corporate sponsors, and future enrollment in the BSA. Its beliefs have always been at the forefront of everything the BSA does. Many of the local troop meetings are held at and supported by churches. BSA's beliefs have been clearly stated in guidebooks, bylaws, and the oath, so the Welshes' case does not bring forth any information that your members and supporters do not already know.

In addition to the strategies addressing the BSA's public image and negative press, you have a few options to maintain the stability of the BSA. You could reach out to similar civic organizations that may have had comparable experience with such issues. The BSA and like-minded organizations have the statistics to prove the success of their missions based on their existing principles. BSA has longevity and the majority opinion on its side, in comparison to the opposing views of atheists.

Should you discover that the BSA is losing corporate sponsors as a result of the lawsuit, you could actively seek corporate sponsors from among companies that espouse religious or ethical beliefs. For example, companies such as Hobby Lobby and Chick-fil-A openly display their Christian beliefs. The BSA could look into joint advertising efforts with such companies.

Phase IV — Future Plans

The Supreme Court ruled in favor of the BSA, and the Court of Appeals upheld the right of the BSA and all private organizations to set membership standards in accordance with the First Amendment-protected "freedom of association" (Welsh, 1993). The ruling has essentially provided the BSA an opportunity to publicly reaffirm its values and beliefs. It is now the organization's responsibility to make sure those values and beliefs are clearly communicated.

It is imperative to do what you can to ensure that the BSA holds fast to its mission, Scout Oath, and Scout Law and doesn't allow itself to get pulled into an exercise of defending a moral question. Responses from the BSA should be of one singular theme: "The BSA respects those who do not share its belief in God, and would not ask others to alter their belief in order to become members of the BSA. There is, however, an overriding belief that the 'duty to God' is fundamental to Scouting. The principals set forth in the BSA mission, the Scout Oath, and the Scout Law are central to the goal of teaching the values of self-reliance, courage, integrity, and consideration to others."

Phase V — Resolution and Conclusion

Case law has settled the matter for now. Your organization is steadfast in its opinion that one cannot have a duty to God without a religious belief. The idea of the BSA welcoming atheists as members and leaders might currently seem to be a difficult bridge to cross, but at some point, the BSA may have to cross that bridge. When that time comes, this particular issue can be handled and should be resolved with mutual respect and common sense.

Since the Scouts' inception, there have been shifts in what society tolerates or accepts in matters of race, gender, or sexual orientation, and the extent to which equal rights are afforded in these matters.

The media perpetuates public relations issues. If the BSA continues to be embroiled in controversy, the media will ensure that the organization will remain in the public's eye. Handling public relations is one thing, but preserving the image and mission of the BSA in the face of negative publicity is another and far more important consideration. The BSA needs to carefully respond to any public relations issue. As a long-standing, well-established organization, it does not want to appear to either praise or defend itself at the first sign of any potential public relations issue.

The BSA cannot ignore the impact on its organization where social issues are concerned. There may come a time when it has to consider severing its connection between "duty to God" and membership, and perhaps such a break would allow the organization to welcome atheists with the hope of having a positive influence on them through the teaching of BSA skills and values.

Chapter 3

Boy Scouts of America — Gay Scoutmaster Court Case — 2000

Phase I — Situation

You are a senior-level administrator of the Boy Scouts of America (BSA), one of the largest and most prominent values-based youth development organizations in the United States. The BSA provides programs for boys that build character, train them in the responsibilities of participating as citizens, and develop them into leaders. For more than a century, the BSA has helped build future leaders of this country by leading boys in educational activities and instilling lifelong values. The BSA believes that helping youths is a key to building a more conscientious, responsible, and productive society (Boy Scouts of America, 2013). The mission of the BSA is to prepare young people to make ethical and moral choices over their lifetimes by endeavoring to instill in them values such as duty to God and country, obeying the Scout Law, and embodying a string of wholesome adjectives, including keeping "myself physically strong, mentally awake, and morally straight" (Boy Scouts of America, 2013).

James Dale was an Eagle Scout and assistant Scoutmaster for the Monmouth County, New Jersey, Boy Scouts and was considered an outstanding representative of the BSA. In 1990, members of your organization's leadership read in a newspaper that Dale was gay. Shortly thereafter, Dale received a letter from the Monmouth Scout Council informing him that his membership in the BSA and service as an assistant Scoutmaster had been revoked because of his sexuality.

Dale — who rapidly became popularly known as “a gay activist” — responded with a request for justification of the revocation of his membership, to which the Monmouth Scout Council responded that the BSA forbids membership to homosexuals, and as an openly gay man, he had demonstrated his inability to live by the Scout Oath and Scout Law.

Questions that should be asked by the administrator at this phase:

1. What effect might Dale’s public admission of his homosexuality and the BSA response to that have on your organization?
2. Apart from Dale coming out as homosexual, he embodied the qualities Scouting seeks to instill and led other young men and boys to do so as well. How will you justify revoking the membership of a man who had fulfilled his duties and seemingly followed the tenets of Scouting well enough to have risen to the levels of Eagle Scout and assistant Scoutmaster?
3. Will the BSA’s response to Dale affect corporate sponsorships and monetary contributions?
4. The BSA is a well-respected organization, but could Lesbian, Gay, Bisexual, Transgender (LGBT) organizations and others who oppose the BSA’s stance on homosexuality use the BSA’s response to Dale to their advantage in the public eye?

Potential Issues for Public Relations

The immediate concern will be the reaction from individuals, the media, and organizations that support and are fighting for equal rights for homosexuals. The pressure those organizations exert should dictate the extent and type of response from the BSA.

Unlike the BSA, its counterpart for training girls and young women for leadership roles, the Girl Scouts of America, has had a diversity policy and nondiscrimination clause in place since 1980 (James, 2012). At the very least, this fact will lead to accusations of prejudice and unfairness, which the BSA must answer to. That Dale was popular and highly thought of by the boys whom he led and, perhaps more importantly, by their parents will present another challenge that you and your organization will have to approach and attempt to persuade of the correctness of your decision. In addition, for several decades, the American public — with the exception of conservative Christians — has grown increasingly accepting of homosexuality in general and gays and lesbians in leadership roles and as parents in particular.

You must determine how to best balance upholding the values of Scouting against the certain accusations that the Scouts are an outdated, bigoted, wrong-headed organization that violates human and civil rights and dismisses the talents and abilities of a healthy minority population as “unwholesome.” In addition to attempting to soften or even erase the appearance of intolerance in the organization as a whole, you should expect — and endeavor to counter — widespread defections by Boy Scouts at the troop level, as parents who disagree with the decision for various reasons pull their boys out of the organization. This could in turn lead to a decrease in monetary contributions and corporate sponsorships by organizations that might sense a turning of the tide and pull out of their affiliation with Scouts to avoid appearing to discriminate against gays and lesbians.

Finally, you must consider the possibility that Dale will not walk away quietly from this dismissal and could file a lawsuit against the BSA.

Phase II — First Issue

According to Lambda Legal, from which came Dale's attorneys, a complaint was filed on Dale's behalf for his reinstatement in the BSA in New Jersey Superior Court on July 29, 1992. It was the first case to invoke New Jersey's Law against Discrimination (LAD) based on several categories, including sexual orientation, in places of public accommodation.

In 1995, the lower court ruled against Dale, in what Lambda Legal termed "a harshly worded opinion peppered with biblical allusions and references to 'sodomy' and 'buggery.'" The opinion stated that the BSA had consistently excluded any self-declared homosexuals and that the LAD was inapplicable, according to the Oyez Project (www.oyez.com) because the Boy Scouts was not a place of public accommodation. The court also concluded that the Boy Scouts' First Amendment freedom of expressive association prevented the government from forcing the Boy Scouts to accept Dale as an adult leader.

In March 1998, the New Jersey intermediate appellate court ruled that Dale's expulsion violated LAD, the first-ever appellate court victory in the United States against the Boy Scouts' anti-gay policy. According to Oyez, the appellate court held that New Jersey's public accommodations law applied to the Boy Scouts "because of its broad-based membership solicitation and its connections with various public entities, and that the Boy Scouts violated it by revoking Dale's membership based on his homosexuality. The court rejected the Boy Scouts' federal constitutional claims."

The case then went on to the New Jersey Supreme Court on appeal by the BSA; in August 1999, that court unanimously upheld the appellate court ruling that the anti-gay Scout ban violated LAD (*BSA v. Dale*). The New Jersey Supreme Court determined that the BSA had not demonstrated it was a sufficiently "private organization" to warrant First Amendment "freedom of association."

The US Supreme Court, on June 28, 2000, in a 5–4 vote, ruled that "as a private, expressive group, the Boy Scouts has a right to exclude from its leadership positions those who are openly gay" (*BSA v. Dale*). The majority opinion stated that BSA "believes homosexual conduct is inconsistent with the values it seeks to instill in its youth members."

Questions that should be asked by the administrator at this phase:

1. In view of the Supreme Court decision, should the BSA screen its current leadership to identify those who are openly homosexual?
2. What impact, if any, will the Supreme Court decision have on the relationships between the BSA and its various shareholders?

Potential Issues for Public Relations

The Supreme Court ruling will undoubtedly have an impact on how your organization is perceived by the public. Stances that appear discriminatory in any form are susceptible to public scrutiny and may be viewed negatively by the media. Corporations and charities, such as the United Way, that are conscious of and concerned about their own public image, may view the ruling as being too controversial or contrary to that of public opinion and decrease or eliminate their monetary contributions to the BSA.

Alternatively, some individuals and religious groups will view the ruling and stance on homosexuals by the BSA as morally and religiously correct. They will provide the support for positive media coverage and a possible growth in memberships or increase in monetary contributions. The BSA will need to critically analyze its position on the issue of homosexuality and how that stance influences its membership enrollment, fundraising, and ultimately its organizational mission.

Phase III — Second Issue

In the years following the Supreme Court's decision, many in the United States have wrestled with the perceived "immorality" of homosexuality versus the protection of equal rights for all, including gays and lesbians. The BSA partners with, and is strongly supported by, religious organizations, including the Baptist, Catholic, Episcopal, Lutheran, Methodist, and Presbyterian churches and the Church of Jesus Christ of Latter-day Saints (BSA Religious Partners). These religious institutions hold strong to the view that homosexuality is morally incompatible with their beliefs and teachings.

On February 6, 2002, the National Executive Board of the BSA passed a resolution expressly excluding homosexuals from membership because, among several reasons, "membership is contingent upon one's willingness to accept the values and standards" of the BSA, and "as a national organization whose very reason for existence is to instill and reinforce values in youth, the BSA's values cannot be subject to local option choices but must be the same in every unit."

The resolution went on to state that "homosexual conduct is inconsistent with the traditional values" of Scouting, so "an avowed homosexual cannot serve as role model" for Scouts. The statement concluded that the BSA respects the right of others to adhere to different values than theirs, but the national leadership believes that the BSA "is entitled to expect persons and organizations with different values and standards" to respect those it holds (BSA National Executive Board Resolution, 2002).

As the United States becomes more tolerant and accepting of gays and lesbians, their equal rights are being legally enforced. States continue to enact laws granting equal protection under the law for civil unions and gay marriages. The military policy "Don't Ask, Don't Tell" (DADT), which was enacted in 1994, prohibited discrimination against closeted gay and lesbian service members, yet also barred openly homosexual individuals from military service. The Supreme Court ruled the policy unconstitutional in 2011.

In 2010, the BSA, under pressure from both internal and external forces to reconsider its position on homosexuals, formed a secret committee to conduct an extensive internal review by 11 "volunteers and professional leaders to evaluate whether the policy was in the best interests of the organization," according to a BSA press release from its headquarters in Irving, Texas. The committee "included a diversity of perspectives" and engaged in "extensive research and evaluations," and in July 2012 reaffirmed its policy of barring openly gay boys from membership and gay or lesbian adults from serving as leaders (Eckholm, 2012).

The official policy reads a bit like a Boy Scout version of DADT: "While the BSA does not proactively inquire about the sexual orientation of employees, volunteers or members, we do not grant membership to individuals who are open or avowed homosexuals or who engage in behavior that would become a distraction to the mission of the BSA" (BSA Membership Standards Resolution).

In response, gay rights leaders pointed out that the BSA is out of step with the progress toward gay equality that many other organizations — like the Girl Scouts, 4-H, the Boys and Girls Clubs, and the military — are making. Richard Ferraro, vice president for communications with the Gay and Lesbian Alliance against Defamation, called the BSA "one of the last cultural institutions to have discrimination as part of their policy," and expressed concern that "prohibiting or ejecting gay children or leaders sends a dangerous message to all children. ... It's policies like this that contribute to bullying in schools" (Eckholm, 2012).

In April 2012, Jennifer Tyrrell, a lesbian parent and den mother to her son's Tiger Scouts group, was forced out because of her sexual orientation.

A few months after the reaffirming statement's release, two members of the BSA executive board, James S. Turley, chairman and chief executive of Ernst & Young, and Randall L. Stephenson, chairman and chief executive of AT&T, vowed to push to end the exclusion policy. An AT&T spokesman reissued a previous statement on behalf of Stephenson: "We don't agree with every policy of every organization we support, nor would we expect them to agree with us on everything. Our belief is that change at any organization must come from within to be successful and sustainable" (Eckholm, 2012).

Questions that should be asked by the administrator at this phase:

1. How will you handle potential dissention within the BSA's executive ranks regarding the historical position on homosexuals' participation as members and leaders?
2. In evaluating its position on homosexuals, should your organization be beholden to the religious groups that have a long history of supporting the BSA?
3. What are potential strategies to mitigate any negative press resulting from the continuation of the BSA's position regarding homosexuals?
4. How will this stance on homosexuality influence your stakeholders?

Potential Issues for Public Relations

A division within the rank and file of any organization can be a public relations nuisance; however, a division within the executive level of the BSA can be devastating to your efforts to put forth a unified message to the public.

The public relations decisions and strategies that the BSA utilizes to handle a socially controversial topic within its executive level will be an important test of the ability of the BSA to thrive in the future. The potential damage involves alienation of a large segment of the population whose views on homosexuality and human rights will have an impact on the public perception of organizations such as the BSA. The influence of these perceptions will be seen in membership rates, donations, and overall financial support.

As a BSA executive, it will be imperative for you to navigate the historical position of the BSA in regard to homosexuals in Scouting, as well as be conscious of the changing social, political, and monetary environments that influence your organization.

Phase IV — Third Issue

In response to social and political pressure on the BSA to again reconsider its position on homosexuals, while addressing the leadership of the BSA in May 2013, Bishop Gary E. Stevenson, presiding bishop of the Church of Jesus Christ of Latter-day Saints, said:

> I am very aware of the controversial moral, legal and policy issues that face this great organization. … I believe it constructive counsel for each of us to pray that divine direction manifest itself upon those who have the weighty responsibility to lead this organization properly. … When the societal and political winds come, and they surely will, scouting cannot unhinge itself from this fundamental principle.

Stevenson's plea was made on the same day that a vote was taken to once again address the position of the BSA and homosexuals within its membership and leadership. Based on growing influences from within the Scouting organization — both those who agreed with the policy and those who supported a change — the BSA leadership chose to conduct an additional review of the organization's long-standing opposition to allowing gays and lesbians to serve in the organization and its impact on Scouting's mission. The Scouts agreed to consider a proposal "to allow local charter organizations to decide for themselves whether to accept gay members and leaders" (James, 2012).

Questions that should be asked by the administrator at this phase:

1. This additional review comes soon after issuing a reaffirmation of your organization's position on homosexuals; what conclusions, if any, can you draw from it?
2. If there were a change in the BSA's position on homosexuals, how might this affect the culture and mission of the BSA?
3. How might a change in position affect the religious institutions and other organizations that have historically supported the BSA?
4. In the event of such a change, how should the BSA justify the appearance that it is abandoning its Supreme Court victory in 2000?

Potential Issues for Public Relations

Currently, regardless of the decision your leadership makes regarding its position on homosexual members and leaders, the potential public relations issues are critical. These issues to consider include the media's influence, your image, influence on your current and potential membership base, and both your stakeholders and shareholders. It will be important to address public reactions to your decision and be mindful of the opposing viewpoints between conventional religious morality and equal rights for homosexuals.

Phase V — Resolution and Conclusion

On May 23, 2013, 1,400 voting members of the BSA's National Council approved a resolution to remove the restriction denying membership to youths on the basis of sexual orientation alone, but "a change to the current membership policy for adult leaders was not under consideration, thus, the policy for adults remains in place" (Boy Scouts of America Statement, 2013).

This policy change was effective January 1, 2014, providing the BSA adequate time to implement this policy throughout its organization. The 2013 BSA statement said, in part, that the BSA will not sacrifice its mission, or the youths served by the movement, by allowing the organization to be consumed by a single, divisive, and unresolved societal issue. "While people have different opinions about this policy, we can all agree that kids are better off when they are in Scouting. Going forward, our Scouting family will continue to focus on reaching and serving youth in order to help them grow into good, strong citizens. America's youth need Scouting, and by focusing on the goals that unite us, we can continue to accomplish incredible things for young people and the communities we serve."

This resolution can be viewed as the BSA's recognition of tolerance and inclusivity — at least toward its members, if not its leaders — or as a concession to social and political pressure. "The controversial policy change spurred strong reactions from all sides," according to a *New York Daily News* article. "Some supporters argue the policy, which leaves a ban on gay adults intact, doesn't go far enough, while conservative groups claim the 103-year-old youth organization has abandoned its core values. … 'Any sexual activity outside the context of the covenant of marriage between one man and one woman is sinful before God,' conservative scouting alternative Trail Life USA said in a statement" (Murphy, 2014).

Chapter 4

Alcoholics Anonymous — Midtown AA Scandal — 2007

Phase I — Situation

You are an advisory board member for the non-profit organization Alcoholics Anonymous, whose mission is to assist in the recovery of alcoholics. You have held this role for one year with another year left in the leadership position. You have been entrusted to be an adviser for the twelve-step program, but recently there have been complaints by other Alcoholics Anonymous chapters that one chapter is not following the guidelines set forth by the Alcoholics Anonymous World Services Advisory Board (Summers, 2007). Several former members are stating that the group encourages them to have sex with other Midtown members, cut off all contact with friends and family, and are given a rigid schedule on when to attend Midtown meetings (Summers, 2007). What are you going to do about the real or perceived public image for your organization?

Questions that should be asked by the advisory board at this phase:

1. What powers or authority does the advisory board really have over the local chapters?
2. If the advisory board does have some power or authority to intervene, what actions should be taken?
3. How much liability will the advisory board be responsible for since the chapter is using the Alcoholics Anonymous name?

4. What responsibility do you have for the members attending that chapter?
5. Should the advisory board ask law enforcement officials to launch an investigation into the chapter?
6. Should the advisory board file an injunction for the chapter to stop using their organizational name?

Potential Issues for Public Relations, Civil Litigation, and Criminal Charges

Alcoholics Anonymous has been in existence since the mid 1930s with a mission of helping alcoholics become sober (Alcoholics Anonymous, 2002, 2012). If the information is true about the Midtown chapter operating as a cult, this is in violation of the Alcoholics Anonymous Preamble, which strictly forbids such behaviors in any of the chapters. If the information about the Midtown chapter's actions are true, the advisory board has a duty to order the chapter to stop using Alcoholics Anonymous' name in order to prevent an extremely bad public relations situation with doctors, counselors, and other recovery professionals who have already begun to stop referring patients to Alcoholics Anonymous until the advisory board intervenes (Summers, 2007). Clearly, this is not what the advisory board would want in the form of public exposure. The advisory board may operate in a decentralized organization, but that does not mean that the advisory board should avoid being proactive.

Even though the advisory board has limited oversight of the chapters, it still could be held liable if an organization that uses the Alcoholics Anonymous name causes harm to members attending the Midtown chapter. If the advisory board fails to act on knowledge or suspicions known to the board, the non-profit can be held accountable through civil litigation and even criminal prosecution. If information is brought to the advisory board's attention, they should ask law enforcement to investigate the chapter if the accusations include criminal behavior within the chapter.

Phase II — First Issue

It is 2007 and *Newsweek* has just run an investigative report on the Midtown chapter with what appears to be damaging information that could harm the organization's image and reputation. The article appears to have interviewed several people that state the Midtown chapter is operating in a cultlike fashion (Summers, 2007). In addition, there are now recovery professionals that are writing open letters to the recovery professional community highlighting disturbing behavior by the Midtown chapter, and doctors are now hesitant to refer patients to Alcoholics Anonymous (Summers, 2007).

Questions that should be asked by the advisory board at this phase:

1. Will the Midtown chapter's alleged actions and current reputation negatively affect the national Alcoholics Anonymous organization?
2. Should the advisory board take any action even though the advisory board's power is very limited currently on what can be done to intervene?
3. Up to this time period, the advisory board has taken no action nor issued any statement on the situation at the Midtown chapter except to say that, "Chapters rise and fall." Do you feel as an advisory board that this is essentially a way to distance the national organization of Alcoholics Anonymous from the Midtown chapter?
4. Should the advisory board look into having some oversight over local chapters when allegations of illegal activity could be occurring?
5. Is there any liability to the advisory board?
6. What are the ethical implications for the advisory board?

What Could the Advisory Board Do?

The action or inaction of the advisory board is determined by its membership of the advisory board. To go forward with a possible intervention or to do absolutely nothing is completely up to the advisory board members. The advisory board members do not have to answer to the public legally, since they are not funded by any type of tax dollars and its existence is not tied to any type of public charter. The advisory board members are also not bound by stakeholders in any type of financial situation since every chapter is locally funded. The issue of alleged improper or illegal conduct by a local chapter, therefore, is more of an ethical issue that the advisory board can either confront or ignore. Both options do have risks associated with actions that can be taken.

If the advisory board does intervene, it could be considered an incorporated organization that has the power to mandate other issues to all of the local chapters. The disadvantage to taking this approach is that it opens up the possibility of being liable for anything that a local chapter may do that is illegal or can result in civil damages from litigation. Additionally, the idea of remaining anonymous disappears for anyone in a leadership role at the local chapter level. This appears to be the reasoning behind Alcoholics Anonymous remaining unincorporated as an organization. It is hard to litigate against what does not exist as an official organization.

The downside to not intervening is the ethical quandary of having knowledge that members could in fact be harmed under the national organization banner of Alcoholics Anonymous. By not taking action against a local chapter such as Midtown, the advisory board is allowing members to be harmed by a local chapter that is not abiding by the national twelve-step program. Inaction can also damage the organization's national reputation, which will discourage would-be members from joining local chapters that are correctly promoting Alcoholics Anonymous' messages and methodologies to helping individuals get sober.

Another option that was not apparently pursued by the advisory board (at least it was not apparent from any of the Midtown reports released) would be for the advisory board to publicly denounce the Midtown group's actions. The advisory board could then openly recommend other chapters that are reputable that are located close to the Midtown chapter. Furthermore, the advisory board can contact recovery specialists in the area and ask them to refer patients and clients to other local chapters instead of the Midtown chapter.

Phase III — Second Issue

The Midtown Alcoholics Anonymous group has been banned from holding meetings in the church it had been using (NBC4.com, 2007). At the moment, your national office has had a complete hands-off approach by stating, "Each group is autonomous and follows its own conscious" (NBC4.com, 2007). Currently, the Washington, D.C., police and city prosecutor's office state that there is not an ongoing investigation into Midtown's activities (NBC4.com, 2007).

Questions that should be asked by the advisory board at this phase:

1. Does the advisory board have some ethical or moral obligation to take action against the Midtown chapter?
2. Should the advisory board ask the police or city prosecutor's office to begin an investigation?
3. Do you feel the advisory board's hands-off approach serves the national organization of Alcoholics Anonymous properly?
4. Do the Midtown chapter's actions harm the relationship between the national organization and the religious organizations that host Alcoholics Anonymous meetings?

Relationships with Religious Organizations

The advisory board should be somewhat concerned about not only the well-being of its members in the Midtown chapter, but also the relationships that are maintained with religious organizations that are currently hosting Alcoholics Anonymous meetings. Religious organizations that have now banned the Midtown chapter from meeting in their churches may now be less likely to host future chapters or recommend Alcoholics Anonymous to individuals that could benefit from being involved with such an organization. Publicly, the national organization's reputation may suffer if the public begins to take a dim view on the advisory board's hands-off approach as uncaring or unresponsive to alleged cultlike activities. While the advisory board may be taking a hands-off approach and may be free from potential litigation, it may also suffer from negative publicity and declining membership.

Phase IV — Third Issue

You have been informed that the "leader" of the Midtown chapter that was suspected of promoting cultlike activities has died (Fisher, 2007). However you are not sure if the chapter will continue its questionable practices now that the leader who instigated these activities is gone (Fisher, 2007).

Questions that should be asked by the advisory board at this phase:

1. Should the advisory board take a public stand on the issue of the Midtown chapter?
2. Should an advisory board member or members visit the Midtown chapter to see how its meetings are conducted?
3. If any advisory board members do visit the Midtown chapter's meeting, should they be open to the members about their visit or should the advisory board members infiltrate the open meeting anonymously?
4. Ultimately the question remains: Should the advisory board do anything at this point?
5. If cultlike activities have occurred at the Midtown chapter, does the advisory board bear any type of moral or ethical responsibility for what occurred to its members in that local chapter?

Does the Advisory Board Really Want to Know?

Once an organization truly understands what is occurring underneath its name and therefore it auspices, what are the moral and ethical obligations? With the dispersed and nebulous nature of Alcoholics Anonymous, it is very difficult for anyone to successfully litigate or bring criminal charges against the advisory board, since it officially has chosen to have no oversight over the local chapters. Granted, if the advisory board were to choose to incorporate the organization, it would have to put controls in place for proper oversight of the local chapters.

The issue therefore becomes this: What does the advisory board feel is its ethical and moral obligation to its membership? It has been established in the organization structure that there may not be anything official that the advisory board could do to the Midtown chapter, but there are other actions that the advisory board could take that would be unofficial and could allow the national organization to operate as it was intended. The first item that comes to mind is to find out exactly what is going on in the local chapter. This can be done with the advisory board member attending a couple of meetings either openly (which may dissuade future behavior from occurring) or covertly as a new member. If illegal actions are occurring, then this should be reported to law enforcement officials. If the behavior or culture of the local chapter is in direct violation of the national organization's twelve-step program, then the advisory board can use public relations to denounce the local chapter's actions and contact recovery specialists in the area to refer people to chapters that are in good standing with the national organization. The advisory board can also establish a list of chapters that are known to be in violation of the twelve-step program and make this list public. While these steps are not punishing in nature, the steps are intended to provide safety and guidance for its membership. These action steps also provide some reassurance to the public that the advisory board does care about its membership and the twelve-step program.

Recommendations and Concluding Remarks

This case study is unique in that Alcoholics Anonymous is not structured like a traditional organization. Decentralized organizations are at risk of individuals taking advantage of the fact that there is no true accountability if a local chapter behaves unethically. Organizations that have no formal structure or oversight should consider what options are available to them that do not rely on traditional litigation or law enforcement officials.

The advisory board members appeared to have taken no action to discover if the allegations about the Midtown chapter had any basis in truth. There are methods that the advisory board could have taken to discover what was occurring in the Midtown chapter that still would have preserved anonymity. Researchers frequently use unobtrusive observation methods to collect data either by being a nonparticipant observer (simply watching) or by being a participant observer. By using either of these techniques, the advisory board could have obtained a more clear and concise picture of what behaviors and actions were taking place at the Midtown chapter.

While the alleged actions of the Midtown chapter are considered reprehensible, the actions do not appear to be illegal, according to the penal code. The sexual conduct appeared to be consensual among adults of legal age. Even civil litigation actions would probably have had no results in stopping the alleged actions from occurring in the Midtown chapter. The main question, however, remains whether the advisory board was ethically bound to take action if it felt the twelve-step program was being used in a corrupt manner to recruit sexual partners. The only people that can answer that question are the advisory board members themselves.

Chapter 5

United Network for Organ Sharing — Falsifying Lists of Patients Needing Organs — 2008

Phase I — Situation

You are a director at the United Network for Organ Sharing (UNOS), which is a private, non-profit organization that has a contract with the federal government to manage the nation's organ transplant system. The UNOS mission is to make organs more readily available and more efficiently transported. It aims to do this through uniting the community by means of education, technology, and policy development in order to benefit patients. Every organ match is monitored to ensure that organ allocation policies are followed; a national transplant waiting list is maintained, along with a database with all dates pertaining to each transplant event that takes place in the United States. The purpose of the organization is to develop policies that make optimum use of the limited number of organs available for transplant (United, 2013).

An online database, UNET, collects, stores, analyzes, and publishes all data having to do with the waiting list of patients, the matching of organs, and the transplants. The system maintained by UNOS enables hospitals, and doctors who perform transplants, to register patients, match available organs with patients, and manage the time-sensitive data every step of the way (United, 2013).

Notwithstanding the scope of UNOS, there are some areas of organ transplantation that are outside of its control, specifically, the falsifying of records to circumvent the protocols and controls established by UNOS and federal data submission regulations.

Questions that should be asked by the directors at this phase:

1. What are your main priorities in terms of transplantation?
2. Do you have the resources and expertise to meet your mission adequately?
3. How will you interact with hospitals when regulating the transplantation process?
4. What protocols does the organization have to address the actions of other organizations or people that fall outside of the control of UNOS?

Potential Issues for Public Relations

With UNOS providing such a wide range of services and being under contract with the federal government to administer those services, the public perception may be one of complete control over all processes relating to organ transplantation. You may face potential public relations issues in overcoming the perception that the organization is responsible for matters that are technically outside of its control, such as dealing with the falsifying of records or circumventing federal data submission regulations.

Phase II — First Issue

During a routine audit in 2005, you discovered doctors and officials at St. Vincent Medical Center (St. Vincent) incorrectly matched a Saudi Arabian national with a liver that should have been reserved for a higher priority patient elsewhere. Priority on the transplant list is based upon factors such as the time it takes to travel between the donor and the recipient, the time the recipient has been on the list, the donor's blood type, and the recipient's medical urgency. The Saudi Arabian national who received the transplant was listed as 52nd on the transplant list. A patient at UCLA Medical Center was higher on the transplant list at the time this incident occurred. In addition, the Royal Embassy of Saudi Arabia paid a full $339,000 for the transplant and hospital stay, which is 25 percent to 30 percent higher than the amount insurance and government programs would have normally paid the hospital.

The audit revealed hospital staff members and doctors apparently ignored protocol and falsified numerous documents in an effort to hide their misdeeds. In response to the circumstances and allegations, Dr. Douglas Hanto, chief of the transplant division at Beth Israel Deaconess Medical Center, said that it was "totally unconscionable" to move one patient up on the donor list over another for any consideration other than medical (Ornstein, 2005).

Questions that should be asked by the directors at this phase:

1. Why did it take you two years to identify the breach in protocol and falsification of records?
2. Should your organization consider more frequent or unannounced audits?
3. Have there been other incidents, within St. Vincent or at other hospitals, involving breach of protocol or falsification of organ transplant records?
4. How will you work with state and federal officials to ensure both fairness and integrity in the organ transplant process subsequent to these findings?
5. What impact could this incident have on potential organ donors?
6. Should you consider suspending the liver transplantation program at St. Vincent pending completion of reviews and investigations by all entities concerned (i.e., internal hospital review, UNOS review, and federal review)?

Potential Issues for Public Relations

This incident will undoubtedly receive considerable media coverage, be it general — in the reporting of the facts — or sensational — in the reporting of the circumstances surrounding the incident and potential legal issues that may arise. St. Vincent will more than likely receive a good deal of negative publicity concerning this matter.

There may be legal issues involving the actions of hospital staff and doctors or lawsuits from patients who were compelled to spend a longer time on the waiting list, resulting in potential further medical or emotional problems.

The public relations issues of St. Vincent may very well directly reflect on UNOS, if the perception by the general public is that the hospital is responsible for a lack of corporate or institutional control in this situation.

Based on the audit and allegations regarding falsifying of documents with the involvement of hospital staff and doctors, St. Vincent will have to deal directly with the fallout from this incident, while UNOS will likely have to address the consequences indirectly. The issue of UNOS's competency in fulfilling its mission as the preeminent organization in governance and monitoring of organ donations in the United States may come into question. You will have to be prepared to counter any questions and negative public relations issues related to your involvement, governance, and monitoring of the organ donation process as it relates to this incident.

The credibility of UNOS could be at risk. As a director in the organization responsible for overseeing the nation's organ transplant system, it is imperative for you to ensure that the public at large has a high level of confidence about the services provided, and that the federal government is not put in a position of having to question whether UNOS can adequately perform the requirements under its federal contract. A loss of credibility can result in severe damage to the organization's image and ability to effectively perform its mission, and could result in the loss of its contract with the federal government.

As a director, you should focus on how to clearly state the role and responsibility of UNOS in this incident and separate that role and responsibility from the actions of St. Vincent, its administrators, staff, and doctors, and identify the best way to portray that distinction to the public. Additionally, you should ensure proper documentation is in existence for the organization to have clear roles, responsibilities for oversight, appropriate indemnification for organization personnel performing their duties properly, and that make certain the organization is held harmless when operating within proper guidelines set forth by the organization. You must make a decision, within the authority of UNOS under the government contract, regarding what actions can be taken to punish or sanction St. Vincent as a deterrent against similar incidents in the future.

Phase III — Second Issue

The St. Vincent liver transplant program was created in 1995. Since its creation, and prior to the audit that uncovered the irregularities, there had been 184 liver transplants performed, with 22 of those being performed during the year before the audit. As a result of the audit findings, in 2005, the liver transplant program at St. Vincent was suspended. At the time of the suspension, 75 patients were on the hospital's waiting list (Ornstein, 2005).

In 2006, the federal government indicated it was considering an investigation into possible criminal activity by hospital administrators, doctors, and officers in connection with the breach of protocol and falsification of records. In 2006, UNOS publicly sanctioned St. Vincent, and as part of the sanction, UNOS required St. Vincent to notify 4,000 patients of the punishment designating the hospital a "member not in good standing." The public sanction was unusual in that sanctions in the past were always conducted privately (Ornstein, 2006).

Insurers removed St. Vincent from their list of preferred providers or stopped referring patients for liver transplants at St. Vincent altogether.

Questions that should be asked by the directors at this phase:

1. What repercussions from the federal government, if any, can you expect as a result of the St. Vincent incident?
2. How should hospital staff and doctors who are found to be part of the breach of protocol or falsification of records be handled?
3. How can you determine the extent to which those involved contributed to this situation? When that is determined, how can this information be used to establish disciplinary action?
4. Should executive officers and administrators at St. Vincent be at risk of losing their jobs?
5. What recommendations should you make as options for the patients who are on the liver transplant waiting list at St. Vincent?

Potential Issues for Public Relations

The public relations challenge for UNOS is to avoid the negative attention and image that is being given to St. Vincent. In order to accomplish this, UNOS must show that the actions of St. Vincent were outside of the scope of its oversight and responsibility.

Phase IV — Resolution and Conclusion

The liver transplant scandal and its aftermath proved far-reaching for St. Vincent. The liver transplant program was suspended. Doctors Richard R. Lopez, Jr., and Hector C. Ramos, director and assistant director of the liver transplant program, respectively, volunteered to, or were forced to, resign, with both facing potential criminal charges. St. Vincent has seen a considerable reduction in patients being treated, and faces the possibility of losing federal funding. The negative public relations have been considerable and are ongoing.

UNOS has worked with the US Department of Health and Human Resources — Organ Procurement and Transplant Network to establish a plan of corrective action to be followed by St. Vincent. This plan will also be used as a guide in future related matters to ensure the type of misconduct, breach of protocol, and falsification of federal data submission that will be mitigated or eliminated (HHS, 2006).

Dr. Max Fox, associate director of the Oklahoma Bioethics Center and former chairman of the ethics committee at UNOS, said it best: “Having a system that the public views as equitable and views as worthy of their trust and their investment is really critical to securing the needs of 90,000 people that need transplants.” In light of the St. Vincent scandal, UNOS must continue to build and strengthen the public’s trust in its ability to deliver on its mission.

Chapter 6

World Health Organization — Vaccine Scandal — 2009

Phase I — Situation

You are a top-level administrator of the World Health Organization (WHO), which is a part of the United Nations (World Health Organization, 2012). Your organization is responsible for monitoring illnesses worldwide as well as working on solutions to prevent pandemics from occurring across the globe (World Health Organization, 2012). In the past, some illnesses have been eradicated from the globe by taking an aggressive and universal vaccination program and containment strategy to all of the world's populations (i.e., smallpox) (World Health Organization, 2012). Smallpox was eradicated after World War II between 1966 and 1980, in large part because of the United Nations and national governments cooperating to resolve a common problem (World Health Organization, 2012). Pandemics can be extremely deadly to populations, as shown by the Spanish flu in 1918 that killed between 50 million and 100 million people between 1918 and 1919 (Taubenberger and Morens, 2006).

The H5N1 bird flu, which appeared in 2003, had shown potential to spread rapidly with deadly consequences for the public because there was no vaccine available at that time (Nebehay, 2010). You feel that your organization should be prepared for the next major virus. There is a new virus strain designated as the H1N1 flu, which is more commonly known as swine flu. Your organization is aware of the fact that the H1N1 flu first appeared in Mexico and has resulted in 117,770 people being killed in 213 countries over the past year (Nebehay, 2010). Your organization is supposed to monitor the H1N1 flu and work on a solution to prevent the virus from being spread to other parts of the world. What should your priorities be?

Questions that should be asked by the administrator at this phase:

1. What should your priorities be for your organization?
2. What type of resources can you allocate to the new H1N1 flu?
3. How will you allocate your resources for all of the other issues that the organization currently faces in light of this new H1N1 flu?
4. How will you communicate the concerns of the H1N1 flu to the public and other professional organizations that test for H1N1 flu?
5. How will you interact with other governmental agencies about preventing the spread of the H1N1 flu?
6. Does your organization have the expertise and experience to lead such a project?

Potential Issues for Public Relations

WHO will need to earn the public and government entities' trust if it is going to succeed in its mission of preventing the spread of disease and illness around the world. Your organization needs to be factual and accurate about the predictions of what the spread of the flu could potentially be without exaggerating the possible impact on the world's populations. In addition, the organization will need to be conscious of the costs involved in creating a vaccine for the H1N1 flu, since there are other diseases and viruses (i.e., Ebola) that need research as well to prevent any strains from spreading. As a top-level administrator, you need to understand how real the threat may be so that you can allocate personnel and funding appropriately. How your organization does or does not contend with the H1N1 flu will be a barometer for public opinion about the effectiveness of your organization.

Phase II — First Issue

Your agency has now been involved in the first pandemic in 40 years (Nebehay, 2010). However, you realize that your organization is not certain how deadly the virus is compared to the previous H5N1 bird flu, which killed 364 people and had a 60 percent fatality rate since 2003 (Nebehay, 2010; World Health Organization, 2014). Your organization has released a statement that does not convey the uncertainty of how deadly or widespread the H1N1 flu will be on the world's population, which could lead many governmental officials to believe that the epidemic could be catastrophic to their populations (Nebehay, 2010). Pharmaceutical companies such as GlaxoSmithKline and Sanofi-Aventis have already begun to produce vaccines that governments around the world are already stockpiling (Nebehay, 2010). The vaccines are extremely expensive, and many developing nations will have a difficult time affording new drugs for the potential epidemic (Nebehay, 2010).

Questions that should be asked by the administrator at this phase:

1. How will your organization work with government organizations and pharmaceutical companies to ensure that the population that is the most vulnerable will receive the vaccine?
2. Should you indicate publicly that your organization is uncertain how deadly the virus will be on the population?
3. Are you concerned about the potential conflict of interests that may occur with the pharmaceutical companies?
4. Will your organization attempt to subsidize the costs of the vaccine for poorer countries that will probably have very limited medical resources?
5. Will you stress a targeted approach to highly at-risk populations to get the vaccine first as opposed to what some governments are choosing to do, which is to stockpile the vaccine?

Potential Issues for Public Relations

A non-profit organization should always be wary of any type of situation that could be construed as a conflict of interest. If a non-profit organization is seen enabling a particular party to benefit either monetarily or politically, then the non-profit organization may lose credibility, respect, and negotiating prowess with government entities and the public. In this case study, the non-profit organization is making statements on how deadly or how much a virus could potentially infect the world's populations when in fact there is a great deal of uncertainty about how accurate those statements will be as the event unfolds.

In this case, there will be a certain amount of organization drift that occurs from what may happen (the theory) versus what actually occurs (reality). In this situation the theory is a driving force in what is actually occurring. The theory is that the potential for a virus infecting the population with a deadly (at least 60 percent fatality) rate has been seen with the H5N1 bird flu could be repeated by the H1N1 swine flu. The reality is that the statement has actually impacted both private and public sectors with economic factors. The public sector is impacted by several governments buying expensive stockpiles of vaccines for an illness that may or may not occur in their respective countries.

The costs could be staggering to a developing country with limited resources that have dense populations that could be at risk. The government of such a country has a choice: risk not buying a vaccine and potentially expose the population to a devastating illness (according to a non-profit organization), which could wipe out up to 60 percent (maybe even more) of your people, or prepare for the pandemic, which may require budget cuts in several social programs that are needed by the people in your country. As an administrator of such an organization, there needs to be an understanding about how such statements will influence governments' decisions and the consequences that those decisions could have on the population of underdeveloped nations.

To illustrate the impact upon private sector organizations, the non-profit organization's statements have now created a lucrative market. The organization should be concerned about how they are perceived by not only the public, but also government entities. If the non-profit organization is perceived as being either "in bed" with the private sector corporations or incompetent in their ability to predict and react to pandemics correctly, then any future statements that the organization makes (no matter how valid the statement is) could be called into question by the very entities that the organization relies on so heavily to protect the world's populations. Administrators should be cautious in how they approach certain situations to ensure that there is no appearance of conflict of interest and that the organization is competent to handle wide-ranging crisis.

Phase III — Second Issue

Your organization is now discovering that the H1N1 flu is not nearly as deadly as previously stated (Nebehay, 2010). Governments now have stockpiles of unused vaccines that were extremely expensive to purchase from pharmaceutical companies, and certain developing countries are now extremely critical of your organization (Nebehay, 2010). Only 31 of poorer developing countries have received any supplies of the vaccine, and even then those countries received very limited quantities from your organization (Nebehay, 2010). Some countries are now stating openly that patents on such vital vaccines should be lifted so that they may manufacture their own vaccines in times of crisis (Nebehay, 2010).

Questions that should be asked by the administrator at this phase:

1. How will you address the public about the impact of the N1H1 virus now that it is known not to be as deadly as initially stated by your organization?
2. How will you address the logistical issues that have created a shortage of vaccine for the poorer nations' populations?
3. How will you address the perception of a conflict of interest with the pharmaceutical companies?
4. How will you address the issue of countries wanting the lifting of intellectual property rights from critical pharmaceuticals so that they may produce their own supplies in times of crisis?

Potential Issues for Public Relations and Logistics

WHO overstating how deadly a strain of virus the H1N1 would be cause of the organization to lose credibility. The lack of adequate supplies of vaccine undermined how effectively it can lead in times of a pandemic crisis. The administrator overseeing logistics for WHO should be analyzing the reasons why the vaccine was not delivered to the developing nations that needed it the most. Although it is important to provide information as quickly as possible, and the public will be clamoring for this information, it is equally necessary to ensure that the information provided is as accurate as possible and that any announcements will not induce panic. It would also behoove WHO to work with the pharmaceutical companies to ensure that commercial licensing agreements with the governments of developing nations are in place prior to the next outbreak so that these governments can produce the necessary vaccines in their own country to meet the critical need. By taking this approach, the pharmaceutical companies can safeguard their intellectual property, make some royalties off the production of drugs in countries that have the license (or WHO could pay the royalties itself), the cost of the drugs could be controlled, and the drugs could be distributed in a more timely fashion. This arrangement could also prevent governments from stockpiling supplies of vaccines that may or may not be used. By acting as an advocate for such a licensing arrangement, WHO can dispel any perception of having a conflict of interest with the pharmaceutical companies.

Phase IV — Third Issue

Since the outbreak of the pandemic, it has been discovered that only one dose of the vaccine is required instead of the two doses of vaccine that was originally recommended (Nebehay, 2010). This has resulted in overproduction of the vaccine, unnecessary costs incurred by governments, and an oversupply of vaccine in some countries that were not as heavily impacted by the disease, while underdeveloped countries continue to have limited access to supplies (Nebehay, 2010).

Questions that should be asked by the administrator at this phase:

1. Was the vaccine not thoroughly tested before it was shipped to other countries, since only one dose was required instead of two?
2. What, if anything, should WHO do about the oversupply of vaccine in some countries and the insufficient supply of vaccine in other countries?
3. In the future, what should WHO do about planning for vaccine distribution?
4. Should WHO revise how it is communicating with the public and government entities, in light of the issues regarding public statements made by WHO that induced governments to stockpile vaccine dosages?

Potential Issues for Public Relations and Logistics

The massive amount of oversupply affected the United States economy by more than $260 million, which was lost when 40 million unused vaccine dosages expired

(Strobbe, 2010). This amount will be almost doubled when 30 million more vaccine dosages expire at a later date (Strobbe, 2010). Another reason that there was an oversupply of vaccine was due to production that occurred well after the H1N1 flu epidemic was more or less over (Strobbe, 2010). While the United States can absorb costs of unused vaccines, the public taxpayer is still paying the bill for the vaccines being purchased. These funds could have been used to keep other programs budgeted and funded during the same time period. Other countries that are not as wealthy as the United States will be hard pressed to take such heavy financial losses.

Phase V — Resolution and Conclusion

The number of deaths that have occurred from the H1N1 virus is closer to 284,500 people, which was much higher than originally reported (MyHealthNewsDaily, 2012). Additionally, most of the H1N1 virus cases occurred in African or Asian nations, with 59 percent of the deaths coming from those two continents. (MyHealthNewsDaily, 2012). High-risk populations for the H1N1 virus tended to be younger people, with 80 percent of the deaths reported occurring in people who were under 65 years old (MyHealthNewsDaily, 2012).

Questions that should be asked by the administrator at this phase:

1. Were the countries in Asia and Africa able to get supplies of the vaccine to their at-risk populations?
2. If not, did the deaths occur developing nations or more established countries?
3. How will you resolve the issues in logistics and affordability in underdeveloped countries?

Recommendations and Concluding Remarks

WHO will need to resolve issues in predicting pandemics accurately, develop a plan to communicate effectively with governmental entities and the public, and resolve the problem of distributing vaccines to countries that are poor or underdeveloped. If WHO can successfully set up a licensing arrangement for critically needed vaccines to be produced locally by government entities, this could resolve some of the logistical issues. To preserve the organization's credibility and reputation, WHO will need to improve its communication and predictions on pandemics. Administrators of non-profit organizations should take these lessons to heart because their organizations are capable of causing multiple ripples through the public and several government entities.

Chapter 7

Susan G. Komen for the Cure — Planned Parenthood — 2011

Phase I — Situation

You are a member of the board of directors at the Susan G. Komen Foundation (Komen, 2013). Komen is involved in breast cancer research, education, screening, and treatment. Its mission is to eradicate breast cancer as a life-threatening disease through early detection and effective treatment. Komen funds studies that have had a huge impact on advances in the fight against breast cancer. There has been a 33 percent reduction in deaths due to breast cancer in the United States, an increase in the survival rate for women who have been diagnosed with early stage breast cancer, plus an increase in dollars allocated to research (Komen, 2013).

The Susan G. Komen Foundation is associated with more than 130 corporations as sponsors or partners, including American Airlines, Bank of America, Caterpillar, the Dallas Cowboys football franchise, Dell, Ford Motor Company, Leggett & Platt, Major League Baseball, Macy's Inc., NBC Universal, Ralph Lauren, True Religion Brand Jeans, Walgreens, and General Mills (Komen, 2013).

One of the organizations the foundation provides grant funding to is Planned Parenthood Federation of America (Planned Parenthood). Planned Parenthood and its affiliates serve 5 million women, men, and adolescents per year in approximately 800 clinics throughout the United States. Abortion represents approximately 3 percent of the services provided by Planned Parenthood.

Many of the clinics do not directly provide abortions; however, abortion and abortion funding has long been a contentious political issue. Supporters of Planned Parenthood believe there has been a move by conservative politicians in recent years against abortion and even contraception. There are strong political efforts to prevent groups tied to abortion providers from receiving public or federal funding. Notwithstanding a law that prohibits federal funding from being used for abortions, Planned Parenthood is being targeted by those with anti-choice political agendas (Somashekhar, 2012).

By association, Komen has also become a target. Komen provided grants totaling approximately $680,000 to Planned Parenthood affiliates in 2011 and approximately $580,000 in 2010. Approximately 170,000 breast exams have been paid for by grants from Komen in the past five years (Memmott, 2012).

Most of the services offered by Planned Parenthood are related to prenatal care, pregnancy testing, sexually transmitted diseases, and cancer treatment and prevention, and only 3 percent are related to abortion. Even so, Planned Parenthood is perhaps the most visible target of political efforts to promote the pro-life agenda and challenge abortions (Lowen, 2013).

Questions that should be asked by the board at this phase:

1. What is the opinion of each of your corporate sponsors and partners about the grant funding of Planned Parenthood? Do the politics of abortion influence their support of your organization?
2. In an effort to stay politically neutral, should you consider not providing grant funding to any organization with ties to abortion?
3. What actions can you take to keep the public's focus on your services as the catalyst for research and for advancements in the fight against breast cancer as opposed to a giver of grants that then fund abortions?

Potential Issues for Public Relations

Although the amount of grant money given to Planned Parenthood is a relatively small part of its grant allocation budget, the political portrayal of Komen is that of a substantial contributor to Planned Parenthood. Komen is being drawn into a potential political and public relations problem because of its grant funding to Planned Parenthood and Planned Parenthood's ties to abortion.

Phase II — First Issue

There has been considerable pressure applied to Planned Parenthood, and by association to Komen, to cease any and all ties to abortion. To those who oppose abortion, Komen's association with Planned Parenthood is an implied approval of abortion.

LifeWay Christian Resources, owned by the Southern Baptist Convention, recalled its "Pink Bible" promotion. Sold in retail outlets, a portion of the sales from the Pink Bibles went to Komen to be used in its grant program. LifeWay cancelled the partnership because Komen gave grant funding to Planned Parenthood (Memmott, 2012).

In 2005, South Carolina's Catholic diocese decided to pull out of a local Komen fundraiser. This was the beginning of the Catholic Church's opposition to Komen in the United States. Four more dioceses — in Arizona, Indiana, Florida, and Missouri — spoke out, over the next four years, or stopped monetary donations primarily because of Komen's affiliation with Planned Parenthood (Morgan, 2012). The Atlanta Archdiocese of the Catholic Church said, "Support for Komen amounted to direct cooperation with evil" (Wallis, 2012), in its vituperative denouncement of a local Komen affiliate.

Americans United for Life (AUL), a non-profit organization considered to be the nation's top pro-life legal team, released a 30-page report in 2011 that accused Planned Parenthood of misusing federal funds, along with a host of other illegal activities. The purpose of the AUL report was to give Congress ammunition to investigate Planned Parenthood and to revoke its federal funding. Congress, indeed, opened an investigation requiring Planned Parenthood and its affiliates to produce 12 years of audit reports and other documentation (Bassett, 2011).

Leading up to the 2012 presidential elections, the Republican presidential candidates opposed funding for Planned Parenthood. At some point, all referred to Planned Parenthood as "an abortion provider" or "the nation's largest abortion provider" (Peoples, 2011).

There are a large number of monetary donors and potential donors who are members of religious groups, political groups, or other organizations who object to one particular grant recipient of Komen: Planned Parenthood.

Questions that should be asked by the board at this phase:

1. What would be the advantages and disadvantages of severing your ties with Planned Parenthood?
2. Could the grant funding to Planned Parenthood be better used by clinics specifically devoted to cancer screening and treatment? If so, can you identify alternative service providers in geographic areas currently serviced by Planned Parenthood?
3. How has the opposition to abortion, and by association (rightly or wrongly) to Planned Parenthood and Komen, affected monetary donations you have received?
4. Will monetary donations from your supporters be enough to offset any reduction in monetary donations from those opposed to you?

Potential Issues for Public Relations

The obvious public relations issue is Komen's association with Planned Parenthood and, as a result, growing negative publicity, fueled by political agendas. With the timing squarely within the national political election cycle, more questions and pressure are being put on Komen to discontinue its affiliation with Planned Parenthood. Does Komen value its relationship with Planned Parenthood enough to withstand an onslaught of negative publicity and political pressure from those who oppose abortion?

Phase III — Second Issue

The corporate response to the pressure, direct and indirect, from political and religious groups resulted in your board of directors, in the spring of 2011, beginning a review of grant funding guidelines.

It must be noted that, in January 2011, after an unsuccessful run for governor of Georgia, Karen Handel joined Komen as a consultant and was subsequently hired as a senior vice president for public policy. Her platform while running for governor included advocating for defunding of Planned Parenthood.

On November 29, 2011, your board unanimously voted to adopt new funding guidelines, excluding organizations that were under investigation. Under the new guidelines, to be effective January 1, 2012, if an applicant or its affiliates were found to be under investigation for financial or administrative issues by local, state, or federal authorities, that applicant would not be eligible to receive a grant from Komen. Once cleared of impropriety, an organization and its related affiliates would be able to regain eligibility (Timeline, 2012).

On November 30, 2011, Mollie Williams, senior managing director of community health programs, who oversaw the distribution of more than $93 million in grants, resigned in protest. In December 2011, the Komen board approved a memorandum to be distributed to affiliates denying any connection between the pressure from groups opposed to abortion and the decision to change the grant guidelines.

Komen's president, Elizabeth Thompson, personally informed Cecile Richards, president of Planned Parenthood, of the decision to no longer provide grant funding on December 16, 2011.

Then, on January 31, 2012, the Associated Press reported Komen had discontinued funding to Planned Parenthood. The reason stated was that Komen had adopted new funding guidelines for community grants, excluding eligibility for those organizations under investigation.

On February 2, 2012, Nancy Brinker released a video defending the November 29, 2011, decision and stated that the decision had been miscategorized by critics, and by February 3, 2012, the media reported details about Handel and Brinker's commitment to defund Planned Parenthood and Brinker's connection with and donations to the Republican Party.

The following day, Komen reversed its decision to exclude funding for Planned Parenthood by revising the noneligibility standard to apply only to those organizations under "criminal" investigation (Timeline, 2012).

Questions that should be asked by the board at this phase:

1. How have the events of the past year, specifically the decision to stop funding Planned Parenthood, and subsequent changes to continue funding, affected your relationships with corporate partners and sponsorships?
2. Should consideration be given to terminating the employment of Handel, as her political views may not be compatible with the Komen mission?
3. Should a policy be implemented for review of executive level employees and board members regarding their political views, political activity or connections, and the impact those views or connections may have on their job performance and the mission of Komen?
4. How do you address the appearance of inconsistency and lack of corporate leadership resulting from your organization's actions involving Planned Parenthood over the past year?
5. Are there any organizations currently receiving funding that would be affected by the new guidelines?

Potential Issues for Public Relations

Throughout its history, Komen has successfully maintained the appearance of political neutrality, which was a great asset in allowing people from all backgrounds, religions, and political persuasions to feel comfortable in their support of Komen's mission. The potential public relations issue presents the real possibility of a change in public perception. The perception may very well move from Komen being politically neutral to being politically motivated, regardless of the motivating issue. That would put Komen in a position of being constantly attacked from those with a political agenda. As a result of the circumstances and response to the Planned Parenthood situation, there could be a perception of ineptitude on the part of the leadership within Komen, and questions about whether Komen can remain politically neutral in performing its mission.

Perception can quickly turn into reality, and corporate sponsors and partners may defect, causing considerable damage to Komen's ability to raise funds to advance its mission.

As a board of directors, your options are to live with the actions that have been taken thus far, and ride out the public's and corporate partners' responses to those actions, or to take immediate steps to rebuild trust in Komen's leadership and its commitment to fulfilling its mission, free of political influence.

Phase IV — Third Issue

The consensus of public opinion about Komen's handling of the matter of grant funding to Planned Parenthood was probably best stated by Peg Yorkin, chair and cofounder of the Feminist Majority Foundation, when she said, "Who would want to stay with them? What they've done is incredibly dumb" (Duant, 2012).

The negative publicity resulting from the chain of events from November 29, 2011, through February 3, 2012, was widespread, with considerable negative media coverage and massive negative social media coverage. As a result, there were calls for boycotts of Komen fundraising events and damage to its image. It seems there was public anger and confusion over the decision to stop and then to reinstate funding, both within a very short period of time.

There was an exodus of executives, including Handel resigning her position effective February 7, 2012; Eric Brinker, son of Nancy Brinker and a member of the board of directors, resigning his position in March 2012; Dr. LaSalle Leffall, chairman of the board of directors, resigning his position effective March 31, 2012; Dr. Dara Richardson, CEO of Komen's largest affiliate, Greater New York City, resigning her position effective April 30, 2012; Christine McDonald, CEO of the Oregon and Southeast Washington affiliates, resigning her position effective April 30, 2012; and Katrina McGhee, executive vice president and chief marketing officer of Komen, resigning her position effective May 4, 2012 (Hrywna, 2012). In addition, Elizabeth Thompson, president of Komen, resigned her position effective September 2012, and there were calls for Nancy Brinker to step down.

In a statement, executive vice president and corporate reputation practice head of Harris Interactive Robert Fronk said, "Susan G. Komen for the Cure has in many ways represented the 'gold standard' among non-profits measured in our study, consistently reporting high scores for quality, the willingness to recommend and, most importantly, trust. Now, Komen finds itself near the bottom of the pack on all of these items" (Scandal, 2012).

Questions that should be asked by the board at this phase:

1. In view of defections from the board, executives, and affiliate leadership, should you consider hiring an outside consultant to identify potential replacements?
2. What actions should you take to rehabilitate your image? Should consideration be given to hiring an outside public relations firm?
3. Should you consider establishing a crisis communication plan?
4. How can you convince your corporate partners that future decisions in forwarding your mission will be free of political influence in order to fulfill the mission of the organization?
5. Should you hire an outside fundraising consultant, or bring in new hires, in house, to introduce new fundraising ideas?

Potential Issues for Public Relations

The public relations issue is one of rehabilitation of image, brand, and trust. This Planned Parenthood misstep was exacerbated by the public perception that Komen's decisions were politically motivated. For more than 30 years, Komen has been a top charity. There is a history of good works to draw upon in an effort to repair the public relations damage, provided work is done to defuse the notion that its actions were political, and external voices are organized to help remind people of Komen's legacy (Arnold, 2012).

Phase V — Resolution and Conclusion

Many of Komen's corporate partners are reluctant to leave because their own philanthropic identity is tied up in the partnership. Of its 196 corporate partners, nearly all indicated they were going to remain, but many expressed concern about the political connections of executives and decision makers within the organization and the influence of politics on the mission of fighting breast cancer.

Karuna Jaggar, executive director of Breast Cancer Action, said, "That's an opportunity for Komen, right now, as it evaluates its own giving, to take a look where it's getting its money and the standards it's going to apply to that, not only the standards that its applying to the gift-giving" (Terkel, 2012).

Komen suffered a considerable decline in the perception of its leadership, its brand equity declined, its image was tarnished, and support for its signature fundraiser, "Race for the Cure," suffered. The organization must continue to address the perception of its leadership capability. This has to be accomplished in the appointment of executive level management, affiliate management, and board members to replace those who have resigned.

Komen's actions in response to pressure resulting from its association with Planned Parenthood revealed how public opinion appeared to reveal issues with the executive board's decision making, since the organization changed positions on certain policies. It also appears that they were not prepared to deal with the impact of social media (i.e., Facebook and Twitter). Cecile Richards said, "I absolutely believe the exposure on Facebook and Twitter really drove a lot of coverage by mainstream media. I've never seen anything catch fire like this" (Lynch, 2012).

The dysfunctional handling of crisis management must be rectified. Hiring an outside crisis management firm or hiring an in-house crisis management specialist can accomplish this. Social media management must also be addressed, not only in handling negative press through that medium, but as a source of positive promotion directed by Komen.

The focus should be on the mission to erase breast cancer through research, education, screening, and treatment. There should be a complete separation between personal political preferences and outside pressure, political or otherwise, in advancing its mission moving forward.

On June 17, 2013, Judith A. Salerno replaced Brinker as CEO. From a public relations and perception standpoint, this may be the ultimate change that allows Komen to move forward and regain its status in the world of non-profit organizations, provided it can reestablish the commitment to its mission.

Chapter 8

Lance Armstrong Investigated by Federal Prosecutors — Public Relations Damage — 2011

Phase I — Situation

You are a director of a large non-profit organization that has a mission to raise funding for cancer research and awareness. Your organization was founded in 1997 by Lance Armstrong, who is a cancer survivor and a sports celebrity for winning multiple Tour de France titles between 1999 and 2005 (Livestrong, 2012). Since 1997, your organization has raised $325 million to support the organization's mission (Livestrong, 2012).

While the fundraising for cancer research and to raise cancer awareness has been strong, the organization has had several media reports about the founder that have been less than helpful to the organization's image. Throughout the history of your organization, the founder's personal life has been in the tabloids with his divorce from his wife in 2003 (Silverman, 2006) and his yearlong relationship with a celebrity that ended in 2004 (Fox News, 2009). In 2007, a story was published that the founder had tested positive for erythropoietin (EPO) in 1999 (Selthoffer, 2007). This is not the type of image that your organization needs for fundraising efforts. You believe strongly in your organization, the organization's mission, and the belief that the funding is truly bettering society by funding research to combat cancer.

Questions that should be asked by the administrator at this phase:

1. How will you adjust fundraising efforts in light of the negative press that the founder is currently facing?
2. What is your strategy for carrying forth the mission of the organization?
3. Are there strategies that the director can pursue that may alleviate some of the negative press that the founder has been facing?

Potential Issues for Public Relations

It is always beneficial to have a celebrity as a founder of the organization if the celebrity has a good public image. However, if the celebrity generates negative publicity, funding could be jeopardized and the organization can suffer, particularly if the public determines that its donation can go elsewhere, in this case, the eradication of cancer. In the case of organizations that combat cancer, there are not only several non-profits competing for funding, but also private and governmental entities as well that solicit funds from all types of donors (i.e., American Cancer Society, University of Texas M.D. Anderson).

Maintaining a positive image for the organization is critical to encourage donors to continue to support the organization, particularly since the image of this organization is closely intertwined with the founder. One strategy that the director may pursue is find another celebrity (or group of celebrities) to vocally support your organization's fundraising efforts for cancer research and awareness, which may offset some of the negative publicity that the founder has been facing.

Phase II — First Issue

You learn that more negative media reports are about to be released about the founder of your organization. Your founder has been linked by reporters to a doctor that has once been banned in Italy for providing performance-enhancing drugs to cyclists (Associated Press, 2011). You are concerned that the image of the founder associating with such a controversial individual will damage your organization's image and limit your ability to raise funds. As the top administrator of the organization, you will need a plan to lessen the negative impact of the reports on donations to your organization.

Questions that should be asked by the administrator:

1. How much public relations damage could be caused by these reports?

2. As the director of the organization, should you discuss the matter with the original founder?
3. What type of action is needed by the organization to negate the news reports?
4. How much will these reports affect your donations, and does a new tactic for bringing in different donors need to offset any potential decline in donations to the organization?

Phase III — Second Issue

The negative media reports are continuing to be an issue. As the director, you have now learned that Lance Armstrong is under investigation for possible performance-enhancing drug involvement (Levinson and Novy-Williams, 2011). The nature of the allegations can severely hurt the organization, whether or not the allegations are proven true by the investigators. You begin to formulate strategies that will assist the organization in weathering the coming storm of negative media attention and public perception problems. You wonder how the organization's image can be separated from the founder's public image if the negative public image cannot be overcome and donations dry up over the public relations issue.

Questions that should be asked by the administrator at this phase:

1. What other potential negative news reports could possibly be generated about the founder?
2. Should the organization begin to distance itself from the founder?
3. What strategy should the organization take in regard to public relations?

How Much Damage Can the Organization Incur?

Donations and credibility of the organization can be seriously hampered if the public associates a negative image with the founder. As stated by Fredrix and Liedtke:

> Yet everything the seven-time Tour de France champion has created is now threatened by a new opponent: a federal investigation. Philanthropy experts say the foundation, in particular, is at risk of losing future donations if the namesake and chairman is dragged down in scandal. (2010)

Since the founder and the organization are tightly coupled, there is a high probability that donations will be negatively affected:

> At least 10 percent to 20 percent of that support might be lost if the allegations prove true, said Doug White, academic director at New

> York University's Heyman Center for Philanthropy and Fundraising. ... White said he based the estimate on other major charities that have faced public discredit. Livestrong may be in even greater danger because "he is that charity," White added. (Levinson and Novy-Williams, 2011)

What Doug White does not address is the possibility that even if the founder is dropped from the investigation, a negative public image can still persist because there was no positive outcome. Without a positive outcome, it will be difficult to overcome doubts that donors may potentially have about the celebrity and the organization that bears his name. However, if the organization maintains a strong mission, good personnel, and manages its financing well, this issue can be overcome. An example would be the recent bad publicity that Tiger Woods received that did not appear to negatively impact his Tiger Woods Foundation, which focuses on education (Fish, 2012).

What Options Are Open to the Director?

The director of the organization has several options if donations begin to severely decline. Launching a positive public relations campaign to support the image of the founder is an option. However, if the campaign is unsuccessful or other issues with the founder are raised by external entities, this strategy could backfire and place the organization in an even worse public relations position.

Another option open to the director is to change the name of the organization and create a naming rights policy for the organization. While changing the name of the organization may be difficult, it is still a viable option to support the organization's mission and yet distance itself from negative public perception. The branding of the organization will have to start over from scratch and compete against other established organizations for the same donor dollars. This strategy may have a good, long-term effect, but in the short term it could severely hurt the organization.

The director has the option of giving the founder less of a role in the organization. This can provide the organization with the appearance that it operates independently of the founder and may eventually decouple the organization from the founder's public image.

> "They are not going to be able to thrive if the person who is the spirit behind it is in trouble," said Ken Berger, CEO of Charity Navigator, which analyzes more than 5,000 non-profits in the U.S. "It is just going to devastate them." (Fredrix and Liedtke, 2010)

However, the founder at present appears to be able to convince donors to give to the charity. His disappearance from the face of the organization may hurt short-term donations.

The other option is to do nothing and operate the organization as usual and see how donations fare. The donations may drop off temporarily and then go back to their pre-crisis levels over a short amount of time. Only time will tell on how the public will react to the celebrity's status.

Phase IV — Third Issue

You are now beginning to see a high volume of news articles and investigative reports that show the founder in a negative tone. Many of the founder's former teammates and friends have made damaging allegations that the founder used performance-enhancing drugs while he was competing (Gifford, 2012). Other reports accuse the founder of being a bully, which casts his personality into a very negative light (Sager, 2011). In addition, there is some speculation on whether or not the founder was guilty of witness tampering in a federal investigation (Stokes, 2011). While corporate donations are up, individual donations appear to have dropped since the federal investigation started (Gifford, 2012).

Additionally, a reporter has pointed out that since 2005 the mission of your organization has changed from researching cures for cancer to funding programs for awareness of cancer (Gifford, 2012). This change in mission and scope could impact how potential donors will feel about donating funds to the organization. The donors to and sponsors of your organization should be made aware of where and how those financial donations are being expended with regard to the organizational mission. Now there are two issues to contend with: First, how will you combat your founder's negative image to increase donations to your organization; and second, how will you promote and clarify the change of your organization's mission to donors?

Questions that should be asked by the administrator at this phase:

1. What public relations strategies should be put into place at this point to lessen the negative reports that are being dispersed throughout the media about the founder?
2. Does there need to be a change in strategy now that the organization's focus has changed?
3. With the change in focus for the organization, does there need to be a different mix of personnel within the organization?
4. What will be the pitfalls of changing the focus of the organization from cancer research to cancer awareness?
5. How will the organization separate itself from other cancer awareness nonprofit organizations to get donations from both individuals and corporations?

Options Open to the Director

The director will need to restate that the organization is focused on its mission of raising money for cancer research and will need to avoid being intertwined with negative publicity toward the founder. The director will need to make sure that all money has been accounted for and state publicly how donations are being expended (marketing, research, etc.) Additionally, if the organization's mission has changed, the perception of how donors' money is being spent may alter how much donors are prepared to give toward the organization's new focus. While making people aware of cancer is important, it does not have the perceived impact of funding research to eradicate cancer. If individuals or corporations begin to perceive that their donations are not being allocated in the manner they were led to believe, the organization will have an issue with credibility. The director should attempt to convince the founder to tone down the rhetoric in the media so that additional negative media reports will not be as forthcoming in the future. As long as the founder continues to spar with the media, the negative reports will continue, as well as an increased possibility of an Internal Revenue Service (IRS) audit or the launching of a state attorney general's investigation. This is a contest the founder will ultimately not be able to win and, in fact, can cause further damage to his foundation's fundraising efforts.

Phase V — Fourth Issue

The director has learned that even though the federal investigators are closing their investigation, the U.S. Anti-Doping Agency is ramping up their investigation on whether or not the founder used performance-enhancing drugs in the sport of cycling (Murphy, 2012). How should the director proceed with the organization in light of another potentially damaging investigation?

Questions that should be asked by the administrator at this phase:

1. What impact will the U.S. Anti-Doping Agency investigation have on Livestrong?
2. What happens if the U.S. Anti-Doping Agency rules against the founder?
3. Is legal action against the U.S. Anti-Doping Agency worth the time, effort, and money?

Issues Raised

This case study brings up the potential worst-case scenario for a non-profit organization that does not result in any civil liabilities or criminal charges. Unfortunately, an organization that is so closely tied with its founder can be negatively impacted if its founder is targeted negatively by the media, law enforcement, legal community, and the general public. Donors are not immune to this type of negative publicity and the top administrators of such a non-profit organization will need to see how they can limit any negative connotation of founder's image from hurting the organization's donations or mission. How the founder and top administrators interact and plan for overcoming any such issues will be the keys to success in generating a positive position for the organization in relation to the public.

Phase VI — Resolution and Conclusion

Lance Armstrong attempted several maneuvers to nullify the U.S. Anti-Doping Agency's investigation by stating that this was the jurisdiction of the International Cycling Union (ICU) and apparently by asking U.S. Rep. Jim Sensenbrenner to lean on the U.S. Anti-Doping Agency to drop their investigation (Cohrs, 2012; Rovell, 2012). The U.S. Doping Agency ended up winning in court against Armstrong, which forced him to go through arbitration (Rovell, 2012). On August 24, 2012, Armstrong announced that he would not fight the charges in arbitration with the U.S. Anti-Doping Agency (Rovell, 2012). On the same day, the U.S. Anti-Doping Agency announced they would strip Armstrong of his seven Tour de France titles and issue a lifetime ban for doping activities (Rovell, 2012). The International Olympic Committee announced that it would review whether to strip Armstrong's bronze medal that he won in the 2000 Olympic Games (Rovell, 2012). The ICU President Pat McQuaid said he was "shocked and angry" by the information and evidence in the U.S. Anti-Doping Agency's report (Telegraph, 2012). Armstrong would eventually be stripped of the Olympic bronze medal, forced back to court against SCA Promotions, has lost endorsements, and, at the time of this printing, is being litigated by the federal government for violations of the False Claims Act (Vinton, 2014).

Recommendations and Concluding Remarks

The authors would highly recommend that the administrators of the non-profit organization return to their original mission and fund research that will potentially cure cancer. Just funding areas that promote the awareness of cancer does not have the same perception as actually working to resolve an issue.

Additionally, the authors would recommend that the administrators distance themselves from the founder, unless the founder's public perception increases favorably. As stated by Salter:

> "Even if Armstrong isn't ultimately charged, a prolonged investigation that sullies the foundation's public face could take a toll on its fund-raising and, most important, its credibility. Will corporate sponsors and donors differentiate between the founder and his foundation? While Ulman awaits the outcome, he's being forced to wrestle with a critical question about his boss: Is Livestrong's greatest asset also its greatest risk?" (Salter, 2010)

To put a new face on the organization, the director may have other survivors of testicular cancer be more involved with public relations for the organization, as well as have other celebrities endorse the organization's mission. With the current negative media reports that are attributed to the founder, it may do well for the organization to get more funding from independent sources and possibly change the name of the organization if a negative stigma begins to be attached to the Livestrong name. The news stories that show the founder in a positive light should be highly distributed to offset some of the negative media reports that are currently circulating. Since the founder does visit cancer patients on a regular basis and has a good disposition for the media when making these visits, the founder could make more visits to these types of environments and end media interviews for anything else that does not involve Livestrong.

A negative public image can cause an immense amount of damage to a non-profit organization, which will dissipate funding from both corporations and individuals. To combat a negative public image, the administrators in charge of a non-profit organization will need to find a way to change the public image (and the organization) to a positive image, which will increase funding for the mission of the organization. Since resources are finite and there are only so many non-profit organizations that will be able to tap into donor generosity, administrators will need to find a way to separate themselves from the pack of non-profit organizations that have similar causes and missions.

III

MISMANAGEMENT OF FUNDS AND EMBEZZLEMENT

Chapter 9

American Cancer Society—Embezzlement—2000 and 1980s

Phase I — Situation

You are a senior level administrator at the American Cancer Society. The American Cancer Society, which was established in 1913, is a nationwide voluntary health organization dedicated to eliminating cancer. The society is organized into 12 geographical divisions of both medical and lay volunteers operating in more than 900 offices throughout the United States, including Puerto Rico. Its home office is located in the American Cancer Society Center in Atlanta, Georgia. Its activities include providing grants to researchers, running public health advertising campaigns, and organizing projects such as the Relay for Life and the Great American Smokeout. It operates a series of thrift stores to raise money for its operations (Irmawan, 2013).

However, as with all large non-profit organizations, they are not without challenges in managing the activities of the organization, its people, and its satellite operations. The vast size of the organization and the amount of funds that flows annually through the organization pose substantial challenges in financial control and image management. We are going to step through two different financial control crises that illustrate how difficult it is stay on top of all your board members, personnel, and financial processes to ensure the running of a stable and highly ethical organization.

In the 1980s, an employee of a New York branch was indicted for a tax fraud scheme that allowed individuals to fraudulently claim charitable tax deduction contributions, much of which had been returned to them. In 2000, the chief administrative officer of the American Cancer Society of Ohio pleaded guilty to embezzling $7 million from the organization (Bird, 1985).

Let us look at the board, appointed executives, and their organizational controls and processes to see what we can learn about these financial crimes to understand how to prevent and avoid such financial mismanagement in our non-profit organizations. In the New York chapter incident, the former head of fundraising for the American Cancer Society's New York City branch, Miriam Grubard, was indicted for masterminding a scheme that enabled contributors to take nearly $4 million in illegal tax deductions. Federal officials said contributors wrote checks to the American Cancer Society and then received cash kickbacks for 90 percent of the amount of the checks. The contributors would deduct the full amounts on their income tax returns, using the canceled checks to support their claims. Grubard was dismissed in July 1984. In the 1960s, according to the indictment, Grubard took direct charge of fundraising of the Bernice Leavitt-Joseph Tookel Memorial Branch of the American Cancer Society, the largest branch in New York City. The indictment charged that Grubard had carried out the scheme through annual fall dinner-dance casino parties. The authorities said the manipulations reached their height from 1979 to 1983. The contributors involved in the scheme were indicted with helping Grubard with tax evasion, and five others were named in the indictment as taking the fraudulent tax deductions. The tax fraud was uncovered by a staff person under the American Cancer Society's whistleblower policy, who worked with Grubard for a short while. Grubard was convicted of fraud, the American Cancer Society was not accused of wrongdoing, and none of the directors were found to be violating their fiduciary duties (Bird, 1985).

The second case involved the embezzlement of $9.7 million by Daniel Wiant, the chief administrative officer of the Ohio division of the American Cancer Society. In May 2000, the FBI alerted the American Cancer Society that Wiant had transferred $6.9 million to an Austrian bank account. Prior to the large transfer, Wiant, had written checks totaling $650,000 to personal bank accounts he had set up. The amounts were expensed as consulting fees. After the revelations of the transfer, an American Cancer Society spokesperson had said that their financial procedures were already in place to prevent embezzlement of funds (Tribune News Services, 2000). However, every time there is a breach of the organization's internal controls, it always warrants another review to see if there are ways to strengthen the internal controls even further.

Questions that should be asked by the administrator at this phase:

1. What type of recordkeeping did the national office require in American Cancer Society branches or divisions?
2. Where were the internal controls to document the amount of the donations and their deposit in the American Cancer Society bank accounts?
3. What were the separation of duties between the people soliciting, collecting, and depositing the donations?

4. Why were the reports of the amount raised at the annual dinner-casino events not reconciled to the bank reports of the American Cancer Society's New York City branch?
5. Why did the person performing the monthly reconciliation of bank accounts not catch these fraudulent transactions?
6. What might be the impact on the organization if this tax fraud scheme had been widespread throughout the entire American Cancer Society?
7. In the Wiant matter, why did the financial controls in place to prevent Wiant's embezzlement not detect the illegal transfer of funds?
8. Where were the procedures such as audit committee reviews or budget committee cost and expenditure controls needed to prevent these of embezzlement schemes?
9. Should new background checks have been performed on employees?
10. Should a periodic review of internal controls be performed?
11. In the Wiant case, how did one employee transfer so much money without anyone else having to approve the transaction? Should a dual signature or authorization be required on amounts that are over a certain threshold?

Potential Public Relations Issues

The fact that high-level personnel such as Grubard and Wiant were involved in these criminal activities could result in significant negative publicity, lack of trust, considerable scrutiny of the organization, and a long-term public relations recovery. It would undoubtedly have a negative impact on the American Cancer Society, the local American Cancer Society offices, and their ability to successfully fundraise to continue the organization's mission.

Initially, the American Cancer Society can anticipate damage to the image of and trust in the organization by such criminal activity from a high-level fundraising official of the New York City division of the American Cancer Society, and from the chief administrative officer of the Ohio branch. An investigation should be initiated, perhaps first internally, focusing on an audit of the organization's accounting practices and policies, a full reconciliation of the organization's committed donations versus collected revenues in the Grubard matter, and a full review of the organization's internal controls in the Wiant matter. Depending on the depth of the initial findings, it may be necessary for an outside independent investigator to take over the process to avoid any appearance of a cover-up and to ensure an objective investigation.

Phase II — First Issue

In the matter of Grubard, it was clear that the American Cancer Society had an employee that had been trained or instilled with the idea that matters that did not appear to be ethical or illegal were to be reported only to higher officials to protect the organization. The American Cancer Society's policy of reporting misconduct was well-ingrained into the organization's personnel. In the matter involving the Wiant case, a much stronger response was needed on the part of the American Cancer Society. The American Cancer Society expanded its procedure for background checks of employees (HROT, 2014). It also engaged PricewaterhouseCoopers, one of the large accounting firms, to conduct a fraud audit and to review the organization's internal controls (Bird, 1985).

Questions that should be asked by the administrator at this phase:

1. How could the issue of recordkeeping and accounting discrepancies go unnoticed or unchecked by the organization?
2. What internal procedures, if any, were or are in place for the review of consulting expenses submitted by Wiant, and who approves those reports?
3. Does the American Cancer Society use an outside firm to conduct audits of financial reports and accounting practices? If not, should you consider using such a firm?
4. Is the American Cancer Society's culture of accountability and transparency well established?
5. Is everyone in the organization adequately trained in the values and code of ethics of the organization?
6. Do the board members understand their fiduciary responsibilities?
7. Does the organization have a whistleblower policy?
8. Is the American Cancer Society's established whistleblower policy not well understood by the board members and staff members?

Potential Issues for Public Relations

Public relations issues concerning the lack of control of division offices could have a negative effect on the ability of the American Cancer Society and its local offices to effectively work with their local corporate partners and to secure donations.

Phase III — Third Issue

The board of directors should look at its role in this matter; what fault lies with the board? Should the board have taken a stronger role in supervising its personnel and state divisions? The American Cancer Society had to admit that it was unaware that Wiant had a criminal record that included a two-year prison term in Hawaii (Epstein, 2010). Wiant was in charge of the computer and financial systems at the Ohio Division of the American Cancer Society (Epstein, 2010).

Questions that should be asked by the administrator at this phase:

1. Do all the board of directors and officers know their obligations and act on them for the good of the organization? Are there regular board orientation sessions?
2. Has the board developed a culture of accountability and transparency?
3. Is the statement of values and the code of ethics ingrained into the entire organization?
4. Does the organization have a process to thoroughly review candidates before making a hiring decision?
5. What kind of due diligence did the American Cancer Society preform on all its hires?
6. Did it check the credit history of its employees?
7. Did it check the educational attainment of its employees?
8. Did it check the criminal history of its employees?
9. Did it check the references for all its employees?
10. Is a clear description given of the audit committee's duties?
11. Are there sufficient financial controls to prevent employee misuse or funds?

Potential Issues for Public Relations

When a board's ability to oversee its organization's operations comes into question, the public will increase its scrutiny of the organization. The board will need to implement damage control through effective public relations to demonstrate that corrections have been made and that effective oversight measures are in place in the organization.

Phase IV — Resolution and Conclusion

After Wiant's arrest, the American Cancer Society board of governors implemented an aggressive approach to shore up its financial and internal controls to prevent employee misuse of funds and criminal behavior. The actions taken by the board after the Wiant matter included the following:

1. It expanded its procedures on background checks on employees.
2. It engaged the accounting firm of PricewaterhouseCoopers to conduct a fraud audit and to review the organization's internal controls.

Chapter 10

United Way — Misuse of Funds by Executives — 1992

Phase I — Situation

You are a senior-level administrator at the United Way of America (UWA). The UWA is a non-profit organization that serves as a service and training center for local United Way offices throughout the United States. The aim of UWA and its local offices is to identify and resolve local issues, in partnership with community-based institutions such as schools, financial institutions, businesses, development corporations, and faith-based organizations, with a focus on education, health, and basic income and needs.

Under the guidance of William Aramony, president of UWA from 1970 to 1992, the annual donations grew from $787 million in 1970 to more than $3 billion in 1990, with UWA overseeing a US network of 2,100 independent local United Way agencies that, in turn, supported 47,000 charities through fundraising and donations (Pederson, 2001).

In late 1990, amid ongoing separation issues involving Aramony and his wife, an anonymous letter was received at UWA, on UWA letterhead, alleging misuse of UWA money and other improprieties by Aramony (Glaser, 1994).

Questions that should be asked by the administrator at this phase:

1. Should there be a formal investigation of the allegations against Aramony, and, if so, what form should the investigation take (i.e., internal, external, criminal)?
2. What might be the impact on the organization if these allegations are found to be true?
3. Other than Aramony, are there other members of your organization who should be held accountable in the event these allegations are true?
4. What are the advantages and disadvantages of making the allegations public at this time?
5. Should law enforcement be contacted at this time? Or should there be an internal investigation first, and by whom should it be conducted?
6. Should the organization's insurance carrier be contacted?
7. Should legal counsel be contacted?

Potential Public Relations Issues

Aramony, the high-profile corporate face of the organization, could very well be embroiled in a public scandal concerning his marriage and improper or criminal activities involving organizational funds. Such a scandal, especially if it involves criminal activity, could result in significant negative publicity, considerable scrutiny of the organization, and a long-term public relations recovery. It would undoubtedly have a negative impact on UWA, the local United Way offices, and their ability to successfully fundraise to continue the organization's mission.

Initially, UWA can anticipate damage to the image of and trust in the organization, and if the allegations, including criminal activity, prove to be true, the damage could be devastating: withdrawal of corporate partners and sponsorships, substantial reduction in donations, and even closure of some local offices. An investigation should be initiated, perhaps first internally, focusing on an audit of the organization's accounting practices and a full reconciliation of the organization's collected revenues and expenditures. Depending on the depth of the initial findings, it may be necessary for an outside independent investigator to take over the process to avoid any appearance of a cover-up.

In the event of possible criminal improprieties, federal law enforcement agencies should be contacted to perform a thorough criminal investigation. Consideration should also be given to suspending or relieving Aramony of his duties, pending the outcome of the investigation(s).

Phase II — First Issue

Internal and external independent and criminal investigations were initiated. The independent investigation found evidence of sloppy recordkeeping and accounting discrepancies. The results of the independent investigation were made public in February of 1992.

In the aftermath, local offices began to disassociate themselves from UWA, and some of the larger offices withheld dues to UWA. Donations dropped sharply. Regional branches across the country reported canceled pledges, and donation drives fell short of expectations (Sontag, 1992). The media attention became overwhelming and overshadowed the good work being done by UWA and its local offices.

Questions that should be asked by the administrator at this phase:

1. Why did recordkeeping and accounting discrepancies go unnoticed or unchecked by the organization?
2. What internal procedures, if any, were or are in place for the review of expense reports submitted by Aramony, and who approves those reports?
3. Does UWA use an outside firm to conduct audits of financial reports and accounting practices? If not, should it consider using such a firm?
4. Does UWA have a code of ethics? If not, should one be established?

Potential Issues for Public Relations

Public relations issues concerning potential strife between UWA and its local offices could grow, which would have a negative effect on the ability of the local offices to effectively work with their local corporate partners and to secure donations (Sontag, 1992).

Phase III — Second Issue

Under the weight of the results of the independent investigation and reaction from local offices and the public, Aramony resigned his position; however, the criminal investigation is continuing. Regarding his resignation, Aramony told the UWA board, "I did not pay enough attention to detail or to the way some of my actions could have been perceived and my personal style could have been perceived by certain people" (Shepard, 1992).

Local offices withheld dues pending resolution of the matter and experienced backlash by way of decreasing donations. The leadership of local offices was faced with the need to reassure donors that their monetary donations would be used toward the mission of UWA and not for the personal use of officers or executives of UWA.

Questions that should be asked by the administrator at this phase:

1. What is the process in place to fill Aramony's position?
2. What steps will be taken to address the concerns of corporate partners regarding possible misuse of UWA money by Aramony?
3. How will the concerns of donors in regard to the safety of their donations be addressed?

4. What support will be given to local chapters struggling to meet campaign goals due to the negative perception of UWA as a result of the Aramony matter?
5. How is the organization going to repair its image and reputation during this time of negative publicity and public opinion?

Potential Issues for Public Relations

Amamony's resignation was beneficial for the organization for the long term. However, in the short term, the his resignation served to increase the media scrutiny and negative publicity surrounding possible impropriety involving donations to local offices and UWA. The increased scrutiny and negative publicity can only increase questions and decrease donations. You must determine how to provide better accountability of funds used by executive-level personnel; however, the most pressing matter at this time is to identify and secure a replacement for Aramony as UWA's president.

Phase IV — Third Issue

The board of directors should look at its role in this matter and determine how it could have provided oversight in carrying out its fiduciary duties. Should the board have received and reviewed some form of reporting regarding executive expenditures?

Questions that should be asked by the administrator at this phase:

1. Did the board authorize Aramony's travel and expenditures?
2. Does the board have appropriate policies and procedures in place to authorize executive-level compensation and expense accounts?
3. What are the legal responsibilities of the board in overseeing the performance and evaluating the position of the president, and what process should be implemented to carry these out?
4. Are board members with conflicts of interest appropriately excluded from the decision-making process to avoid perceived and actual conflicts of interest?

Potential Issues for Public Relations

Questions concerning the lack of oversight by the board add to the increased scrutiny of UWA. With the top executive and the board of directors under question, it is imperative for UWA to use effective public relations to manage and improve its image.

Phase V — Resolution and Conclusion

After Aramony's resignation, the UWA board of directors launched a nationwide search for a new leader and hired Elaine Chao as president and CEO. She came to the position with a reputation for integrity in serving as director of the Peace Corps and proven skills leading large, complex organizations.

One of her first orders of business was to cut her own salary in half, and she declined all perks and special benefits. She worked with volunteers and professionals within the UWA and local offices to restructure the governance framework of the organization, establish a code of ethics, eliminate bloated expense accounts, install financial controls to create transparency in the organization, and personally visit local offices throughout the country to carry the message of reform and accountability (Chao, 2013).

Also under her leadership, the board of directors has been expanded from 37 seats to 45 seats, with 15 seats allocated for members from local offices. The board is also required to meet four times a year instead of the previous two times a year. Six oversight committees have been established, including one ethics committee, and first-class travel has been banned (Marshall, 1993). Chao has said, "My goal at the United Way was to create a new reverence for integrity and respect for supporters."

As a result of the criminal investigation, Aramony was indicted on 53 criminal counts ranging from fraud to engaging in the interstate transportation of fraudulently acquired property to money laundering to filing false income tax returns. He was found guilty on April 3, 1995, his conviction was upheld on appeal for 23 counts, and he was sentenced to 84 months in federal prison (Shapiro, 2011). The UWA is hoping Aramony's sentencing will bring to a close a period of prolonged embarrassment to UWA and allow a new chapter to begin (Arenson, 1995).

Chapter 11

NAACP — Misuse of Funds Question — William F. Gibson — 1995

Phase I — Situation

You are a board member of the National Association for the Advancement of Colored People (NAACP), which was founded in 1909 and is America's oldest and largest civil rights organization. The organization has always fought all forms of racial segregation and discrimination. In addition, it has demanded equal rights for all Americans regardless of race or color. The primary goal of the organization was the full participation of African-Americans and other minorities in the promise of the American dream. The NAACP has 400,000 to 450,000 members and a staff of 181 employees (Berg, 2014).

In the post-civil rights era, the NAACP lost some of its focus and prominence in American society and the political life of the country. Especially in the 1990s, the NAACP went through a period of internal crisis that seemed to threaten its existence. In an attempt to stem the loss of members and to attract more young people, Executive Director Benjamin Chavis-Muhammad tried to open up the association to Black Nationalism. He repeatedly met with Louis Farrakhan, the leader of the Nation of Islam (NOI), and agreed with him on the need for black unity, despite Farrakhan's well-known rabid anti-Semitism. The advances to then NOI sparked heated controversy with the association, and its supporters among the Jewish community were incensed and threatened to withdraw. When Chavis-Muhammad admitted that he had misused funds for personal purposes, he was ousted in 1994. It was determined that the association had accumulated a large debt and was teetering toward bankruptcy. Some commemorators of the day even called for the dissolution of the NAACP and reorganization under a new name (Berg, 2014).

The board of the NAACP hired the accounting firm of Coopers and Lybrand to conduct an audit of the organization's expenditures and financial management controls from January 1989 through August 1994. The audit revealed a large number of questionable expenditures and lack of spending controls over top officers in the organization (Terry, 1995). The findings of Coopers and Lybrand audit of NAACP officers included the following:

The NAACP paid expenses charged to the corporate credit card by the chairman of the board and the executive director without obtaining and analyzing any detailed supporting documentation or backup. Expense records were disorganized and in disarray. No NAACP employee had the authority to question charges by the chairman and executive director (Terry, 1995).

In 1993 and 1994, the board of director's travel costs "were seriously overrun by $80,000, yet no corrective actions were taken." Additionally, Coopers and Lybrand (1995) discovered NAACP officers did not take responsibility for having oversight responsibilities over the personal charges to corporate credit cards made by NAACP executives and employees (Terry, 1995).

Cash advances of up to $12,000 were made to NAACP officers. In one case, a $10,000 cash advance was made in April for a July convention. In another instance, Dr. William F. Gibson, board chairman, received a $10,000 travel advance that was actually a personal loan, later repaid with $300 interest. The audit report stated loans to board members were prohibited in New York state, where the NAACP is incorporated, and there was no written board policy regarding this matter (Terry, 1995).

There was excessive spending, such as the executive director racking up more than $120,000 in limousine rental charges during his tenure. It was found that limos transported Chavis-Muhammad, the executive director, aides, and non-NAACP employees around Washington, DC, and New York at a cost of hundreds of dollars a day (Terry, 1995).

Dr. Gibson stayed in a $1,083 a night suite at a Beverly Hills hotel in the fall of 1994 and ran up a total bill of $4,827 for three nights.

A 14-person NAACP delegation traveled to South Africa in the summer of 1993. Everyone traveled business class, and the NAACP paid $2,700 each at the last minute for three passengers to upgrade their seats from economy class (Terry, 1995).

The auditors recommended 29 ways to improve the NAACP's financial management.

The organization was found to be $3.8 million in debt and in desperate need of contributions to meet its payroll (Bock, 1995).

In addition, Chavis-Muhammad was alleged to have sexual harassment and discrimination charges against him from a former aide. He was accused of using NAACP funds to make a payment to the former aide to silence her after she claimed that she was involved in an adulterous relationship with him. Dr. Gibson was also alleged to have known of the sexual harassment of employees at the organization and the payment to the former aide to induce her to drop legal actions against Chavis-Muhammad. The board of directors was never informed of the expenses being incurred by the executive directors, the chairman of the board, and the other board officers (Bock, 1995). These financial issues were never brought to the attention of the budget committee, the audit committee, or the board.

Questions that should be asked by the board at this phase:

1. Why were the roles of the board chairmen, executive director, and staff not better defined?
2. Why were the budget committee, the audit committee, and the board not informed by the board officers or the staff of these expenditures and the extent of the budget deficit?
3. Why weren't the executive director, the finance officer, and the finance committee members working closely with these officials to stay ahead of the organization's financial condition?
4. How was it that the audit committee was not selecting and adequately supervising the external auditor that conducted the annual financial audit of the organization?
5. Since the audit committee is charged with establishing and overseeing internal controls, why did that not occur?
6. Why did the annual financial statements from the outside auditors give the board no hint of the growing deficit and excessive financial spending?
7. Why did the board fail to use the budget as a management tool to keep budgets realistic and balanced?
8. Why was the board not taking action when the executive director and financial staff did not provide variance reports and cash flow reports to the finance committee and the board?
9. Why was the end-of-year financial report not aggressively reviewed and acted upon to keep the organization fiscally healthy?
10. Since the organization is incorporated in New York, why wasn't the board aware that personal loans to board members were prohibited under state law?

Potential Issues for the Board to Consider

When you have a national organization with the size, stature, and breadth of the NAACP, it is vital that you supervise and hold accountable the executive director and organization officers to the highest standards of ethics. The chairman of the organization has held his position for almost a decade, and it might be appropriate to consider term limits for board officers and board members to provide new leadership on a regular basis. The informal relationship that developed between the executive director and the chairman was too casual to insure good financial stewardship of the organization. The NAACP treasurer's report had been declared too vague when discussing the organization's deficit position. Some of the organization's financial problems stemmed from the group's annual Image Awards program that showed that, while the show had not lost money, it had experienced financial losses from the show's ancillary activities like ticket sales and the sale of advertisements and souvenirs, a clear demonstration of weak financial controls by the board, since the board ran these operations. The organization's weak financial condition also shed light on the fact that the organization lacked financial ratios such as liquidity ratios, cash reserve ratios, current ratios, asset ratios, target liquidity ratios, and funding ratios that all non-profits employ and which the NAACP board members could have used to quickly evaluate its fiscal health.

When there are issues with the chairman of the board, the board officers, and the executive director, the board members must take it upon themselves to demand answers and to investigate matters of management and finances to insure the viability and longevity of the organization. Board members are charged with insuring the organization's finances, and they have a fiduciary responsibility to the donors and members of the organization.

In addition, the board members should have been conducting regular job reviews of the executive director to provide constructive feedback and a development plan for improvement. The members of the organization at their annual meetings should have demanded better answers regarding the organization's finances.

Phase II — Board Action

The executive director was fired after secretly committing up to $332,400 in NAACP funds to settle a sexual harassment claim. At the 1994 annual meeting of the NAACP, Dr. Gibson was removed from office by a one-vote margin and replaced by Myrtle Evers-Williams.

The board voted unanimously that the expenses of Dr. Gibson and all NAACP officers must be line items in the budget, and must be reported to the full board at every meeting. They also initiated a selection process to identify and hire a new executive director for the NAACP. All the organization's corporate credit cards were revoked, and the 64 board members would in the future have to pay their own way to the board meetings (Bock, 1995).

Phase III — The New Road Ahead

Evers-Williams was faced with turning a deeply divided board into a cohesive and effective policymaking board. In addition, she had to rebuild the executive staff and find a competent executive director for the organization who had knowledge of and appreciation for the NAACP history. She also had to repair the organization's tarnished image and quickly reduce its debts so that it could fight for the civil rights and social programs that the organization believed in for the next century. The first step in her long to-do list was choosing an executive director capable of restoring the organization's integrity and winning for it the respect that made it the flagship of the civil rights movement for much of the last century. Everyone was aware that it was the executive director, rather than the chairman who built the NAACP's, public persona and reputation as a legendary fighter for all Americans' civil rights (Berg, 2014).

Phase IV — Resolution and Conclusion

In 1995 Kweisi Mfume, a prominent Democratic congressman from Baltimore and former chairman of the Congressional Black Congress, was elected the new president of the NAACP and its new executive director. Under the leadership of Mfume, the association managed to consolidate its finances and reestablish good relations with its historic allies among liberal groups.

Recommendations and Concluding Remarks

There were many signs that the organization was in distress and that the executive staff, the elected leaders, and many of the board members were not truly paying attention to what was going on in this renowned civil rights organization. It had lost focus on its primary mission of removing the barriers of racial discrimination and prejudice from American life. The NAACP needed to make changes to its financial and asset controls if the organization had hopes of maintaining credibility with the public, making operations more efficient and effective, and being able to work with the confidence of its members, the media, the public, and elected and appointed government officials at all levels. If problems were not addressed with the asset and financial management, the NAACP ran the risk of providing its critics with the ammunition to thwart its efforts to accomplish all the organization's civil rights goals.

Non-profit organizations must realize that just because an organization has non-profit status does not mean that proper controls should not be in place. Quite the contrary, because a non-profit organization is usually heavily reliant on donations or some type of subsidies, it becomes imperative that the organization protects what it currently has as well as what it can potentially have in the form of revenue streams. The question becomes, "Who would want to donate to an organization that has demonstrated that it cannot manage or use its funds in an appropriate manner?" The NAACP now finds itself attempting to answer that very question to its membership, friends, allies, supporters, elected officials, and opponents. This case study in particular should highlight how it is important for board members and administrators to preserve administrative and financial accountability of non-profit organizations if they are to remain effective and viable long into the future. While the good management of the organization is highly important, its reputation in the community and the world is just as important as competent staff and a great balance sheet.

Chapter 12

American Red Cross — Hurricane Katrina — 2005

Phase I — Situation

You are an upper-level administrator for the American Red Cross. The American Red Cross has an organizational mission to assist in emergency situations and support victims in natural disasters as well as providing community support and educational services (American Red Cross, 2012). The organization has been in existence since 1881, has responded to thousands of disasters, and has half a million volunteers in addition to 35,000 employees (American Red Cross, 2012). The American Red Cross educates more than 9 million people yearly in CPR and swimming/water safety programs, as well as other programs (American Red Cross, 2012). Overhead costs are roughly 9 percent out of every donated dollar, and the American Red Cross collects blood supplies from approximately 4 million donors (American Red Cross, 2012).

During 9/11, your organization had been criticized for diverting some donations designated for the 9/11 disaster that totaled $200 million out of $1.1 billion raised (Associated Press, 2005). Your organization has worked extremely hard to rectify the situation. All donations designated for the 9/11 fund were restored, and the president of the organization resigned due to the controversy (Associated Press, 2005). The organization has now decided to expand its emergency response role to include areas that the organization had not ventured into before, like short-term financial aid (Associated Press, 2005). It is 2005 and a massive hurricane named Katrina has just hit the Gulf of Mexico coastline, primarily from Louisiana to Mississippi. There is massive damage and carnage wrought throughout the area, with people stranded in their homes and injured, wholesale shortages of supplies, limited numbers of trained personnel on the ground to fix or repair infrastructure, and a complete lack of adequate transportation. With electrical, communication, and water lines inoperable, the area will be in a state of confusion and chaos. What should your organization do to respond to the disaster successfully?

Questions that should be asked by the administrator at this phase:

1. Does the organization have logistical support to handle an increase in roles that the organization is now involved in?
2. How will the organization handle financial controls in regard to the donation allotment that should be specific to this response?
3. How will the organization manage such a large number of staff and volunteers in a large-scale disaster response?
4. How will your organization work with other non-profit organizations?
5. How will your organization work with government entities?

Potential Issues for the Administrator to Consider

When a disaster such as Hurricane Katrina is impending, there is no way to predict accurately what impact it will have on a given area or population. The storm may hit the coastline and have almost no effect if the storm loses power and becomes a tropical storm. Moreover, the storm could change direction and hit an area of the coastline that is sparsely populated and contains few structures that could be damaged. In Hurricane Katrina's case, however, the storm hit a very large and densely populated area of the country that had not been completely evacuated. The storm caused severe flooding, electrical outages, food and water supply shortages, and strained medical resources. The American Red Cross has traditionally filled a needed role in assisting first responders and government entities in times of crisis. Unfortunately, the American Red Cross has delved into new arenas of operation that will require some trial and error with organizational operations before the newly expanded roles work seamlessly with other aspects of the organization.

With a wide array of staff and volunteers, the American Red Cross's upper administrators will need to be more coordinated than ever to organize disaster response efforts successfully in the different facets of operational venues. Upper administrators should also be concerned about making sure financial controls are in place to ensure that donations earmarked for this relief effort are correctly allocated. In some cases, it may be more appropriate to subcontract work to other non-profit organizations that are more experienced or more efficient at providing the population in need with services that are critical for disaster response efforts. Working with governmental entities will require effective communications to ensure that the organization is providing services that are truly needed and are doing so in a timely fashion. Good communication will hopefully prevent any duplication of efforts from other non-profit organizations and prevent any inefficiencies in the disaster response effort.

Phase II — First Issue

The American Red Cross has been responding actively to Hurricane Katrina's victims' needs. There are now some complaints being brought to the upper administration about how the funding for the relief efforts is being spent. There are some complaints from smaller organizations that your organization should share the funding, since the American Red Cross's efforts have not been equitable or well-organized in some of the areas that need relief (Associated Press, 2005). Some are now beginning to criticize the organization for not being flexible enough and not offering long-term financing for reconstruction purposes (Associated Press, 2005). In addition, your organization is receiving complaints that the organization served white areas better than African-American areas in the first few days of the disaster (Associated Press, 2005). As an administrator, how do you propose to resolve or address these criticisms of your organization's performance?

Questions that should be asked by the administrator at this phase:

1. How many of these criticisms are real and how many are perceived?
2. Are the resources earmarked for the disaster relief getting to where they are most needed?
3. Should the American Red Cross reconsider how it defines its role and mission in regard to funding disaster response by delving into the new role of long-term financing for reconstruction?
4. How will you address the issue of serving some segments of the population inadequately based on ethnicity?

Potential Issues for the Administrator to Consider

The issue of serving different segments of the population in different manners should cause some concern for the administrators. In this particular case, the American Red Cross responded that it was difficult to gain access to areas where the African-American community was located (Associated Press, 2005), presumably due to storm damage to infrastructure. If that is the case, the American Red Cross should learn from the disaster and develop resources that would allow it to access impoverished or heavily damaged areas at a faster pace, particularly since an impoverished population will probably have limited resources to evacuate or be self-sufficient for very long. The obstacles that the American Red Cross faced during this time period could also stem from a lack of coordination with government officials. The organization should review its efforts to see if there are any improvements that could be made for future disaster response operations.

The American Red Cross's upper administration should conduct a full assessment of its logistics capability to get resources and services to areas that were insufficiently supplied during Hurricane Katrina. The American Red Cross may find it beneficial to liaise with other types of non-profit organizations so that a coordinated and more efficient disaster response approach can be realized.

As an upper-level administrator for the organization, you should be cautious about expanding the role of the organization into new ventures where the organization may not have the expertise or experience to successfully support such endeavors. If a new role is to be attempted, the organization may want to attempt a pilot program first to see where potential problems may be realized. Initiatives like long-term financing can present several challenges that can be better met by consulting with professionals familiar with financing, perhaps keeping a few on retainer with the organization to ensure that any financial program devised is properly vetted before it is rolled out to the public.

The American Red Cross should assess the performance of the organization during any disaster response intervention. This assessment should consist of operational aspects of delivery of resources and services, communications between governmental entities and other non-profit organizations, and the performances of administrators, staff members, and volunteers. There should also be a periodic review of the organization's policies and procedures, as well as an audit from an outside firm on all donations and operational expenses, if this task is not being currently conducted. An outside entity should also be retained to conduct unbiased appraisals of the organization's operational conduct and organizational leadership.

Phase III — Second Issue

Your organization had issues with some governmental officials when one particular relief center appeared to handle victims like cattle after demand far outstripped the abilities of the volunteers to handle (Associated Press, 2005). There were also two other issues that have now been brought to your attention. The first was the American Red Cross telephone hotline being completely clogged with callers (Associated Press, 2005). The second issue was that the federal government reimbursed the American Red Cross for expenses (paid with donor funds) associated with lodging refugees when the American Red Cross shelters became overwhelmed and victims were placed in hotels (Associated Press, 2005). It would appear that there are more issues with the organization than with inappropriate allocations of funds during the 9/11 situation. What actions do you think will rectify the organization's operational capability and image?

Questions that should be asked by the administrator at this phase:

1. Do you have a problem getting the correct number of volunteers to assist staff members at your relief centers?

2. Why is your phone hotline system facing so many issues?
3. How do you feel about the donors' money going toward temporary housing and then having the federal government reimburse the organization for those expenditures? Does your organization have an ethical obligation to disclose that information to the donors? What should you do with the reimbursement funds received from the federal government?

Potential Issues for the Administrator to Consider

As an upper-level administrator for the organization, it is your responsibility to notify the donors that their funds went to house temporarily displaced people in motels when the shelters become overpopulated and that the federal government did indeed reimburse the organization for those costs. The organization (providing it wants to avoid the earlier experience of the 9/11 donor money issue) should reallocate the reimbursement from the federal government to a fund that will assist victims of Hurricane Katrina and maintain complete transparency with donors about these plans.

The telephone hotline system needs to be reevaluated if it is inadequate during large emergencies. This may require an assessment of what type of telephone system the American Red Cross is using, what type of menu system should be used with the telephone system, whether online access should be promoted more heavily, and how many trained volunteers and employed staff members need to be trained on the telephone hotline system. If the volume is extremely high, this may require the administration of the American Red Cross to consider hiring an outside firm or temporary staff members to assist in fielding all of the calls coming into the organization. There needs to be a contingency plan in place in case the telephone hotline becomes overloaded. While staff members and volunteers can show patience, it is not often the case with victims who need information quickly in order to get to safety or obtain scarce resources.

The administration will need to review how its relief centers are staffed and managed. Earning a negative perception from governmental officials is not helpful to the organization's mission, and this complaint should be reviewed thoroughly. An assessment may need to be taken on how many volunteers and staff members are required for facilities with certain occupancy capacities. This issue is not only a problem for staffing reasons, but also for fire code occupancy rates, which, if violated, could create an unsafe environment for everyone in the facility.

Phase IV — Third Issue

The Hurricane Katrina disaster response is now over, and there has been new information on some alleged improprieties that have occurred during the relief operation. The new accusations consist of misappropriated supplies by volunteers that could have resulted in millions of dollars in theft when American Red

Cross policies were not followed (Stephanie Strom, 2006). Additionally, there were felons among the volunteers during the disaster response, which is against American Red Cross policies (Strom, 2006). Among the items that were misappropriated were a computer that could be used to add money to debit cards, rental cars, generators, and 3,000 air mattresses that were donated by a private company (Strom, 2006). Due to these latest allegations, Sen. Grassley from Iowa is now threatening to revoke the organization's charter unless drastic changes are made to put in controls for financial assets and an inventory control (Strom, 2006). This senator is a committee chairman and has quite a bit of political power and can cause the organization a great deal of problems. It would be wise to address these concerns quickly and effectively.

Questions that should be asked by the administrator at this phase:

1. What type of financial controls were in place that were not effective during the Hurricane Katrina disaster response?
2. Which type of financial controls needs to be put in place to supplement policies and procedures that apparently were not followed during the crisis?
3. What types of inventory controls are in place for the organization?
4. Who is responsible for keeping the inventory for the organization? How are they kept accountable when inventory is missing?
5. What needs to be done to satisfy the senator's requirements and reassure the legislator that all steps are being taken to rectify the current state of affairs?

Potential Issues for the Administrator to Consider

The administrator has to know how his or her organization is supposed to function. If there is no clear understanding on how the policies and procedures are supposed to work for the organization, there is no hope of enforcing or improving those policies. The administrator should put mechanisms in place that will hold certain key staff members accountable for both inventory and financial assets. To make those staff members accountable, the organization will not only have to increase the number of internal audits in its organization, but also the number of outside audits that occur on a quarterly basis with regular reports going to the upper administration and governing board of the organization.

The upper administration and the governing board, for that matter, should take the senator's threats to heart and make sure that every type of control is put in place to rectify a bad situation. For this type of criminal conduct to occur on such a wide scale would indicate that the organization did not have the proper mechanisms, policies, or procedures in place to combat misappropriation of inventory and financial assets. A revocation or rewriting of an organization's charter should be seen as more than just a threat; it could be a reality that can cause the organization irreparable harm to its image.

Phase V — Resolution and Conclusion

In 2005, the president of the American Red Cross, Marsha J. Evans, resigned in the face of alleged shortcomings of the organization (Strom, 2005). During the Hurricane Katrina crisis response, the organization failed to accurately account for evacuees in need of housing, did not have enough blankets on hand at shelters, and issued some debit bank cards that failed to function (Strom, 2005). Critics point out that the ever-changing leadership at the top and the board at the American Red Cross has led to "an underinvestment in telecommunications, technology and other infrastructure" to assist the organization in carrying out its mandate (Strom, 2005). Also in 2005, 49 people working as contractors at an American Red Cross call center during the Hurricane Katrina Relief effort were indicted for wire fraud (CNN, 2005).

Recommendations and Concluding Remarks

The American Red Cross will have to make changes to its financial and asset controls if the organization has hopes of maintaining credibility with the public, making operations more efficient and effective, and being able to work with the confidence of government officials at the local, state, and federal levels. If problems are not addressed with the asset and financial management, the American Red Cross runs the risk of gaining opponents among elected officials to its operation and mission to assist in disaster response. Non-profit organizations must realize that just because an organization has non-profit status does not mean that proper controls should not be in place. Quite the contrary, because a non-profit organization is usually heavily reliant on donations or some type of subsidies, it becomes imperative that the organization protect its revenue streams. The question becomes: "Who would want to donate to an organization that has demonstrated that it cannot manage or use donations effectively?" The American Red Cross will now find itself attempting to answer that very question to potential donors, existing donors, and legislators that now see two distinct situations (9/11 and Hurricane Katrina) where the organization has had issues with donations, financial controls, or asset management. This case study in particular should highlight how important it is for administrators to address potential shortfalls in policies and procedures and prevent these types of issues from occurring with an organization's operation and mission.

Chapter 13

Gloria Wise Boys and Girls Club — 2005

Phase I — Situation

You are a member on the board of directors at the Gloria Wise Boys and Girls Club of America. As an independent organization affiliated with Boys and Girls Clubs of America, the Gloria Wise Boys and Girls Club (Gloria Wise) has a mission "to enable all young people, especially those who need us most, to reach their full potential as productive, caring, responsible citizens," with a focus on character development and ensuring a safe environment for underprivileged youths while providing them with the building blocks for a brighter future (Boys and Girls Club of America, 2012).

The New York City Department of Investigation (DOI) received an anonymous letter from someone who described themselves as an employee, which began an investigation into allegations of theft, financial mismanagement, absent employees, executives receiving bloated salaries, and embezzlement hidden by the use of separate accounts (Hearn, 2006).

Questions that should be asked by the board at this phase:

1. What plans are in place, or should be put in place, to develop a response to the general public in regard these allegations?
2. Considering the allegations, how should the board respond to corporate partners and sponsors?
3. Who should represent Gloria Wise in cooperating with the New York City DOI in regard to their investigation? The board? Corporate counsel? Others?

Potential Issues for Public Relations

Media scrutiny will develop surrounding these allegations. The fact that the New York City DOI has already initiated an investigation means the media will soon report this issue. The longer the investigation, the more likely the media reporting will be focused on the negative aspects of the findings. Gloria Wise will have to be prepared to withstand and respond to the scrutiny and negative press.

The New York City DOI's investigation of Gloria Wise is enough to cause major damage to the image of the organization's management and executives, and to influence stakeholders, donors, and corporate partners/sponsors to question the organization's ability to appropriately handle monetary donations. Any significant negative hit to its image or fiduciary trust can result in Gloria Wise being forced to shut down, or at least reinvent itself, possibly under a new name and leadership.

An immediate decision must be made regarding the status of those executives involved in the investigation (i.e., suspend those involved pending the results of the investigation, and formally terminate those involved from their association with the organization). Directors, on behalf of the organization, must provide the public perception of working with the investigators and taking steps to mitigate any further activities by those who are the subjects of the investigation.

Phase II — First Issue

The investigation revealed considerable inappropriate and criminal activity centered around or controlled by a small group of individuals. A review of some of that activity shows that Charles Rosen, executive director and member of the board of directors, received $69,000 that was not listed on Gloria Wise's financial or tax reports. Jeffrey Aulenbach, deputy executive director of operations, received $87,370, and Lorraine Corva, deputy director of programs, received $60,801. These payments also were not made with board approval, and the money was used for Aulenbach and Corva's personal gain.

Rosen created four separate bank accounts under the names "Co-op City Tennis Club Program," "The Bronx International Express Track Program," "The Bronx Queens Basketball Program," and "The Bronx Youth Soccer Program." These false programs were established to secure contracts with New York City agencies: the Department for Youth & Community Development, the Department for the Aging, and the Department of Education. Some of the funding for these false programs came from the city of New York. The bank accounts were not listed on the account, financial, or tax records of Gloria Wise. Payments were made from Gloria Wise to these false accounts, allegedly for youth programs and athletic training events, but they were then given to executives of the organization.

Rosen made four loans totaling $875,000 from Gloria Wise to Radio Free America (aka Air America), a startup commercial broadcast radio company. The loans were made without the approval of the board of directors. Of additional concern was Evan Montvel-Cohen, director of development, who though primarily responsible for Gloria Wise fundraising, was also a director at Radio Free America. It was revealed that Montvel-Cohen was rarely present and performed few actual duties at Gloria Wise, but he was paid a full-time salary.

Rosen and a combination of the above-mentioned executives routinely falsified records and documents in an effort to substantiate or cover up their actions. Hillen Valentine, secretary and a member of the board, Octavio Cruz, treasurer and member of the board, and Jeanette Graves, president and member of the board, may have had knowledge of some or all of the activity and were complicit in the actions of Rosen, Aulenbach, Corva, and Montvel-Cohen (Hearn, 2006).

Questions that should be asked by the board at this phase:

1. How will you respond to corporate sponsors and donors in light of the results of the investigation?
2. Was it typical for the board to have so little oversight in executive matters?
3. What actions are you going to take against those involved in the embezzlement and misuse of funds?
4. What steps should be taken to ensure similar incidents do not occur in the future?
5. What is your strategy moving forward to rehabilitate your image within the community?

Potential Issues for Public Relations

A significant lack of trust and confidence in Gloria Wise is the critical consideration for public relations issues. The actions by the executives of Gloria Wise provide an unstable and untrustworthy framework for the organization. It will be difficult and challenging to rebuild trust from corporate partners, donors, and the community. The revelations uncovered in the investigation will certainly result in increased media scrutiny and negative press; therefore, preparation to effectively manage the scrutiny and negative press is mandatory.

With the results of the investigation being made public, as well as the extent of inappropriate and potential criminal activity regarding the embezzlement and misuse of funds of the organization, the damage to the image of and trust in the executive level management of the organization could be felt for many years to come. This mistrust is likely to permeate all levels of involvement with Gloria Wise, so you should expect intense scrutiny as a board for possible complicity in the matter, as well as accusations of neglect of your duties as board members.

Being able to solicit and secure donations under such circumstances could be an impossible task.

Phase III — Second Issue

It is apparent that the board of directors was passive and superficial in its review and approval of the financial dealings of executives, failed in its oversight of the management of the organization, and did not live up to its fiduciary responsibility. The business records, contracts, and documents/certifications filed with government agencies reflected whatever the executives wanted, without regard to accuracy, actual events that took place, or authenticity.

The board met monthly but generally deferred to the dominant executive director, Rosen, a fellow board member. Board members accepted his statements without question and were obviously not prepared to govern an organization of the size and complexity of Gloria Wise, which allowed Rosen's unethical and irresponsible actions to continue (Hearn, 2006).

Questions that should be asked by the board of directors at this phase:

1. What did members of the board know and when did they know it?
2. Should there be an independent search to identify and fill board positions?
3. Should the board reconstitute itself and adopt policies and procedures to prevent the issues revealed in the investigation from occurring again?
4. Should the board secure the services of an independent accountant to review or prepare a financial statement and ensure compliance with applicable accounting standards?
5. Should the board establish or appoint an audit committee to monitor the organization's compliance?
6. Should the board be included in a conflict of interest policy applicable to board and staff members?

Potential Issues for Public Relations

Increased scrutiny and calls for a boycott of the organization can reasonably be foreseen. Misappropriation of organizational funds by executive-level employees and an ineffective board that failed in its duties could mean it will be years before the community, donors, and corporate sponsors feel comfortable supporting Gloria Wise.

How this public relations issue is managed will go a long way to determining if Gloria Wise will be a viable organization in the future. If there is no trust in the ability of the board of directors, there will be no support of the organization from the corporate community. Without that support, the organization would be a shell of itself and quite possibly no longer exist. The damage could be irreparable.

At this point, the directors should concern themselves with strengthening the board by offering appointments to people who are highly qualified and experienced. Once the board is strengthened and competent, it will be in a position to properly oversee the management and governance practices of the organization.

Phase IV — Resolution and Conclusion

All executives involved in the investigation resigned from the organization or were terminated: Montvel-Cohen in May 2004, Rosen in June 2005, Aulenbach in August 2005, and Corva in September 2005. Rosen and Aulenbach pleaded guilty to charges of grand larceny, forgery, and obstructing government administration, but through a plea deal served no jail time (Maloney, 2007).

Through efforts of the New York City DOI, $250,000 of the $875,000 loan to Radio Free America was returned to Gloria Wise. The contracts with the Department for Youth & Community Development, the Department for the Aging, and the Department of Education, in addition to contracts with the New York City Housing Authority, were terminated. Gloria Wise lost its affiliation with Boys and Girls Club of America (Lombino, 2006).

Once a competent board is in place, the creation of a finance committee is recommended. The finance committee would have the responsibility of implementing a sound, written fiscal procedure and following it at all levels of the organization, emphasizing compliance and enforcement. The finance committee would obtain and review the required documents and report to the board. The documents should include opening and closing balances of all bank accounts, cash flows, major expenditures and liabilities, payables and receivables, a list of all consulting payments with justifications, any emergency payroll advances, and compensation and perks to executives.

By implementing best practices in transparency, accountability, and independence, the board will be in a position to grow a culture of compliance throughout the organization. Wrongdoing such as that perpetrated by the Gloria Wise executives could be prevented or, at least, quickly detected if there were a board in place that would take compliance seriously and was genuinely committed to oversight (Sieminski, 2006).

Chapter 14

Oral Roberts University Scandal—Ethical/Financial Corruption — 2007

Phase I — Situation

You are a member of the board of trustees for Oral Roberts University, a higher education institution that was founded by televangelist Oral Roberts (Associated Press, 2007). The university is located on a 263-acre campus in Tulsa, Oklahoma, with an undergraduate enrollment of 2,676 students (fall 2011), 583 graduate students (fall 2011), and a 15 to 1 teacher-to-student ratio (Oral Roberts University, 2012). Your institution offers 60 undergraduate majors, 14 master's level programs, and two doctoral degrees in an effort to be a leading Christian university (Oral Roberts University, 2012).

Currently, your institution has more than 30,000 alumni. The Green family has donated more than $60 million to the university. Your institution is working to upgrade technology capabilities, as well as facilities across your campus (Oral Roberts University, 2012). Currently, there are six colleges at Oral Roberts University: the College of Arts and Cultural Studies, the College of Business, the College of Education, the College of Nursing, the College of Science and Engineering, and the College of Theology and Ministry (Oral Roberts University, 2012).

In 2005, your institution raised $76 million in revenue (Associated Press, 2007). You are extremely concerned when you hear that the current president of Oral Roberts University, Richard Roberts, has been accused of illegal contributions to political entities, as well as misappropriation of funds that were raised through donations (Associated Press, 2007).

Questions that should be asked by the administrator at this phase:

1. How will you investigate the allegations?
2. If these allegations are true, how will this impact the operations of your institution (i.e., potential shortfalls in funding)?
3. How will the allegations themselves impact the applications, admissions, and enrollment of the university?
4. If the allegations are true, how will this impact the ability to raise donations among donors and alumni?
5. How do you propose to hold administrators accountable if misappropriations have occurred?
6. Should you contact law enforcement officials at this point in time?

Potential Issues for the Administrator to Consider

If the allegations have supporting evidence that misappropriations could have occurred, then the administrator should contact external entities for a possible criminal investigation. For a non-profit organization, it is critical that revenue is protected, since not only is it donor money, but there is also money that is being paid by students in the form of tuition and fees that have to be accounted for accurately. If administrators suspect that misappropriation of funds is occurring, there should be an audit of the organization's financial records, and the appropriate law enforcement official should be contacted. Missing and inappropriately expended funds could negatively impact operations of the university from academics to facility management. Failure to investigate or report possible violations is not only illegal but also does the donors, staff, faculty, and alumni a disservice. If the various stakeholders feel that the money that they expend on university services or donate to the university is being misappropriated, this could be a negative impact upon the institution's abilities to raise funding for projects and could potentially harm enrollment and retention.

Phase II — First Issue

The details of the alleged misappropriation of funds appear to be several that have been detailed in a lawsuit by three former professors who were recently terminated from their positions (Associated Press, 2007). Richard Roberts has been accused in the lawsuit of using donor money to complete home remodeling projects, using the institution's private jet for personal use, and buying two cars for the president's wife, Lindsey (Associated Press, 2007).

More specifically, the lawsuit details that the president asked a professor to use his students and university resources to work on a county commissioner's election campaign, which is a violation of state and federal statues for how a non-profit organization can operate (Associated Press, 2007). The lawsuit alleged that up to 50 students worked on the campaign and that the professors were terminated from their positions when they released a document to the board overseeing the institution that reported moral and ethical issues with the president and his family (Associated Press, 2007). Additionally, the president's wife had allegedly spent large amounts of funds on personal clothing, awarded scholarships to her friends' children, and used university-owned cell phones to send inappropriate text messages (Associated Press, 2007). These are extremely troubling and potentially damaging allegations to the institution that were documented in the lawsuit. What do you do now?

Questions that should be asked by the administrator at this phase:

1. If these expenses are accurate, did any of the staff know that these expenses were occurring?
2. If the staff did know these expenses were occurring, were these issues reported to anyone inside or outside the university's administrative structure?
3. If the allegations are true and students as well as university resources were used for an election campaign, what are the potential legal repercussions for the organization?
4. Could these allegations lead to a criminal investigation of the organization and its leaders? If so, what will be the backlash against the institution with donors, alumni, and students?
5. What would be the best avenue to investigate the legitimacy of the alleged offenses?
6. If the alleged offenses are valid and accurate, what actions should be taken?

Potential Issues for the Administrator to Consider

If any of these allegations are proven to be accurate, the organization could host a number of investigations from law enforcement officials and government agencies (i.e., Internal Revenue Service). This does not include the current civil litigation the organization is facing for an alleged unjustified termination of employees, which could result in the organization losing funds due to lawsuits and bring about new lawsuits by donors if the misappropriation of funds is proven to be true.

There should be a set of controls put in place to prevent misappropriation of funds, which would consist of a series of checks and balances to be established between the president and the board. For example, if the president wanted to spend over a certain amount of money on a particular item, he/she would need to provide written justification and obtain board approval before such expenses would be processed. Additionally, there needs to be a mechanism put in place where staff members can report misappropriation of funds without fear of losing their positions.

Phase III — Second Issue

With the students and staff of your organization now publicly condemning the alleged actions of the president and his family, and with more allegations about improper conduct surfacing, you are concerned that the scandal will become public (Willard, 2007-1). You are learning that if staff disagreed with or voiced concerns about President Roberts, they would be dismissed from their positions (Willard, 2007-1). Students attending Oral Roberts University who voiced concerns with the university could be (and were) expelled when certain topics were broached about Roberts (Willard, 2007-1). This culture of fear has kept several employees and students from voicing their concerns to the appropriate officials (Willard, 2007-1). Roberts has also been seen endorsing Randi Miller's mayoral campaign in front of four thousand attendees at the university chapel during a chapel service (Willard, 2007-1).

Questions that should be asked by the administrator at this phase:

1. How will you contend with discontent from the employees and the students?
2. How will you attempt to insulate the organization from future lawsuits, sanctions, or fines?
3. If the allegations of the president's actions are true, how will you get the organization back on track to follow the mission statement that the university should be following?

Potential Issues for the Administrator to Consider

If the students and employees are this upset over the breaking scandal and conduct of the administration, this will seed deeper problems within the organization, which could lead to its ultimate demise. An administrator needs to be aware of the issues that are being brought forward by paying customers (i.e., students) as well as their employees, both of which are the lifeblood of the organization. Any donor or alumni viewing this type of discontent from afar will be much less likely to donate to the organization if the alleged type of behavior is condoned or no action is taken to prevent its reoccurrence. The board needs to launch a full investigation and disclose all of its findings if there is any hope for the university administration to retain or restore its credibility with students, employees, and alumni.

Phase IV — Third Issue

Your president goes on "Larry King Live" and states that he and his wife have done nothing improper (Willard, 2007-2). Roberts has also refused requests to step down and has denied any wrongdoing, but he has taken a temporary leave of absence from his post at the university (Willard, 2007-2). Your board has decided to do whatever is necessary based on what the investigation uncovers (Willard, 2007-2). Roberts has filed a legal action to place a gag order against the three professors who have filed suit and has also filed an action to disqualify the professors' attorney from the hearing (Willard, 2007-2). You are up to your neck in legal action at this point. What actions do you want to take next?

Questions that should be asked by the administrator at this phase:

1. As a board member, what are you going to propose in regard to your president?
2. What actions will you take to limit the public relations damage that is occurring at your institution?
3. What steps can you take to avoid being entangled any further in a legal quagmire?

Potential Issues for the Administrator to Consider

At this point, the public relations for the university is a complete disaster. The board should attempt to rein in the president or threaten to remove him from his position if he does not cease and desist from any more public statements. There is very little the board can do except to follow up on any type of audits and work on improvement with policies and procedures to prevent situations of this type from occurring in the future. The legal processes will have to play out in court, and there is no gain in making any public statement from the board's point of view other than to say that appropriate action will be taken when the investigations are concluded.

Phase V — Fourth Issue

The faculty has voted "no confidence" in the president's leadership, and the provost has threatened to resign if Roberts was allowed to continue as president (Branstetter, 2007). In the face of this, Roberts resigned his position as university president (Branstetter, 2007). Yet another lawsuit has been filed against the university, and this time it is a student who contends that his degree has been devalued (Branstetter, 2007). Your university is $52 million in debt, and students are leaving the university (Branstetter, 2007). There is an active investigation by an external firm that should have a report to the board fairly soon (Branstetter, 2007). You will now have to conduct a search for a new president of the university, and you will still be contending with the fallout from this very public scandal (Branstetter, 2007).

Questions that should be asked by the administrator at this phase:

1. How do you persuade students to come back to your university?
2. What will you look for in a new president?
3. How will you contend with the large debt that is now facing the university in light of the scandal?

Potential Issues for the Administrator to Consider

Enrollment and donations will need to be the first things that the board will have to address. These may be two areas that a new president will need to be able to rectify if hired for the position. The new president will need to have credibility with the alumni, faculty, staff, and students. In addition, the president may need to add to his or her staff a skilled budget administrator to contend with the large amount of the debt that the university has now incurred. In short, the board and the new president will need to take a hard look at every operational aspect of the university, reduce costs, and make every possible effort to make operational aspects more efficient and effective with less money.

Phase VI — Resolution and Conclusion

The university would hire a new president. Mart Green made a $70 million donation that kept Oral Roberts University financially afloat (Siegel, 2007). The board at Oral Roberts University officially separated from the Oral Roberts Evangelistic Association in 2007, which was in accordance with the agreement that the university made with the IRS in prior years (Siegel, 2007). According to the chairman of the Board of Regents, both Oral and Richard Roberts were removed from any business decisions with the university (Siegel, 2007). Three Board of Regent members that were being investigated by a senator were dismissed from the board (Siegel, 2007). The lawsuits against Oral Roberts University from its former employees were either dismissed with prejudice or settled in 2008 (The Oklahoma State Courts Network, 2008). Richard Roberts' troubles would continue when he was arrested for driving while drunk on January 24, 2012 (Jones, 2012).

Recommendations and Concluding Remarks

The organization has a chance for a fresh start with the $70 million donation that could potentially satisfy the $52 million debt. With the separation between the university and the ministry, the organization has the opportunity to re-form operationally and to realign with its original mission statement. The Board of Regents will need to exercise more control and oversight over the top executives and have a series of checks and balances that will hold top-level administrators accountable when large, questionable expenses have incurred.

Chapter 15

TOEIC Scandal in Japan — Nepotism, Mismanagement of Funds — 2009

Phase I — Situation

You are a board member of the Institute for International Business Communications (IIBC), which tests individuals on speaking, writing, and comprehension of the English language. Your organization is a non-profit organization that operates primarily in Japan and has a relationship with the US-based Educational Testing Service (ETS). Your organization uses an expensive test on thousands of individuals, and the endeavor generates millions of dollars in revenue. The chairman of the board, Watanabe Yaeji, is a retired bureaucrat of the Ministry of International Trade and Industry (MITI). The board is populated with many other retired bureaucrats from MITI and other business executives. The chairman of the board and many of the other members of the board have no experience or formal training in language teaching or testing. The organization was created with the permission the Ministry of International Trade and Industry and operating under the supervision of MITI, the IIBC assumed responsibilities for the Test of English for International Communication (TOEIC) in Japan (McCrostie, 2010).

In May and June 2009, the Japanese weekly magazine *FRIDAY* accused the IIBC's 92-year-old chairman of nepotism when he appointed the son of his girlfriend to the position of chairman of the IIBC board of directors. To force the appointment, half of the volunteers serving on the board were forced out by Watanabe. The magazine article also questioned why Watanabe only showed up for work about one day a week (*FRIDAY,* 2009).

In August 2009, the online version of the English-language newspaper *The Japan Times* published a two-part series examining the TOEIC's origins and early history, as well as the use of test-taker fees by the IIBC on the Internet. The August 18 article examined the questionable uses of test fees, including a fivefold increase in utility expenses in one year, 13 million yen spent annually on research about adapting to Chinese culture, sponsorship of poetry readings by the Chinese Poetry Recitation Association, and membership fees to join the Beautiful Aging Association, for which Watanabe also happened to be chairman (*Japan Times*, 2009).

The article also questioned the relationship between the IIBC and its for-profit partner International Communications School with which it shared office space. International Communications School is responsible for selling the TOEIC textbooks and administers the TOEIC Japanese language website. Also, one of International Commutations School's subsidiaries is E-Communications, which administers the TOEIC's online application system and provides online TOEIC study materials (*Japan Times*, 2009).

In 2009, Watanabe suddenly resigned from the IIBC, leaving the son of his girlfriend in charge of the non-profit. Watanabe received a 25 million yen retirement payment (*Japan Times*, 2009).

Questions that should be asked by the administrator at this phase:

1. Should there be a formal investigation of the allegations against Watanabe, and, if so, what form should the investigation take (i.e., internal, external, criminal)?
2. What might be the impact on the organization if these allegations are found to be true?
3. Other than Watanabe, are there other members of your organization who should be held accountable in the event these allegations are true?
4. What are the advantages and disadvantages to your making the allegations public at this time?
5. Should law enforcement or the Tokyo Tax Bureau (the non-profit supervising agency) be contacted at this time? Or should there be an internal investigation first, and by whom should it be conducted?

Potential Public Relations Issues

Watanabe, the high-profile face of the organization, could very well be embroiled in a public scandal concerning his relationship with his girlfriend and her son and possible improper use of the organization's funds. Such a scandal, especially if it involves misuse of fees, questionable expenses, and nepotism, could result in significant negative publicity, considerable scrutiny of the organization, and a long-term public relations recovery. It would undoubtedly have a negative impact on the

IIBC, its ability to successfully continue administering the test, and maintenance of the organization's mission.

The IIBC can anticipate damage to the image and trust in the organization if the allegations, including misuse of funds and high salaries for non-profit executives, are proven to be true. If the allegations are true, the damage could be devastating: withdrawal of corporate partners that require the use of the tests by their employees, resulting in a substantial reduction in revenue and the organization's continued existence being endangered (McCrostie, 2010).

An investigation should be initiated, perhaps internally at first, focusing on an audit of the organization's accounting practices and a full reconciliation of the organization's collected revenues and expenditures. In addition, the organization's conflict of interest and nepotism guidelines may need to revised or updated. Depending on the depth of the initial findings, it may be necessary for an outside independent investigator to take over the process to avoid any appearance of a cover-up. In the event of possible tax violations and other improprieties, Japanese national civil and law enforcement agencies should be contacted to perform a thorough civil and criminal investigation. Consideration should also be given to suspending or relieving Watanabe of his duties, pending the outcome of the investigation(s) (McCrostie, 2010).

Phase II — First Issue

It was determined that IIBC's budget included several expenses that had little to do with testing English proficiency. The financial reports of the IIBC failed to clearly say how much money was being spent on the Beautiful Aging Association and the IIBC division called Global Human Resources Development (GHRD). The GHRD gathered information from around the world to help the Japanese become better global managers. In a related conflict of interest, IIBC funds were actually funneled through the GHRD to the Chinese Poetry Recitation Association. The IIBC budget documents also showed the salaries received by IIBC executives were very generous when compared to the annual average salaries of Japanese bureaucrats working for independent governmental administrative agencies (McCrostie, 2010).

Due to numerous negative articles and warnings from the Ministry of Trade about excessive fees for the TOEIC tests in 2009, the IIBC refunded test takers who had prepaid for the tests in September. In October of 2009, IIBC announced a reduction in the number of the tests after the Ministry of Trade issued non-binding guidance on the organization's excessive profits and high test fee structure (McCrostie, 2010).

Questions that should be asked by the administrator at this phase:

1. How could the issues of conflicts of interest, high test fees, and generous wages for non-profit executives go unnoticed or unchecked by the organization?

2. What internal procedures, if any, were/are in place for the review of budgets submitted by Watanabe, and who approves those reports?
3. Does IIBC use an outside firm to conduct audits of financial reports and accounting practices? If not, should you consider using such a firm?
4. Does IIBC have a code of ethics? If not, should one be established?

Potential Issues for Public Relations

Watanabe's replacement as board chairman, Murofushi Takayuki, the executive director, Umezawa Naomi, and all the other board of directors were all still with the organization and had all been tainted by the scandal. Their continuing relationship with the organization was still a cause for concern, as they had implemented few, if any, reforms that were needed for IIBC to regain its credibility with the public, its customers, and other stakeholders (McCrostie, 2010).

Phase III — Second Issue

Under the weight of negative news articles and reactions from public officials, public agencies, and the public, Watanabe resigned his position, claiming health issues, while the cloud of the investigation hung over IIBC (McCrostie, 2010).

Questions that should be asked by the administrator at this phase:

1. Should Watanabe's replacement be removed or asked to resign?
2. Should the organization's executive director resign?
3. How are you going to address the concerns of corporate partners regarding possible misuse of funds by Watanabe?
4. How are you going to address the concerns of test takers in regard to the fairness of their test fees?
5. Should all support given to noncore activities, such as funding of the GHRD and BAA, be stopped immediately now that Watanabe has resigned?
6. How is the organization going to repair its image and reputation during this time of negative publicity and public opinion?

Potential Issues for Public Relations

The resignation of Watanabe and the payment of 25 million yen to him on his retirement only serve to increase the media scrutiny and negative publicity surrounding possible impropriety involving the operations of IIBC and its partners. The increased scrutiny and negative publicity can only increase questions and decrease donations. You must determine how to provide better accountability of funds used by the board and executive level personnel.

Phase IV — Third Issue

The board of directors should look at their role in this matter. Should the board have expected some form of reporting regarding the chairman's activities and expenditures and those of the other board members and executive personnel? This growing scandal calls into question the board's oversight of the chairman and the executive director.

Questions that should be asked by the administrator at this phase:

1. Did the board authorize the chairman's use of IIBC funds for activities unrelated to the organization's which was teaching Japanese students become proficient in the English language?
2. What are the legal responsibilities of the board in overseeing the chairman and executive director, and has the board as a whole lived up to its responsibilities?
3. Are any members of the board complicit in Watanabe's actions?

Potential Issues for Public Relations

Questions concerning the lack of oversight by the board add to the increased scrutiny of IIBC. With the new chairman, the executive director, and the board of directors under question, it is imperative for IIBC to use effective public relations to manage and improve its image.

Phase V — Resolution and Conclusion

After Watanabe's resignation, the IIBC board of governors should have launched a search for a new leader. However, it did not do so. It also should have replaced the new chairman, the executive director, and all the board members. In addition, it should have hired or appointed more people with knowledge of language testing and learning. A review of the organization's entire fee structure should have been conducted to ensure that the rates it was charging the test takers were fair and equitable. It most certainly should have ended its relationships with its for-profit partners.

The entire episode came to an unsatisfactory ending, as many of the needed reforms never took place and the organization continues to exist without the true reforms that it needed to reclaim its stature in the nation and with its customers, it governmental partners, and other stakeholders.

Chapter 16

Republican National Committee — Misuse of Funds — 2010

Phase I — Situation

Michael Steele was the first African American chairman of the Republican National Committee (RNC), which is a non-profit that provides national leadership for the Republican Party of the United States. This organization is responsible for developing and promoting the Republican Party political platform, as well as coordinating fundraising and election strategy. It is also responsible for organizing and running the Republican National Convention. Similar committees exist in every state and are allied with the national committee. During Steele's second year in office, he was working diligently to raise funds from individual donors and corporate donors for the Republican Party to compete against the Democratic Party in the 2012 presidential election.

In late March 2010, newspapers reported the use of RNC donor money being spent at a risqué Hollywood nightclub, Voyeur, which features topless dancers and bondage acts. The outing to the club appeared on the RNC monthly Federal Election Commission disclosure report as a $2,000 expenditure. Erik Brown of Orange, California, a Republican consultant and donor, submitted a reimbursement request for $1,946.25 from this club visit on January 31, 2010. He listed the amount as a meal expense at the club, whose interior was inspired by an orgy scene in the movie *Eyes Wide Shut* (Grad, 2010).

Questions that should be asked by the administrator at this phase:

1. Should there be a formal investigation of the allegations of the misuse of funds, and, if so, what form should the investigation take (i.e., internal or external)?
2. What might be the impact on the organization if these allegations are found to be true?
3. Which members of the organization should be held accountable in the club escapade if the allegations are true?
4. How did these expenditures get past the financial controls?
5. How should the media fallout from such actions be managed?
6. What is going to be the impact of these revelations on our conservative donor base?
7. What impact would it have on ongoing political races and future political races?
8. Why did the RNC reimburse Brown for these expenses?

Potential Public Relations Issues

The incident did not help the RNC leadership dispel the notion that they are not high rollers and big spenders. It also made it more difficult for the RNC to attack the Democrats for how government spends taxpayer money when it is spending Republican donor money so recklessly, especially since so many of the Republican donors are of the religious right and evangelical community. While the RNC chairman was not at the nightclub, many felt the RNC should be setting a very high standard of fiscal responsibility. However, the incident at the Voyeur Club showed the country a different picture. It was one of fiscal irresponsibility, with reports of the RNC funding entertainment expenses at a bondage club (Barr, 2010). Such a scandal could result in significant negative publicity, considerable scrutiny of the organization, and a long-term public relations recovery. It would undoubtedly have a negative impact on RNC, and the state organizations, and their ability to successfully fundraise to continue the organization's mission to win elections.

Initially, RNC can anticipate damage to the image of and trust in the organization, and the damage could be devastating: withdrawal of corporate donors and individual donors, and a substantial reduction in donations. An investigation was initiated to answer the many questions following the visit to the risqué nightclub to see what happened, what went wrong, and who signed off on the expenses and why.

Phase II — First Issue

In the aftermath of the nightclub scandal, top donors and committee members for the RNC expressed outrage over the nearly $2,000 spent on meals at the bondage-themed nightclub. Some donors started saying that they might start funding candidates directly or finance political action committees whose views were aligned with the donors' wishes rather than giving the campaign funds to the RNC (Preston, 2010).

The media attention became overwhelming and overshadowed the work being done by the RNC and the state committees to raise funds to win the 2012 presidential campaign and to regain control of both houses of Congress.

Questions that should be asked by the administrator at this phase:

1. How could the issue of recordkeeping and accounting discrepancies go unnoticed or unchecked by the organization?
2. What internal procedures, if any, were/are in place for the review of expense reports submitted by employees and consultants working on the RNC's behalf, and who approves those reports?
3. Does RNC use an outside firm to conduct audits of financial reports and accounting practices? If not, should you consider using such a firm?
4. Does RNC have a code of ethics? If not, should one be established?

Potential Issues for Public Relations

Public relations issues concerning potential misuse of donor contributions to the RNC came at a time when the Democratic National Committee was out-fundraising the RNC. There was tremendous pressure on the RNC to close in on the fundraising level of the DNC and to surpass it to ensure electoral victory in 2012 (Preston, 2010).

Phase III — Second Issue

This nightclub was just the latest of several financial issues related to the chairman's financial stewardship of the RNC. When Steele took over the position, he spent more than $18,000 to redecorate his office. Steele, a former Maryland lieutenant governor, also has received substantial fees for making speeches, even though the RNC pays him a full-time salary (Milbank, 2010).

Republicans have also questioned whether the RNC is overpaying the finance director Steele hired, Republican consultant Robert Bickhart. Bickhart and his firm have taken in at least $411,568 from the RNC since Steele hired him in 2009. That is far more than the roughly $136,000 the RNC has paid Steele during the 2009–10 cycle and rivals President Obama's annual pay of around $400,000 (Babington, 2010).

Steele continued to get into trouble of over misstatements and for his lavish spending. In February 2010, an RNC trip to California included a $9,009 stop at the Beverly Hills Hotel with an additional $6,596 spent at the nearby Four Seasons Hotel. RNC trips to other cities produced bills from a long list of costly hotels, such as the Venetian and the M Resort in Las Vegas and the W Hotel for a total of

$19,443 in Washington, DC. A midwinter trip to Hawaii cost the RNC $43,828, not including airfare. In a February filing with the Federal Election Commission, it came to light that the RNC spent $17,000 on travel by private jet and about $15,000 on limousines (Babington, 2010).

Questions that should be asked by the administrator at this phase:

1. How could Steele reassure the members of the RNC and its donors that he was the right person to lead the organization?
2. How are you going to address the concerns of individual and corporate partners regarding lavish spending by Steele and the RNC?
3. How are you going to address the concerns of donors in regard to the proper use of their donations?
4. Shouldn't every donor dollar be going to the 2010 midterm elections and the 2012 presidential election?
5. How is the organization going to repair its image and reputation during this time of negative publicity and public opinion?

Potential Issues for Public Relations

Some Republican officials and donors complained about Steele's spending decisions, saying the party should devote every available dollar to trying to win House and Senate races in the fall of 2010.

Phase IV — Third Issue

The board of directors should look at their role in this matter. Should the board have expected some form of reporting regarding executive expenditures? This growing scandal calls into question the board's oversight of Steele.

Questions that should be asked by the administrator at this phase:

1. Did the board authorize Steele's travel and expenditures?
2. What are the legal responsibilities of the board in oversight of the position of chairman, and has the board, as a whole, lived up to its responsibilities?
3. Are any members of the board complicit in Steele's actions?

Potential Issues for Public Relations

Questions concerning the lack of oversight by the board add to the increased scrutiny of RNC. With the chairman under scrutiny and the board of directors also under question, it is imperative for RNC to use effective public relations to manage and improve its image.

Phase V — Chairman's Actions

In an effort to reassure party members that he had a good grip on the organization, Steele's chief of staff, Ken McKay, was fired due to the nightclub scandal. Steele blamed McKay for the spending abuses, including the strip club incident. In addition, McKay's deputy was also terminated due to the incident at the California club. Were these actions going to be sufficient to quiet critics and allow Steele to keep his job as chairman of the RNC?

After the nightclub incident, an internal audit found "significant deficiencies" in RNC operations. That report said the tab from the Voyeur was reimbursed with a forged signature but reported it was "questionable" whether Bickhart had reviewed the reimbursement. The report recommended a contract with Bickhart's company — eCapitol Direct — be ended. The audit said the contract could be worth as much as $270,000 on top of Bickhart's salary as an RNC official. The contract was canceled by the RNC board. A new chief of staff was brought in to replace McKay (Babington, 2010).

Phase VI — Resolution and Conclusion

During the 2011 RNC winter meeting, Steele was replaced by Reince Priebus. Reince Priebus became the new chairman of the RNC on January 14, 2011.

IV

CRIMINAL OR UNETHICAL ACTS IN NON-PROFIT ORGANIZATIONS

Chapter 17

Jimmy Hoffa — Corruption of Unions — 1970s

Phase I — Situation

You are a trustee for the International Brotherhood of Teamsters (IBT) in the 1970s. Your organization is a labor union that is responsive to members in the United States and Canada that are employed in the trucking industry (Teamsters, 2012). Your organization was founded in 1903 after Samuel Gompers had convinced two separate groups of team drivers (wagon delivery drivers) to merge and form the IBT (Teamsters, 2012). Your organization, in turn, expanded, and in the coming years would incorporate delivery drivers from many different industries (milk deliveries, gravel haulers, etc.), as well as drivers of motorized vehicles (Teamsters, 2012).

Your organization promotes better working conditions and higher wages for the members in your organization (Teamsters, 2012). During the organization's existence there have been several strikes backed by your union to force management to provide better conditions for employment (Teamsters, 2012). Some of these strikes, like the 1907 strike against Montgomery Ward, were violent and resulted in deaths as well as property damage (Teamsters, 2012). In 1959, the president of your organization, James R. Hoffa, is accused on national television by Robert F. Kennedy, the chief counsel of the Senate Labor Rackets Committee, of being associated with the mafia (Bruno, 2012). What should the trustees do for the organization at this point?

Questions that should be asked by the administrator at this phase:

1. Should the organization call for a special audit on the organization's accounting, policies and procedures to ensure that there is no criminal activity occurring?
2. How will you protect the members in your organization from dubious actions if criminal activity is indeed occurring?
3. What steps should you take to protect the membership's assets?

Potential Issues for the Administrator to Consider

At this point the organization is facing a severe public backlash due to the comments by Kennedy. The leadership should take an active role in investigating if any of these allegations are true and, if so, contact local law enforcement and request that a criminal investigation be conducted on those associated with organized crime. If organized crime was associated with the organization, then there is a likelihood that the membership's assets within the organization are not secure and are vulnerable to use for criminal enterprises or purposes. The organization should take action swiftly to ensure that proper financial controls are put in place and that any loans made of organizational funds are properly documented and are for legitimate purposes. If any leaders of the organization are found to be involved with organized crime, they should be removed from leadership of the organization in accordance to the bylaws and processes in the organization's guidelines. If the organized crime involves the organization, then the proper law enforcement officials should be notified.

Phase II — First Issue

Having Kennedy focusing publicly on your organization is not something that your organization should take lightly, since the Senate Labor Rackets Committee is in charge of determining how much influence organized crime has on labor unions (Bruno, 2012). Kennedy is actively targeting Hoffa for a possible criminal investigation, as well as excising any potential organized criminal activity from labor unions (Bruno, 2012). To further antagonize the situation, Hoffa has engaged in a name-calling campaign against Kennedy and even shoved Kennedy during an encounter in a restaurant (Bruno, 2012). This type of conflict is bringing unwanted attention to your organization (Bruno, 2012). In addition, you suspect that the organization's Central States Pension Fund, which has invested for your members' retirement, has, on Hoffa's orders, loaned money to various underworld figures (Bruno, 2012). How can you protect your organization?

Questions that should be asked by the administrator at this phase:

1. Are the organizational assets safe from criminal activity or criminal enterprises?
2. Should the board ask the president to resign, given the antagonistic relationship between him and a congressional committee adviser who has a substantial amount of political power?

3. Should the organization review the policies and procedures for making loans of organizational funds?
4. How will your organization contend with the media on the issue of organized crime?
5. Should you call in a special auditor to see what loans Hoffa has been allowing from the Central States Pension Fund?
6. How can you tell if members of your organization are involved with organized crime?
7. If you find members who are involved with organized crime, what are you prepared to do to those individuals?

Potential Issues for the Administrator to Consider

If loans are being made to organized crime entities from the Central States Pension Fund, then there may be several individuals involved with the loan activity. This would also indicate that organized crime has infiltrated the organization on such a wide front that the organization should consult with legal counsel and contact law enforcement. The president waging a personal attack campaign on Kennedy will hurt your organization in the long run. Kennedy has the connections and resources to attack the Teamsters from several different criminal investigation standpoints. The more that Kennedy is attacked by Hoffa, the more motivation Kennedy has to mobilize the various resources at his disposal to press for a criminal investigation of the organization and its members. Removing Hoffa from power or giving him strict instructions that he is not to contact Kennedy in public should lessen tensions between the federal government and the organization, since Hoffa is getting the organization into more conflict with the federal government.

Phase III — Second Issue

The Senate Labor Rackets Committee has now discovered that Morris Dalitz requested Hoffa to intervene on behalf of the Detroit Laundry Institute to avert a strike by the Teamsters. In exchange, the Detroit Laundry Institute provided a kickback to Hoffa in the form of a loan (Bruno, 2012). The Senate Labor Rackets Committee also uncovered Hoffa's involvement with the Lucchese crime family in New York City (Bruno, 2012). In exchange for allowing the crime family to set up the labor unions for newspapers and airport trucking in New York City, the newspapers supported Hoffa for the upcoming Teamster elections (Bruno, 2012). There are serious signs of corruption with the upper leadership of your organization. What action steps do you plan to take on these issues?

Questions that should be asked by the administrator at this phase:

1. How should your organization contend with the corruption of its leadership?

2. What should you do to contend with organized crime's involvement with your organization?
3. How do you protect the reputation of the organization when it is currently compromised by associations with organized crime figures?
4. What steps should you take to protect your members' assets?

Potential Issues for the Administrator to Consider

The organization should remove the president immediately, since there are obvious signs of corruption occurring with the organization's assets. The proper law enforcement officials should be contacted to investigate the leadership of the organization and its local chapters. If no action is taken, the organization's reputation and credibility with members, governmental officials, and the public could be damaged. In addition, if no action is taken, the organization's finances and assets will be vulnerable to criminal enterprises and could be used for illegal purposes.

Phase IV — Third Issue

One of the pivotal agreements in your organization's history is the National Freight Agreement that provided standardized protection and benefits to drivers in your union (Teamsters, 2012). The person in your organization responsible for getting the contract agreement in place was Hoffa (Teamsters, 2012). In 1960, Hoffa leads the organization in promoting the election of candidates to office that are friendly to labor unions and to lobby against legislative acts that could potentially harm union operations (Teamsters, 2012). Hoffa has steadily increased membership to approximately 1.5 million members, making the organization extremely strong politically (Teamsters Local 177, 2012). However, in 1964, Hoffa, who is already under investigation by the federal government, is convicted of jury tampering, wiretapping, mail fraud, and conspiracy that results in him going to prison (Bruno, 2012). Before going to prison, Hoffa handpicks Frank Fitzsimmons to take over the Teamsters as president of the organization (Bruno, 2012). What action steps should you take at this point with a new change in leadership?

Questions that should be asked by the administrator at this phase:

1. Has the board independently investigated Fitzsimmons's background?
2. Should the organization call for a criminal investigation of the new president, as well as an audit of finances, policies, and procedures?
3. How will your organization capitalize politically from the signing of the National Freight Agreement, which is a significant milestone for your organization?
4. How will your organization cope with the public relations issues of Hoffa being convicted and going to prison?

Potential Issues for the Administrator to Consider

The National Freight Agreement is significant to the history of the organization and can be used to reform the organization and its leadership to improve their position in the eyes of the public. However, in this case study, the organization has taken no apparent action to distance itself away from organized criminal entities and appears in media reports and with federal elected politicians to be intertwined so tightly with organized crime that it may never be able to dissociate itself from the reputation of being "in bed" with the mafia. The board should scrutinize Hoffa's handpicked successor independently, and if the successor is found to be engaged in the same activities, the organization will need to act quickly to get him out of the organization's leadership role.

Phase V — Fourth Issue

You have a new president for your organization, Fitzsimmons, who has replaced Hoffa (Bruno, 2012). Fitzsimmons has very influential connections with US President Nixon (Bruno, 2012). However, you are suspicious that Fitzsimmons is linked to organized crime (Bruno, 2012). Additionally, it is rumored that Hoffa will attempt to regain control of the union after his release from prison (Bruno, 2012). There are obviously some big concerns for your organization. What action steps do you take as an administrator?

Questions that should be asked by the administrator at this phase:

1. How will you contend with Fitzsimmons?
2. How will you contend with the organized criminal element that is still intertwined with your organization?
3. How will the organization transition under new leadership?
4. With the coming power struggle between Fitzsimmons and Hoffa, how will the organization's assets be protected?

Potential Issues for the Administrator to Consider

With an upcoming power struggle for the top leadership position, the board should make sure the organization and its assets are not used for anyone's personal gain. With the organization in disarray and still involved with organized criminal organizations, the trustees should take action to put extra controls in place that will protect the members and the organization's assets as much as possible and eliminate organized crime's involvement. With additional controls in place, the transition from one leader to another should be seamless. If additional controls are not put in place, the transition could be chaotic and leave the organization's assets vulnerable to criminal activity.

Phase VI — Resolution and Conclusion

Hoffa attempted to consolidate his power and take back his position as president of the union following his release from prison (Bruno, 2012). Hoffa was believed to have a scheduled meeting with two Detroit mobsters about returning as president of the Teamsters when he was allegedly kidnapped and murdered by them (Bruno, 2012). The men allegedly tied to Hoffa's murder and disappearance would eventually be tried and convicted by the government on other, unrelated charges (Bruno, 2012). As of this printing (2015), Hoffa's body has yet to be discovered, and his disappearance is still considered an open case (Bruno, 2012).

Recommendations and Concluding Remarks

This case study is an example of a 501(c)(5) non-profit organization that can use funds for promoting certain candidates for election. As seen in this case study, however, there were large sums of money that the organization possessed that were inappropriately used by organized crime and the organization's president. While the union had successes with Hoffa as its president, including the signing of the National Freight Agreement, the organization became intertwined with organized crime to such an extent that labor unions and organized crime were perceived to have a symbiotic relationship.

To avoid these types of issues, administrators and trustees have a fiduciary obligation to take action against organizational leaders when issues with possible criminal action come to light. Failure to do so invites criminal activity to spread throughout the organization and permeate even lower levels of operation. In this case study, Hoffa was extremely powerful, and the assessment could be made that people inside the organization who wanted to take action were too intimidated to confront the situation (Bruno, 2012).

The organization should have a whistleblower policy to encourage employees and others to report wrongful acts and to put proper controls in place and to make sure that policies and procedures are being carried out to prevent abuse, fraud, theft, or corruption from occurring.

Chapter 18

Tailhook Association — Alleged Sexual Harassment and Molestation — 1991

Phase I — Situation

You are an administrator of a non-profit organization that exists to foster knowledge, generate support, and encourage interested pilots in carrier aviation (Tailhook, 2012). Your organization was founded in 1956 and is currently located in San Diego. The regular membership is open to anyone who has made an arrested carrier landing, and associate membership is open to anyone that supports carrier aviation (Tailhook, 2012). The mission statement for the organization is as follows:

> The purposes of the Association as set forth in the organization bylaws are: "... to foster, encourage, develop, study, and support the aircraft carrier, sea-based aircraft, both fixed and rotary wing, and aircrews of the United States of America; and to educate and inform the public in the appropriate role of the aircraft carrier and carrier aviation in the nation's defense system." (Tailhook, 2012)

Your organization is sponsoring a conference at the Las Vegas Hilton in 1991, with 5,000 members in attendance (*Newsweek Magazine*, 1992). There have been some rumors that at past conventions the Tailhook Association held meetings in "hospitality suites" that contained strippers and porn films for the attendees. At one previous conference, there were allegations of sexual molestation of at least one underage girl (*Newsweek*, 1992). Additionally, there was liquor transported from Florida to the conference using federal tax dollars (*Newsweek*, 1992). Given these rumors, how should management proceed?

Questions that should be asked by the administrator at this phase:

1. There appears to be a pervasive culture that permits a high amount of alcohol consumption at your conference, which leads to other trouble. Is there a mechanism that can be used to curb massive alcohol consumption among your members?
2. Should you be concerned with how the rights of female members are protected while at the conference?
3. The alleged sexual molestation of an underage girl by your members at a conference is disturbing. What steps will you take to prevent are rectify this situation?
4. Should you consider discontinuing the hospitality suites?

Potential Issues for the Administrator to Consider

These issues should concern the administrator greatly. While there is nothing that the administrator can do to prevent boorish behavior outside of the conference, the administrator can make it clear to the membership that such behavior will not be tolerated. The administrator can state that if any member is found to act inappropriately or illegally during the conference, the organization will refer such members to law enforcement officials (if the behavior warrants such action), and the member will be suspended or asked to leave the conference and all membership rights in the organization will be terminated. The bylaws need to reflect this type of organizational response to support the administrators' ability to enforce such policies. Refrain or restrict the use of alcohol at organizational functions, because it could fuel problems among the members. Additionally, consider not sponsoring hospitality suites for your members because misuse of these suites may be a liability to the organization.

Phase II — First Issue

You have just been informed of a case of sexual harassment against one of your organization's female members (*Newsweek*, 1992). The woman, who happens to be an aide to an admiral and a helicopter pilot, was allegedly molested by more 30 male members of the organization when she walked down a hallway (*Newsweek*, 1992). Being associated with this type of conduct is not good for the organization.

Civil litigation and criminal charges could be filed against other members of the organization, and the organization itself could face civil litigation. As the administrator of the organization, what steps are you going to take?

Questions that should be asked by the administrator at this phase:

1. What should be done to investigate the incident in a professional manner?
2. How can the organization show that they are proactive in contending with such an issue?
3. Are there more incidents of this nature that have not been reported?
4. Is this a cultural issue with the organization at the conference?
5. Are officers attending the conference aware of any such instances?
6. Is the hotel aware of any such instances?
7. If these allegations are true, what action should the organization take toward the members who are the offenders, as well as steps to address the victims?

Potential Issues for the Administrator to Consider

The administrator has many different issues to be concerned with, not the least of which is the criminal actions that have allegedly occurred at the conference. The administrators of the association should contact legal counsel, the US Navy criminal investigators unit, and local law enforcement officials to report a suspected criminal act during the conference. Be prepared to provide any documentation that investigators may need during their investigation (attendance lists, etc.). If any members are found to be operating in an illegal or unethical fashion, the organization should be prepared to suspend or expel those individuals from their organization. The administrators, at this point, should also retain an attorney for any civil litigation that may ensue from any victims' claims.

Phase III — Second Issue

The Naval Investigative Service (NIS) has launched an investigation and found that several intoxicated officers allegedly assaulted 26 women, of who 14 were officers (*Newsweek*, 1992). The head of your organization condemned the officers involved in the alleged sexual molestations in a letter, stating that their activities were "far over the line of responsible behavior." This statement has been leaked to the San Diego *Union Tribune* (Center for Military Readiness, 2002). This incident is now becoming a public relations crisis. How will you regain a positive image for your organization?

Questions that should be asked by the administrator at this phase:

1. This situation has now gone public. What should you do in regard to public relations?

2. What strategy with communications should the organization take in addition to the condemnation statement?
3. How much civil liability could the organization potentially face?
4. How will you contend with the alleged victims?
5. How will you contend with the United States Navy, since several members of the alleged offenders that were attending the conference were officers in the United States Navy?

Potential Issues for the Administrator to Consider

The organization is going to have to be proactive to maintain any type of positive public relations image now, especially in spite of the statement to the press. The organization needs to issue a public statement to the effect that:

> We are currently cooperating with federal and local investigators and will comment as soon as the findings are complete and disclosed to us. At this point in time, we are reviewing organizational policies and procedures to address potential issues and rectify any issues that may exist. Any organization member that is found to be conducting illegal activity will be suspended or expelled from the organization.

For the benefit of your organization and the members that were not part of this culture, it is important that the organization is seen as not tolerating criminal behavior at the conference. The board needs to express and restate the mission of the organization and that the conference is for professional development and to promote the field of carrier aviator as a profession in the military. With 4,000 to 5,000 members in attendance at the conference, you should consider how to retain members that were not involved in the activities and successfully recruit new members into the organization. Even if no criminal convictions are made against any of the alleged offenders for activities that occurred at the conference, the organization could have exposure to civil liability if a successful argument was made that the organization facilitated a conference culture that permitted such conduct against female members.

Phase IV — Resolution and Conclusion

The initial whistleblower was awarded a multimillion-dollar suit from Hilton Hotels, since it was hosting the Tailhook conference in 1991 (Knowles, 2011). The scandal eventually led to the resignation of the secretary of the navy (Knowles, 2011). Rear Admiral Riley Mixon was censured for being responsible for the arrangements of the Tailhook convention, which Mixon publicly refuted, since he was in Operation Desert Storm during that timeframe (Center for Military Readiness, 2002). Not a single person was ever court-martialed for the incidents that occurred at the convention (Center for Military Readiness, 2002).

Recommendations and Concluding Remarks

This case study illustrates how an organization can be damaged (i.e., settlement) from criminal activity that occurs during one of its functions. While the organization may not be directly responsible for the criminal actions that occurred at the conference, the organization did not take any proactive steps to prevent sexual harassment or molestation at the conference (i.e., no code of conduct was apparent). The weak response from the organization's top administrator probably did not help the organization's public relations position in the eyes of the public.

While the alleged activities were conducted by navy personnel and officers, the Tailhook organization itself may always be intertwined with what occurred in 1991 and will be hard pressed to ever separate itself from those alleged activities. There are lessons to be learned, and administrators that are in charge of conferences for organizations should take heed of the Tailhook organization since any organization could face such issues and administrators will need a plan to contend with the potential crisis that erupts from such behavior or activities.

Chapter 19

New Life Children's Refuge — Child Adoption Scandal during the Haiti Earthquake — 2010

Phase I — Situation

You are a member of the US diplomatic corps that works with Haiti. It is 2010, and there has just been a massive earthquake in Haiti that has absolutely decimated the entire population and the country (Vu, 2010). Many non-profit organizations have volunteered to assist with the crisis since, Haiti is ill-prepared to contend with such a problem that has impacted so many areas in the country (Rossouw, 2010). One such non-profit organization that has come into Haiti is the New Life Children's Refuge (NLCR) (New Life Children's Refuge, 2010). The group's mission statement is as follows:

> Rescue Haitian orphans abandoned on the streets, makeshift hospitals or from collapsed orphanages in Port au Prince and surrounding areas, and bring them to New Life Children's Refuge in Cabarete, Dominican Republic. (New Life Children's Refuge, 2010)

The group's mission statement is clear that it ultimately wants the orphans to be adopted by families (New Life Children's Refuge, 2010). You have been notified that there is a group of ten missionaries that are with the NLCR that have been arrested crossing the Dominican Republic border with 33 children from Haiti (Vu, 2010). The NLCR is not registered in the United States as a non-profit organization, nor is it registered as an adoption agency in the United States or internationally (Thompson, 2010). The members of the NLCR are currently being held by the Dominican Republic authorities on child trafficking charges (Vu, 2010). The missionaries do not have any paperwork or authorization for transporting the children. The missionaries claim that they were taking the children to a hotel that had been converted to an orphanage in the Dominican Republic (Vu, 2010). Several of the children that were transported are reported to have been traumatized by the experience (SOS Children's Villages, 2010). One of the children had to be taken to the hospital for immediate medical attention (SOS Children's Villages, 2010). This apparently was the second time that the group had been stopped; previously, they attempted to take 40 children to the Dominican Republic but were stopped by a police officer (Vu, 2010). This situation contends with alleged criminal activity, so what are the issues that the non-profit organization should be asking itself currently?

Questions that should be asked by the administrator at this phase:

1. Were the missionaries operating on behalf of the non-profit organization?
2. Did the missionaries have proper authorization to transport the children in the first place, let alone to another country?
3. What attempts were made by the missionaries to make sure that the children were in fact orphans and that there were no parents or relatives around that could take guardianship of the children?
4. How will the non-profit organization contend with the legal authorities in the Dominican Republic and in Haiti?
5. How will you liaise with the government entities that are involved with this case?
6. How will you attempt to protect the missionaries?

Potential Issues for the Director to Consider

The group of missionaries appears to have acted in violation of the law in Haiti, which puts the non-profit organization in a very delicate position trying to protect its personnel. The non-profit organization needs to hire competent legal counsel that is familiar with the local legal system to avoid criminal convictions in a foreign court. The group is affiliated with the Southern Baptist Convention, which has made requests to the US government to get the missionaries free from Haiti, to no avail (Vu, 2010). This should send a message to the non-profit organization and its administrators that the missionaries will need to contend with the Haitian legal system. The non-profit organization's best strategy is to have members that have not been arrested contact key supporters to raise funds for their legal defense.

Phase II — The First Issue

It has now come to light that at least 20 of the children that were transported by the NLCR have parents and are not orphans at all (Vu, 2010). In addition, the Dominican Republic's government asserts that there was no such documentation issued that permitted the children to be transferred across the border from Haiti to the Dominican Republic (Vu, 2010). At least one Dominican Republic official has publicly stated the organization's leader was warned that the missionaries would get into trouble without proper documentation (CNN, 2010). Apparently, the missionaries were well aware that the children in many cases were not orphans and that their relatives were attempting to make sure the children were safe or had a better life (Associated Press, 2010). The US State Department has apparently taken the political position of, "It's their country. The judgment is really up to the Haitian government" (Thompson, 2010). What options are open to the non-profit organization at this point?

Questions that should be asked by the administrator at this phase:

1. What procedures were in place to ensure that the children being transported were actually orphans?
2. Who in the organization should be held accountable for the alleged illegal activities?
3. How will the organization assess its exposure to civil liability and minimize any risks to the same?
4. Should the organization try to gain financial or political support for the leaders of the Southern Baptist Convention for the missionaries that are being held for trial?
5. Why was the NLCR's mission violated with the transportation of children that were known to not be orphans?

Potential Issues for the Director to Consider

The issue of transporting children with parents opens a new dimension into the problems that the NLCR will face. These actions could result in civil litigation against the NLCR, its board, and the missionaries by the parents of the children who were transported. Non-profit organizations should be cognizant of their purpose and operate in accordance with the same. It appears that the children who were intended to be helped by the NLCR may not have been clearly defined or that the missionaries may not have been clearly defined. The Southern Baptist Convention should not be counted on to get the missionaries out of the Haitian legal system through political intervention, since the US State Department appears to have taken a "hands-off approach" toward the matter. It would better serve the members of the Southern Baptist Convention to raise funds for the NLCR's legal defense.

Phase III — Second Issue

The Haitian authorities have released eight of the missionaries, but two of the missionaries, including the head of the NLCR, remain in custody (Romero and Urbina, 2010). Some of the freed missionaries claim that the leader of the NLCR was misled about their operation to Haiti (Romero and Urbina, 2010). In addition, a Dominican adviser to the NLCR is wanted for sex trafficking charges in El Salvador, as well as smuggling illegal immigrants into the United States (Romero and Urbina, 2010).

Questions that should be asked by the administrator at this phase:

1. What can be done, if anything, to get the last two missionaries out of jail?
2. Should the Southern Baptist Convention leadership take a position about how the NLCR has supervised and protected its members?
3. Should the Southern Baptist Convention provide more oversight and guidance to groups that are affiliated with it to protect its members?

Potential Issues for the Administrator to Consider

The danger of being affiliated with a group that is not under direct control or guidance is that if the affiliated group engages in illegal or unethical activity, the reputation of the other group could be tarnished and it will not have the authority to correct the situation. In this case, the Southern Baptist Convention's affiliation with the NLCR has now forced the Southern Baptist Convention in a position of either publically defending the NLCR for its illegal activities (i.e., kidnapping and child smuggling) or completely cutting ties with the organization. Either decision will not reflect well with different segments of the population. Another option for the Southern Baptist Convention is to "assist" the NLCR with diplomatic and legal issues. After the situation is resolved, the Southern Baptist Convention could offer to train the leadership of the NLCR on issues of working with foreign governments and conducting missionary operations. What started as a small non-profit organization being arrested and charged with child trafficking became a situation in which the Southern Baptist Convention leadership is publicly asking the president of the United States to intervene on the NLCR's behalf.

Phase IV — Resolution and Conclusion

Eventually, the ninth missionary was freed, and Laura Silsby of the NLCR was convicted and sentenced to six months of jail in Haiti for arranging illegal travel (*USA Today*, 2010). The NLCR's adviser, Jorge Puello, was wanted by law enforcement officials in the Dominican Republic, El Salvador, and the United States (Lacey and Urbina, 2010).

Recommendations and Concluding Remarks

The NLCR case study shows how a non-profit organization that is not knowledgeable about international law can run into serious legal trouble quickly. The case study also illustrates the dangers of veering away from the original mission and purpose of the organization. The group was led by an individual that, based on the actions that took place and her conviction in Haiti, was ill-equipped to contend with international law or lead volunteers of the organization effectively. It can be concluded that the group was naïve about how it operated, about the people that it relied on (i.e., Puello), and about formulating a plan if problems arose with the local officials.

If an organization is to successfully operate in a foreign country, then it would stand to reason that the organization would have a plan to have funds in reserve for legal counsel, people in the organization who could interface successfully with the foreign government and the US State Department, and have extensive logistics planning, as well as policies and procedures to accomplish their task. Furthermore, the organization appears to have needed additional training as well as connecting with foreign officials before missionaries were sent into the country. The additional problem of the organization not being registered as a legitimate non-profit organization or an adoption agency in the United States (not to mention international registration) poses substantial problems to the organization's legitimacy as a valid non-profit organization.

The Southern Baptist Convention itself appeared to have no contingency plan for an affiliated group that was in trouble with a foreign government. There also appears to be no mechanism for the Southern Baptist Convention to provide any type of leadership or guidance to non-profit organizations with which it is affiliated. This shortfall can present potential problems in regard to public relations for the Southern Baptist Convention. How the Southern Baptist Convention responds next time if an affiliated organization gets in trouble with a foreign government will be interesting to watch.

Chapter 20

Second Mile — Sexual Predator — Penn State University — 2011

Phase I — Situation

You are a member of the board of directors at Penn State University, known as Penn State. Among other things, Penn State is widely known for the quality of its athletics, particularly its football program, led for many years by legendary head coach Joe Paterno. Gerald "Jerry" Sandusky, in his 32 years in Penn State's athletic department, was a former player, defensive coach, and Paterno's one-time heir apparent.

When Paterno did not retire from his position, as some had expected, in 1999, Sandusky retired from the university. His retirement package allowed him to keep an office in the football department, and he was listed as a professor emeritus of physical education. After retirement, Sandusky funded and served as the primary fundraiser for The Second Mile, a non-profit organization providing services to underprivileged and at-risk children and their parents.

Recently, Sandusky has been accused of 48 counts of criminal sexual abuse, over 15 years, involving children. It is alleged that some of the abuse occurred on the grounds of Penn State, and there are allegations that high-level members of the football staff and executives of the university were aware of the alleged abuse for quite some time but overlooked the accusations altogether (Carbone, 2011).

Questions that should be asked by the board of directors at this phase:

1. What should the Penn State University board of directors' initial response be, in light of the accusations, and should media be included at this point, as they will be the ones delivering the news to the public?
2. What processes will you follow to determine who, if anyone, within the athletic department and the executive-level positions had knowledge of the allegations?
3. If members of the athletic department or executive-level positions had knowledge of the allegations, when did they know, and what did they do with that knowledge?
4. What is the relationship between Penn State and The Second Mile?
5. Will these allegations raise any issues with the National Collegiate Athletic Association (NCAA)?

Potential Issues for Public Relations

Any public relations issue for Penn State will be tied to (1) whether any of Sandusky's alleged criminal actions occurred on the Penn State campus; (2) whether, over the 15-year period in which they occurred, any members of the athletic department or executive-level personnel had knowledge of Sandusky's alleged actions; and (3) what, if anything, they did with that knowledge.

If there is any evidence that Penn State personnel were complicit in Sandusky's alleged criminal behavior, or in its cover-up, the scrutiny and negative press will be considerable. There could be a reduction in donations, endowments, and student enrollment, in addition to potential lawsuits directed at Penn State.

Directors must determine to what extent, if any, Penn State personnel were involved in the commission or cover-up of Sandusky's actions.

Phase II — First Issue

Further investigation has revealed considerable evidence against Sandusky, but more troubling is evidence that members of the Penn State coaching staff, including head coach Paterno, were aware of inappropriate activities well before any of the alleged victims came forward. It appears there were Penn State employees and people in leadership positions who knew illegal and immoral behavior by Sandusky was taking place, yet little evidence exists that actions were taken to stop the behavior. In fact, in 1998, after an 11-year-old boy returned from The Second Mile charity home with wet hair, Sandusky admitted to showering naked with the boy and was investigated by the Pennsylvania Department of Public Welfare, but was never charged with any criminal wrongdoing.

It is also reported that janitor James Calhoun observed Sandusky showering with and sexually abusing another male child in 2000. After he reported the incident to his immediate supervisor, nothing else was done.

In 2002, Penn State graduate assistant Mike McQueary observed Sandusky showering with and sexually abusing yet another boy. McQueary alerted the boy's father, in addition to other members of the coaching staff, including Paterno. Neither Penn State police nor any other administrative entity conducted an investigation into this incident. Penn State employees made it clear to the administration that inappropriate and clearly criminal actions were taking place, yet the administration and leadership did not take action (Penn State Scandal, 2011).

Given the degree of this growing scandal, where does the board of directors go from here?

Questions that should be asked by the board of directors at this point:

1. Was the board aware of any of the internally reported allegations before those allegations became public?
2. Are there any legal implications at this point for Penn State?
3. Are there any NCAA implications at this point for Penn State?
4. Does Penn State have a whistleblower policy?
5. Why, even after eyewitness accounts of inappropriate activities, was no action taken against Sandusky? Were threats made? Or was it a matter of apathy or willful obstruction at many levels, including, potentially, your board?
6. How are you going to handle the inevitable scrutiny and negative press that will come from the revelation that members of the athletic department knew of Sandusky's alleged criminal actions, yet apparently did nothing to rectify the situation?

Potential Issues for Public Relations

Now that it is clear that members of the Penn State athletic department were aware of Sandusky's actions over an extended period of time, the investigative reporting will increase. Questions of whether athletics, specifically football, are more important to Penn State than the criminal activity of someone associated with the program will surely be featured. The only way Penn State's public relations issues could get any more negative would be if top-level executives are also involved in the apparent cover-up. This could result in sanctions by the NCAA and could jeopardize federal funding to Penn State.

Phase III — Second Issue

Sandusky was charged with involuntary deviant sexual intercourse, unlawful contact with a minor, indecent assault, endangering the welfare of children, and corruption of minors on November 5, 2011, and was arrested on December 7, 2011 (Curry, 2011). It became apparent that the level of knowledge of Sandusky's child sexual abuse reached the top levels of the executive positions at Penn State, with everyone involved seemingly turning a blind eye to what he'd done.

The appearance of lack of action on the part of Paterno, a very powerful person at Penn State, raises questions about a cover-up for a longtime friend. There is no evidence, even with knowledge of the allegations, that Paterno pressed the issue to get to the bottom of the allegations. He has said, "This is a tragedy. It is one of the great sorrows of my life. With the benefit of hindsight, I wish I had done more" (Chappell, 2012).

Graham Spanier, Penn State president, is accused of participating in a "conspiracy of silence" to cover up the actions of Sandusky; more specifically, he is accused of child endangerment, perjury and criminal conspiracy, failure to report suspected abuse, and obstruction of the administration of law.

Gary Schultz, senior vice president for finance and business, who had oversight of the Penn State police, is accused of child endangerment, criminal conspiracy and obstruction, failure to report suspected abuse, and perjury (Chappell, 2012).

Timothy Curley, former athletic director for Penn State, was indicted for perjury, failing to report possible abuse, and child endangerment.

Questions that should be asked by the board at this point:

1. Should consideration be given to removing Paterno, Spanier, and Schultz from their positions?
2. How are you going to handle the anticipated increase in media attention and coverage resulting from the attention that will come from the involvement of such high-level personnel?
3. There appears to be a lack of institutional control in the handling of the Sandusky scandal. What procedures are in place, or what should the board do to rectify the problem?
4. Should consideration be given to hiring outside legal counsel as a preemptive step in dealing with Paterno, Spanier, and Schultz?
5. How do you manage Penn State's public image, an image that will surely be tarnished, in light of this scandal?
6. How do you respond to your student body, your alumni, and your supporters?

Potential Issues for Public Relations

The lack of action on the part of the Penn State leadership is unacceptable and cause for great concern. The inaction of three members of the Penn State family with the highest-profile positions will have extremely negative public relations implications. Especially with Paterno, any efforts to relieve him of his duties, after what he has meant to and done for Penn State, could be a difficult public relations matter as it relates to students, alumni, donors, and corporate sponsors.

Phase IV — Third Issue

The fallout for the Penn State and its board of trustees is broad, including a $60 million NCAA fine — the largest in its history — and a voiding of its football victories for the past 14 seasons. NCAA President Mark Emmert admonished Penn State, stating it placed "hero worship and winning at all costs ahead of integrity, honesty, and responsibility" (Edith Honan, 2012).

An internal investigation led by former FBI director Louis Freeh reported in July 2012 that Spanier, Schultz, Curley, and Paterno covered up Sandusky's activities from the board of trustees, from the university community, and from authorities. Freeh's investigation began shortly after Sandusky's arrest and delved as far back as 1975, covering more ground than the grand jury report. Freeh and his team conducted 430 interviews and reviewed 3.5 million emails and other documents, revealing an extensive, high-level cover-up, and numerous times Penn State officials might have stopped Sandusky from sexually abusing children but did nothing (Kingkade, 2012).

Freeh's report clearly indicts the board of trustees, as well, stating that it learned about the grand jury's investigation of Sandusky's actions through newspaper accounts. No one on the board was briefed on the matter until April 2011, and then the board took no action, nor was it even briefed again until after Sandusky's arrest.

Citing the experiences of several janitors who witnessed Sandusky raping a child and performing oral sex on another, Freeh said they feared losing their jobs and taking on the powerful Penn State football program. Referring to the board, Freeh stated, "If that's the culture on the bottom, God help the culture on the top." The board "failed in its oversight of the senior university officers and did not create an atmosphere 'where the president and senior officers felt accountable to the board'" (Kingkade, 2012).

The lack of faith in the board and university officials extends even to its credit rating in the wake of the Sandusky scandal. Penn State faces a potential credit downgrade as "Moody's believes that the university is incapable of managing the current sanctions, it is also considering the possibility of future investigations and lawsuits" (Forbes, 2012), in addition to a variety of civil lawsuits the university faces.

Questions that should be asked by the administrator at this phase:

1. Is it appropriate to consider a challenge to the NCAA's sanctions?
2. What steps can be taken to recoup the financial loss from the sanctions?
3. How can you rebuild the public image of Penn State athletics as it relates to the NCAA?

Potential Issues for Public Relations

The public relations issue resulting from the NCAA sanctions is extremely damaging to the institution as well as the athletics department. The reputation of the entire university has been tarnished as a result of the scandal. How Penn State handles the rebuilding of the image of its athletics department and specifically its football program will go a long way to rebuilding the image of the university as a whole.

Phase V — Resolution and Conclusion

Spanier was fired, and Schultz resigned in November 2011. Paterno was fired as head coach and removed from all association with Penn State on November 9, 2011, and he subsequently died of cancer. Dr. Rodney Erickson was named university president in November 2011, and in January 2012, Penn State announced Bill O'Brien would be the new head football coach. Sandusky, who recently turned 70, was convicted on 45 out of 48 criminal counts and is serving out a 30- to 60-year sentence in a maximum-security prison.

Given the new leadership, the university has a chance to renew its image. A new coaching staff, realignment of the athletic department vision, and an expectation of morality and accountability will point the institution in a positive direction. It will be imperative that the president, head coach, and associate coaching staff team members maintain an open line of communication and create a safe working environment. Internally, Penn State must be intentional in creating a workplace where employees are held accountable, trust is reestablished, and security is upheld in reporting inappropriate actions. Policies clearly stating the consequences of how to handle these situations and the reporting process should be strongly upheld.

Compliance to NCAA standards and rebuilding an image of excellence will be the most effective way to promote trust and a renewed favorable public opinion, but it will take time. In the short term, it will be difficult to measure the magnitude this scandal has caused the institution. In the long term, however, it is likely Penn State has the ability to recuperate and regain its former standing and prestige.

Penn State must be diligent about rebuilding its culture and reputation and reforming its governance structure to include more transparency. This process will require assistance from both internal and external forces, from its employees outward, and only time will tell the university's and the athletic program's ability to achieve their goals. Consequently, Penn State may feasibly never fully rebound from the Sandusky scandal.

Chapter 21

ACORN — Voter Fraud — 2011

Phase I — Situation

You are an administrator with the Association for Community Organizations Reform Now (ACORN). ACORN has been a driving force in expanding voter registration, specifically among the more underprivileged areas of the United States (Editorial, 2008).

Since the elections in 2000, in general, the US political climate has been growing more contentious, and presidential elections have seen an increase in partisan political efforts to manipulate votes. During this same period of time, ACORN has intensified its efforts to register more voters.

During the 2008 presidential race, Sen. John McCain's presidential campaign pressed hard to tie Sen. Barack Obama to ACORN, and by association, to voter fraud or voter registration fraud. Charges were made that members of ACORN paid individuals to register to vote. Other charges allege people were registered fraudulently, including using the names of deceased and nonexistent people in Colorado, Indiana, North Carolina, and Nevada (Strom, 2008).

Specifically, in Nevada, there were accusations ACORN associates created an incentive program called "Blackjack." Those who signed up more than 21 prospective voters were allegedly paid $5. The Clark County Nevada Registrar of Voters requested an investigation after noting a high number of forms submitted bearing the names of famous football players and cartoon characters (Friess, 2009).

Questions that should be asked by the administrator at this phase:

1. What have you done to gather information if the alleged fraud actually occurred? If so, how pervasive is it throughout the organization?
2. Are you able to determine if this is the action of the organization itself or of people within it acting of their own accord?
3. What action should be taken against the individuals who are involved if the allegations are proven to be true?
4. What procedures do you have in place to effectively cooperate with those who are investigating the allegations?
5. How will you manage the expected media scrutiny and negative press?

Potential Issues for Public Relations

Senators Obama and McCain both have histories with ACORN; however, Sen. Obama's history is more extensive. This matter concerning alleged voter fraud or voter registration fraud is, in itself, a public relations problem. The fact that it is now being tied into presidential politics makes it significantly more problematic (Suddath, 2008).

It will be imperative to keep the responses to, and management of, the public relations issue above the fray of politics, if at all possible, because the more this becomes a political issue, the longer the public relations problem will persist.

You and the other administrators must do whatever you can to keep the focus on the mission of the organization, and, more specifically, voter registration, without getting pulled into a political quagmire. This may require securing the services of outside crisis management or a public relations consultant for assistance in determining the proper direction to take.

Phase II — First Issue

Between July and August 2009, a series of videos were produced of employees at ACORN offices in Baltimore, Washington, DC, Brooklyn, San Bernardino, and San Diego, California. Hannah Giles and James O'Keefe, conservative activists, pretended to seek advice on how to run an illegal business, and secretly recorded their interaction with the ACORN employees. The videos give the appearance that ACORN employees advised the couple about running an illegal business, hiding prostitution activities, and avoiding paying taxes. Edited versions of the videos were released to the public between September 10 and September 17, 2009.

Sen. Mike Johanns (R) of Nebraska asked the Justice Department to investigate ACORN. He also sponsored a Senate amendment barring ACORN from receiving federal grants (Fessler, 2009).

Questions that should be asked by the administrator at this phase:

1. Should you contact legal counsel at this point so that an investigation can be conducted on the employees who are shown in the videos and gather information about their side of the story?
2. What can be done to mitigate the effects of the videos?
3. Have you considered hiring an independent investigator to look into the backgrounds of Hannah Giles and James O'Keefe and their motives for recording the videos?
4. Have you considered hiring an independent investigator to look into the circumstances surrounding the video recordings at each location and to verify the unedited content of the videos?
5. Should an independent assessment of the organization and its viability be done at this time?
6. Should an independent crisis management or public relations firm be hired to advise and act in the capacity of spokesperson?
7. What are you going to do to protect the government contracts that are in place in light of the public and political scandal that has mushroomed because of the videos?

Potential Issues for Public Relations

Immediately upon the release of the videos, widespread negative publicity and political uproar against ACORN developed. The obvious public relations issue is, how does your organization respond to the videos?

This has resulted in an organizational and political scandal fueled by alleged voter or voter registration fraud. Your public relations response must assure the public that all irregularities and allegations are being taken seriously and addressed as needed.

Government contracts and grants may be voided. Funding sources from all other avenues could cease. Your organization could be rendered ineffective if it appears to have become too politically toxic to remain viable. Individuals within the organization could be subject to criminal charges.

Phase III — Second Issue

Within the current political climate, the allegations of fraud and the release of the videos have resulted in unprecedented scrutiny and investigation of ACORN. Among the actions taken, the US Census Bureau, which had partnered with ACORN to assist in publicizing the importance of the census and to encourage people to participate, revoked that partnership (Sherman, 2009).

The Senate voted to block the Department of Housing and Urban Development (HUD) from giving grants to ACORN, which would affect programs offering counseling for low-income people, instruction on how to get mortgages, and fair housing education and outreach (Taylor, 2009). In addition, the Internal Revenue Service (IRS) has removed ACORN from its volunteer tax-assistance program (Wheaton, 2009).

Independent investigations have been initiated by the Congressional Research Services, commissioned by the House Judiciary Committee, the US Government Accountability Office (GAO) — the audit, evaluation, and investigative arm of Congress — and by the attorneys general of Massachusetts, California, and New York.

There is also mounting evidence of voter registration fraud by individual employees: voter registration cards were made up using fake names, fake birthdays, and even fake Social Security numbers. Some of the individuals involved in these activities have been convicted and sentenced to time in jail (Lawrence, 2008).

Questions that should be asked by the administrator at this phase:

1. What steps will you take to salvage the reputation of the organization?
2. Do you hire counsel to respond to the various investigations that are taking place?
3. Do you hire counsel to challenge the termination of federal grants and act on behalf of ACORN if there is a request for the return of grant funding already provided?
4. If an independent assessment of your organization and its viability has been performed, what are the results of that assessment?
5. How do you plan to promote and accomplish the vision and mission of ACORN under the current circumstances?

Potential Issues for Public Relations

The public relations issue you must consider at this stage is the political assault on your organization. How do you manage it, and what can be done to mitigate the damage that has been caused?

The Proskauer firm was hired by ACORN leadership to conduct its own inquiry into the circumstances surrounding the making of the videos in July 2009; to evaluate the effectiveness of ACORN's new leadership — known as the "reform leadership" — that was hired in June 2008 after news surfaced that a relative of ACORN founder Wade Rathke had embezzled funds, which Rathke attempted to cover up; and to propose short- and long-term solutions for ACORN's management, oversight, and governance (Harshbarger & Crafts, 2009). They issued their report a year and a half later in December 2009.

The videos, according to the report, were perceived as a "third strike" against your organization, following the charges against Rathke and the allegations of voter registration fraud in the 2008 election. Just as the reform leadership was finding its feet and attempting organizational and cultural reform, the video controversy knocked it off them again, pointing up even more serious management challenges. Because the founder and ACORN's leaders did not commit to "basic, appropriate standards of governance and accountability," the report states, ACORN "left itself vulnerable to public embarrassment" (Harshbarger & Crafts, 2009).

The Prokrauer report recommended the following, "as a roadmap to reform and renewal":

> Administrators should immediately implement an independent assessment of the organization, including (1) consolidation, simplification, and centralization of local and national organizational staffing, monitoring, and supervision; (2) implementation of a comprehensive internal governance program and strategy, including internal controls, compliance, and a code of ethics, designed to educate and guide staff, volunteers, and board members; (3) recruitment of an independent ethics officer to oversee and implement the governance and compliance program at the national level; (4) hiring appropriately qualified chief operating and financial officers, a comptroller, and in-house auditing staff; (5) coordination of the dissolution of all extraneous ACORN organizations and representation of the organization's interests in litigation and investigations; (6) requiring all state and local affiliates to agree to oversight by the national staff and board, and adherence to appropriate national standards; and (7) formalizing a strong, independent, national advisory group and charging it with the responsibility of reporting to the national board within six months, and thereafter annually for two years, on the progress of the reform actions plan. (Harshbarger & Crafts, 2009)

Phase IV — Third Issue

ACORN and others raised questions about the truthfulness of the videos in light of potential self-serving editing. As the various investigations concluded, a general consensus can be gleaned from the following reports:

The New York attorney general concluded that the videos were heavily edited to give a misleading impression, and there was no criminal wrongdoing on the part of the ACORN staff in the Brooklyn, New York, office. A law enforcement officer said, "They edited the tape to meet their agenda" (Madden, 2010).

The California attorney general concluded the videos were heavily edited to feature only the worst or most inappropriate statements of the various ACORN employees. While faulting some of the employees for "terrible judgment and highly inappropriate behavior, such behavior did not rise to the level of a law enforcement or governmental concern (Report, 2010).

Questions that should be asked by the administrator at this phase:

1. How can you use the findings of the various investigations to aid in rebuilding the image of ACORN?
2. What actions, if any, are you going to take against Hannah Giles and James O'Keefe?
3. Will you pursue actions begun against those employees who exhibited poor, but not criminal, judgment? Would training sessions suffice in this situation, rather than punitive action?
4. What can you do to ensure that this type of scenario does not take place again at ACORN?
5. What, if anything, can you do to address the political issues that led to this scandal and the mischaracterization of ACORN in the first place?
6. Can the relationships with governmental organizations and other stakeholders be salvaged now that the scandal has abated?

Potential Issues for Public Relations

The findings of these investigations are positive from a public relations standpoint. How can these reports be used for the good of the organization?

Phase V — Resolution and Conclusion

In regard to voter registration fraud, Eric Schnapper, University of Washington law professor, said, "The idea of fake cards turning into real votes is a myth. There are no known instances of fictitious people actually voting. You look at some of the names, Mickey Mouse, Dr. Seuss ... he's not going to show up at a critical precinct in West Virginia or North Carolina" (Lawrence, 2008).

A report from the Brennan Center for Justice at New York University Law School, a nonpartisan organization, supports Schnapper's opinion. Researchers reviewed voter fraud claims across the country and found that most were caused by technical glitches, clerical errors, or human error. Another interesting finding states that a person is more likely to be struck by lightning than to impersonate another voter at the polls (Lawrence, 2008).

Notwithstanding independent investigations to the contrary, ACORN could not overcome the accusations of voter/voter registration fraud and the scandal over videos purporting to show staff helping activists run illegal businesses, hide prostitution activities, and avoid paying taxes. On November 2, 2010, ACORN filed for bankruptcy.

ACORN CEO Bertha Lewis said, "For over 40 years, ACORN has fought the good fight, but a barrage of unmitigated accusations certainly took its toll, and the ongoing political onslaught caused irreparable harm. We have spent our remaining resources trying to dissolve the organization with integrity" (Memoli, 2010).

Chapter 22

Catholic Church — Sexual Abuse Scandal — Ongoing

Phase I — Situation

You are a high-ranking church leader in the Catholic Church. The Catholic Church, also known as the Roman Catholic Church or, simply, the Church, is the world's largest Christian church, with 1.2 billion members. The Catholic hierarchy includes cardinals and bishops and is led by the Bishop of Rome, known as the pope, who has supreme authority over the Church and is considered by Catholics to be, like its doctrine, infallible.

One of the oldest and most powerful forces in Western civilization, the Church has gained public scrutiny in recent years due to its doctrines on homosexuality, birth control, the role of women in the Church, and its handling of cases of sexual abuse by its priests.

The American Psychological Association (2013) defines child sexual abuse as offenses in which an adult engages in sexual activity with a minor or exploits a minor for the purpose of sexual gratification. It involves a dominant adult who forces or coerces a child into such activity. The activity is not solely restricted to physical contact; such abuse could include voyeurism and child pornography.

Historically, the Church has handled matters of child sexual abuse at the hands of bishops, priests, nuns, and other members of the clergy on a local level by the local bishop, refusing to place matters in the hands of civil authorities. Offending clergy are routinely moved from diocese to diocese, where they still have access to children and have often continued to abuse. Church officials have been known to obstruct investigations and prosecutions in an effort to cover up child sexual abuse by leaders of the Church. Church authorities have also been known to reward those who assisted in covering up for abusers and punishing those who tried to bring crimes to light. Perhaps most troubling, Church representatives blame the victims of sexual abuse and raise questions about the motives of those who muster the courage to accuse their abusers (Center for Constitutional Rights, 2013). The Church recognizes sexual abuse of children is an abomination, but it tends to see it as something that should be handled discreetly, internally, and in a way calculated to protect the good name of the Church (Mehegan, 1993).

Scholarly studies of the incidence and prevalence of child sexual abuse first emerged in the 1960s, and then received even more popular attention in the 1980s when a number of child care centers were accused of the sexual abuse of children, according to a report by the John Jay College of Criminal Justice (*The Nature*, 2004), commissioned by the US Conference of Catholic Bishops (USCCB). Because sexual crimes are the most underreported of crimes, it's even more difficult to measure the incidence of child sexual abuse by clergy. However, the John Jay study concluded that in its study range — from 1950 to 2002 — in the United States, 4 percent of priests and deacons in active ministry have been accused of the sexual abuse of a youth (p. 33).

Questions that should be asked by the church leader at this phase:

1. What measures are currently in place to protect the children?
2. Can you determine the scope of child sexual abuse within your own diocese?
3. What disciplinary action is being taken with individuals who are accused of child sexual abuse?
4. What type of assistance, if any, are members of the Church providing to victims of child sexual abuse by clergy?
5. Are whistleblowers and victims treated with respect in your diocese? If not, why not?
6. Should the matter of child sexual abuse be taken out of the hands of local bishops and referred, instead, to the pope for appropriate action and resolution? How could that be initiated?
7. Does the Church have an obligation to report sexual abuse to outside civil authorities?

Potential Issues for Public Relations

The Church's public relations problems in this matter are vast and have reached a global scale. The vast majority of people around the world — inside and outside the Church hierarchy — are all asking the same question: How can Church leaders — who profess to be people of God — justify sexually abusing children? And how could anyone who knew about these crimes participate in a systematic coverup of them?

Phase II — First Issue

In 2003, the *Boston Globe* released an extensive report on child sexual abuse by clergy within the Church in the United States. This report chronicled accounts of abuse, exposed the child sexual abuse scandal, and increased local and national media scrutiny (Cox, 2003). As a consequence of the *Globe* report, USCCB commissioned the John Jay study, which reported a number of disturbing findings in regard to sexual abuse of young people by Church officials:

1. Approximately 80 percent of the victims were male, and 20 percent were female.
2. Approximately 23 percent were 10 years old or younger, 50 percent were between the ages of 11 and 14, and 27 percent were between the ages of 15 and 17.
3. In 72 percent of cases, an investigation was carried out, and of these, 80 percent were substantiated, 18 percent were unsubstantiated, and 1.4 percent were false allegations.
4. In 38 percent of the allegations, the alleged abuse lasted a year or less; in 22 percent, the alleged abuse lasted more than a year, but less than 2 years; in 28 percent, the alleged abuse lasted between 2 and 4 years; and in 10 percent, the alleged abuse lasted between 5 and 9 years. Less than 1 percent of the alleged abuse lasted 10 years or more (Catholic Sex Abuse Cases, n.d., p. 5).

With increasing numbers of alleged victims coming forward, the Church has endeavored to settle with the victims where it feels that the evidence warrants it. In 2003, the archdioceses of Louisville and Boston settled cases involving a total of 792 alleged victims for a total of $112.5 million (Smith, 2003; Wingert, 2010). In 2007, the diocese of San Diego and the archdioceses of Seattle, Los Angeles, and Portland, Oregon, settled cases involving a total of 981 alleged victims for a total of $981 million (Wooden, 2007; Martinez, 2007). The Associated Press estimates the total dollar amount of settlements from 1950–2007 at more than $2 billion. (AP, 2007). Bishop Accountability, the non-profit that documents Catholic child sex abuse cases, reports that figure reached more than $3 billion by 2012 (Schaffer, 2012).

Questions that should be asked by the Church leadership at this phase:

1. Should you continue to handle the child sexual abuse allegations on a local level by individual bishops, or should consideration be given to handling such allegations at the conference or national level, with one directive and one voice?
2. Are you going to institute a clear policy at the conference or national level on how to handle the person who is sexually abused and the abuser? If not, why not?

3. Should you provide psychiatric or psychological counseling/treatment by independent specialists to clergy who have engaged in child sexual abuse activity? If not, why not?
4. Should you press criminal charges against those in the Church hierarchy who sexually abused children? If not, why not?
5. Should you offer psychiatric or psychological counseling/treatment by independent specialist to the alleged victims? If not, why not?
6. What steps are being put in place to serve as preventive measures in mitigating or eliminating such activity from occurring in the future?
7. How will these settlements and legal fees be paid?

Potential Issues for Public Relations

The extent of the child sexual abuse within the Church is becoming clearer and more detailed to the public. Additional transparency will bring more public scrutiny to how these cases were and are being handled by the Church. This is proving to be a major obstacle for the Church to address. The scandal has damaged the image of the Church, faith in its institution, and trust in its clergy. Church members may become disillusioned and leave the Church, which would result in a loss of income from the tithes and offerings of its members.

Phase III — Second Issue

Church child sexual abuse issues are not solely a Church matter in the United States. Ireland, Germany, and Australia offer just a glimpse at the scope of the problem:

One of the many allegations occurred during the tenure of Pope Benedict XVI when he was archbishop of the Munich archdiocese. A priest is alleged to have molested more than 300 children. The revelation threatened the pope's reputation and moral authority, as he had allowed the priest to remain working and involved with children after he learned of the allegations (Gilgoff, 2010).

In Ireland, as of 2002, 50 priests have been convicted of child sexual abuse, with the Church offering $110 million to compensate those who were abused. One of the many allegations involved a three-year ordeal between a 14-year-old boy and a priest who repeatedly raped him (O'Leary, 2013).

The Church in Australia uncovered approximately 620 child sexual abuse cases that have occurred since the 1930s. Since the late 1980s, the Church has been aware of child sexual abuse but failed to comprehend the full scope of the problem. Speaking on behalf of the Church, Cardinal George Pell cited fear of a scandal if it were to admit a cover-up of child sexual abuse allegations (Cardinal, 2013).

Questions that should be asked by the Church leadership at this phase:

1. What is the perspective of the current leadership in the Vatican regarding Church child sexual abuse?
2. Are there clear procedures and guidelines from the Vatican addressing how such matters are to be handled? If not, what will it take to ensure that such strategies are put in place?
3. Does the Vatican actively engage in the oversight of all Catholic churches in dealing with child sexual abuse matters, or is the oversight done on a local level by bishops?

Potential Issues for Public Relations

Sexual abuse of minors in the Church is extremely challenging for public relations. Religious organizations are held to a higher standard and are expected to be, among other things, a refuge and safe place for their members. Within the Church, bishops and priests are looked at as role models and protectors, yet some of those very men are the most frequent sexual abusers of children. It is critical that the Church worldwide reconcile the child sexual abuse that has taken place and is continuing to happen while rebuilding the Church's image and public trust.

Phase IV — Third Issue

Vatican officials feel the resolution of child sexual abuse cases should remain within the Church. They also question why those outside the Church — such as those at work within the legal system — would want to remove the resolution of these cases from Church authority. Some Church officials believe that a general sense of anti-Catholicism in the United States is to blame.

John C. Allen, Jr., senior Vatican correspondent for the *National Catholic Reporter*, said USCCB's reaction has been to call for "swift, sure and final punishment for priests who are guilty of this kind of misconduct," while the Vatican's primary concern is ensuring "that everyone's rights are respected, including the rights of accused clergy" and affirming that it is not acceptable to "remedy the injustice of sexual abuse with the injustice of railroading priests who may or may not be guilty" (*Catholic Sex Abuse Cases*, n.d., p. 11).

Allen goes on to argue that the Vatican and Catholics in the United States complicate the process of formulating a comprehensive sexual abuse policy because of cultural differences. The Vatican considers the American culture's views on sexuality to be "somewhat hysterical," he writes. "There is a lot about the American culture and the American Church that puzzles people in the Vatican," according to Allen, "and there is much about the Vatican that puzzles Americans and English-speakers generally" (*Catholic Sex Abuse Cases*, n.d., p. 14).

The public and the Church in the United States believe the response to the child sexual abuse scandal should be a swift investigation with sure and final punishment for bishops, priests, and clergy who are accused of such acts; however, the Vatican favors a slower response, with the view that everyone's rights are to be respected, including the rights of the accused (SCU Conference, 2003).

Questions that should be asked by the Church leadership at this phase:

1. What steps can be taken to enable the US Church and the Vatican to come to a unified, comprehensive set of procedures and guidelines to address the child sexual abuse in the Church as a whole?
2. Would it be worth considering having secular mediators who deal with similar issues outside of the Church facilitate the discussion between the US Church and the Vatican?

Potential Issues for Public Relations

If there is a perceived conflict between the US Church and the Vatican, the public relations dilemma could be difficult to overcome. In addition, the credibility of the Catholic Church and the public trust in the organization suffers. Though the Vatican has made efforts to prevent and curtail sexual abuse of the young by Church leaders — such as the 2002 dictate to require background checks of all Church employees who have contact with children (*Catholic Sex Abuse Cases*, n.d., p. 16) — change is incrementally slow, and an impatient public seeks justice. Courts have heard lawsuits against the Vatican by abuse victims who see the Church as complicit in their suffering, for example.

As exposure of the problem and public frustration with the Vatican grow, membership in the Church declines, and in the United States, at any rate, the general public is increasingly angry, which in turn can lead to scapegoating of the Vatican itself for its response to the abuse rather than placing the blame on the abusers. It's not difficult to imagine a growing anti-Catholic bias resulting from the public's concerns for the victims and dissatisfaction at the Vatican's policies with regard to the perpetrators.

Phase V — Resolution and Conclusion

At long last, the world is seeing priests accused of sexual abuse being forced to resign, receiving convictions and jail through the courts of civil authority, and, in some cases defrocking at the behest of Church authority. Through a variety of actions, the Church is making an effort to no longer deny and cover up the abuse of children by priests, and to deal with the public and its feelings about the problem.

In the United States, the primary recourse for victims is through lawsuits. According to BishopAccountability.org, settlements of sex abuse cases totaled $3 billion by 2012, thanks to more than 3,000 lawsuits filed against the Church. Within the United States, from 2004 to 2010, the weight of the financial burden of lawsuits has forced eight dioceses to declare bankruptcy. The size and number of settlements of lawsuits has resulted in some dioceses reducing their ordinary operating expenses by closing churches and schools in order to raise funds to pay the settlements (*Catholic Sex Abuse Cases*, n.d, pp. 7–8).

Pope Francis has expressed his desire to have the Church "act decisively" to root out sexual abuse of children by bishops, priests, and clergy and to ensure that the perpetrators undergo due process. He said combating children sexual abuse is important "for the Church and its credibility" (Pope, 2013).

In 2011, the Vatican issued new guidelines on dealing with Church clergy and the matter of child sexual abuse. The guidelines require that bishops and heads of Catholic orders worldwide develop "clear and coordinated" procedures for dealing with child sexual abuse allegations. The guidelines also instruct bishops to cooperate with local police authority and to respect local laws in investigating and reporting to civil authorities; however, those guidelines also reinforce the exclusive authority of bishops in dealing with child sexual abuse cases (Wan, 2010).

In response to decades-long inadequate procedures for reporting child sexual abuse cases within the Church, the USCCB has implemented procedures under the Charter for the Protection of Children and Young People with zero tolerance for failure to respond to allegations of sexual abuse. There is also a requirement for background checks for Church employees, and when a diocese learns of an allegation, authorities must be contacted, an investigation must be conducted, and the accused must be removed from duty (Charter, 2013).

A 2006 study by Jesuit Georgetown University Center for Applied Research in the Apostolate (CARA) found that the lay Catholics it surveyed didn't know what steps the Church has taken, "but 78% strongly approved of reporting allegations of sexual abuse to civil authorities, and 76% strongly approved of removing people credibly accused of sexual abuse of a minor" (Gray, 2006). While this clearly indicates that any and all reforms are welcome, only time will tell how much actual transformation in the Church can occur, given the continued authority of its bishops.

V

ILLEGAL BUSINESS TRANSACTIONS AND FINANCIAL FRAUD IN NON-PROFITS

Chapter 23

LDS Church — Document Buying Scandal — 1981–1987

Phase I — Situation

You are a high-level administrator for The Church of Jesus Christ of Latter-day Saints (LDS). The LDS was originally founded by Joseph Smith in 1830 in New York (The Church of Jesus Christ of Latter-day Saints, 2012). In 1847, Brigham Young led the Mormons to Utah, where the LDS Church established its headquarters in Salt Lake City (The Church of Jesus Christ of Latter-day Saints, 2012). In addition to the religious aspect of the LDS, your organization also engages in charity work and humanitarian aid around the world (The Church of Jesus Christ of Latter-day Saints, 2012). In 2012, the LDS Church had more than 14 million members and 55,000 missionaries around the world (The Church of Jesus Christ of Latter-day Saints, 2012). The organization has decided to purchase historical documents that relate to your organization's faith from a well-known dealer in such documents, Mark Hofmann (Lindsey, 1987). Hofmann, a Mormon who has previously completed his mandatory two-year missionary work in Bristol, England, has "discovered" a transcript from Joseph Smith (Tanner, 1987). Since obtaining original religious artifacts from the founder of your religion is important to your organization, you are considering purchasing the document from Hofmann. The document will not be cheap, since the asking price is approximately $20,000 (Tanner, 1987). What action do you intend to take?

Questions that should be asked by the administrator at this phase:

1. How trustworthy is Mark Hofmann?
2. Is the document authentic?
3. Is the cost of the document worth the asking price to the organization?
4. What background information do you have on the dealer and the actual artifact?
5. How will the members of your organization feel about paying $20,000 for the document?

Potential Issues for the Director to Consider

Anytime an organization is considering buying a document that could involve a large amount of money, the organization should have experts both internal and external to their organization perform due diligence in evaluating a document in question. There should also be a thorough investigation into Hofmann's credentials to see if this is a vendor that can be trusted. The administration should also evaluate whether this money could be better spent on furthering the mission of the organization or offsetting organizational costs that could be used for current operations.

Phase II — First Issue

The LDS Church is reassured of the document's authenticity by an expert in the LDS historical department on handwriting and archival documents (Tanner, 1987). Your organization pays a large amount of money to Hofmann for the document and then announces to the media the document's discovery (Tanner, 1987). With this purchase, Hofmann becomes renowned for the discovery of previously unknown documents, and your organization begins to buy more documents that experts have verified as authentic (Lindsey, 1987). The president of the LDS Church has seen the documents and believes them to be authentic. Other historical experts agree with the organization's president (Tanner, 1987). The organization should consider performing a cost-benefit analysis of obtaining additional documents.

Questions that should be asked by the administrator at this phase:

1. Why are all of these "undiscovered" documents now surfacing through Hofmann?
2. How is Hofmann able to find these previously "undiscovered" documents?
3. Do the experts examining these documents have any conflicts of interest or biases?

Potential Issues for the Director to Consider

The administration of the organization needs to obtain genuine provenance if they are to buy anything of this nature, regardless if the individual is a member of their religion or not. The prudent action to take is to again have experts both internal and external to the organization conduct the necessary due diligence to ensure that the documents are authentic and that the appraised value seems reasonable.

Phase III — Second Issue

Your organization has begun to buy a number of documents and has received other documents through donations. The LDS Church publicizes only some of the documents that they own, while other documents appear to be sequestered, since those particular documents could be sensitive to the LDS Church beliefs and culture (Lindsey, 1987). Hofmann produces a new document that appears to invalidate Brigham Young as a successor to Joseph Smith Jr. (Turner, 1981). The LDS does not want to spend $20,000 for the document, prompting Hofmann to find other customers willing to pay the fee and use the information to embarrass the LDS (Tanner, 1987). Your organization then decides to buy the document for the $20,000 asking price in trade (Tanner, 1987). After the document has been bought, the contents are released to a newspaper, which the LDS Church then confirms (Tanner, 1987). As an administrator, you should have several questions about the motives and methods on which Hofmann operates. What questions should you raise?

Questions that should be asked by the administrator at this phase:

1. Is the document authentic?
2. What are Hofmann's motives for selling the document?
3. Is Hofmann blackmailing the LDS Church?
4. Should the LDS Church pay Hofmann with organizational funds that could be used for another purpose?
5. Are potentially bad public relations worth the money paid for the document?
6. Where has this document been before Hofmann discovered it?
7. Why has no one at the LDS Church known of the document's existence prior to Hofmann's "discovery"?

Potential Issues for the Director to Consider

Again, these documents need to be examined thoroughly and authenticated by numerous experts. Administrators should again be highly suspicious of Hofmann's motives, since the latest group of "documents" appears to have an embarrassing connotation for the LDS Church if they were released publicly. The fact that Hofmann is threatening to sell at least one of the controversial documents to a rival church organization gives the impression that he is attempting to blackmail the organization. The actions by Hofmann should raise red flags with the organizational administration that something is seriously wrong.

Phase IV — Third Issue

Hofmann has now appeared to your organization with a new letter that appears to contradict the history of Joseph Smith and the LDS Church. The new document is known as the "Salamander Letter" and portrays Joseph Smith as a greedy person who acquires money through magical practices (Tanner, 1987). Additionally, the angel that came to Joseph Smith in a vision, as taught in LDS scripture, is instead a vision of a white salamander (Lindsey, 1987). Your Apostle Dallin Oaks has stated that the white salamander is consistent with Joseph Smith's vision, since the salamander is a being that could live in fire (Tanner, 1987). There are now critics outside the LDS that are questioning the authenticity of the letter (Tanner, 1987). As an administrator, what are your concerns?

Questions that should be asked by the administrator at this phase:

1. The documents that Hofmann is now selling to your organization appear to be embarrassing to the LDS organization. Are these documents genuine?
2. Why would critics of the church declare this document as a forgery if they seek to embarrass the church?
3. Is fear of bad public relations driving your organization's decision-making process?

Potential Issues for the Director to Consider

The documents that your organization appears to be buying are numerous, embarrassing in nature, and very expensive. If critics of the LDS are questioning the authenticity of the documents, and they have much to lose if these documents are fraudulent, then the administration should be questioning the validity of the documents as well. Experts and appraisers should be consulted to verify these documents and assign a price to any of the documents that may be legitimate. The LDS should also be open to the public and their membership about what documents they are buying and let their membership use those documents for research purposes. When an organization allows their own fear to dictate how the organization operates, the organization can make bad financial decisions.

Phase V — Fourth Issue

Hofmann is now becoming a regular vendor for your organization for rare and previously undiscovered documents. Hofmann is now peddling a letter from Joseph Smith's mother, which discloses the origins of the *Book of Mormon*, descriptions of visions that the Three Witnesses experienced, as well as other various rare artifacts concerning the Mormon religion (Tanner, 1987). The latest document that

Hofmann has sold the LDS Church was bought by a high-ranking official in the organization for more than $10,000, bypassing the historical department. This new document indicated that Joseph Smith was practicing black magic after his first vision (Tanner, 1987). Like the other cases, after the document was bought by the LDS Church, information has been "mysteriously" leaked to the press about the purchase and the contents of the document (Tanner, 1987). As an administrator, there should be some questioning behind why this type of information is known and being leaked about an "undiscovered" document. What are your next steps?

Questions that should be asked by the administrator at this phase:

1. Where are all of these "undiscovered" documents coming from? There appears to be an endless supply of documents that are coming from Hofmann.
2. The tone of the documents is more embarrassing in nature to the LDS Church. Is this a subtle form of blackmail by Hofmann?
3. Are there controls the LDS should be using when upper administrators are purchasing documents of this type from a vendor?
4. Who is leaking information to the press about these documents and why?

Potential Issues for the Administrator to Consider

Where are the organizational controls and transparency over the spending practices of the leadership, particularly over these documents? The organization needs to have in place a set of organizational policies and procedures that would prevent church leaders from using organizational money without some type of representation or approval from the membership. It should be very apparent to the upper administrators of the LDS that Hofmann is the person that has been leaking information to the media, since he is the one that has been covertly selling the documents to the organization. If an organization is going to purchase artifacts, a confidentiality agreement should be in place and binding. It obviously would not benefit any of the upper administrators to disclose this information, since the organization's leadership is more interested in pretending that certain documents do not exist.

Phase VI — Fifth Issue

When asked why there is a sudden influx of "undiscovered" documents, Hofmann tells the LDS that he actively tracks down all tips and leads for those types of documents (Tanner, 1987). Hofmann is negotiating a sale to the Library of Congress for the Oath of Freeman for which no known copy exists (Tanner, 1987). Hofmann has now come to the LDS Church with an offer to sell the McLellin collection of documents, which could contain seriously negative public relation issues for the LDS Church (Tanner, 1987). What action steps should you take?

Questions that should be asked by the administrator at this phase:

1. Are the documents in the McLellin collection worth the amount of money that Hofmann is sure to ask?
2. Does Hofmann's explanation on the influx of "undiscovered" documents sound reasonable?

Potential Issues for the Director to Consider

Buying documents from Hofmann is getting expensive, and there is still no solid explanation for how these documents are suddenly appearing. The upper administrators should bring in outside experts and appraisers to view any document that the LDS is considering to purchase. The upper administration should be consulting members on whether or not the organization should be spending money on these types of documents or if the money should be allocated for other purposes.

Phase VII — Resolution and Conclusion

During negotiations with the church for the purchase of the McLellin collection, Hofmann revealed that in fact he had no knowledge of where that particular collection resided and would have to "reproduce" a copy of those documents if he were to sell them to the LDS Church (Tanner, 1987). It was eventually revealed that Hofmann was not only guilty of forgery but also of two homicides in an attempt to keep those individuals from revealing that the documents he sold were fake (Lindsey, 1987). George Throckmorton determined that documents previously sold by Hofmann were forgeries (Ramsland, 2012). In 1987, Hofmann pleaded guilty to two counts of second-degree murder and two counts of theft by deception as well as admitting the documents that he had been selling were forgeries (Tanner, 1987). In 1988, Hofmann was sentenced to life in prison. After a hearing, the parole board decided that he would spend the rest of his natural life in prison (Kinkead, 2005).

Recommendations and Concluding Remarks

Hofmann was successful in duping the LDS Church because upper administrators failed to take appropriate actions, such as hiring external appraisers and document experts to review the documents prior to any transactions. The organization also failed to obtain adequate background information and perform due diligence on the vendor or legitimate provenance for any documents that were for sale. After the initial documents were bought, the upper administration made the fatal mistake of falling for Hofmann's personality and wanting to believe he was an honest Mormon with good intentions and never had documents reviewed by experts external to the organization. This last fact alone allowed Hofmann to operate as a confidence man and find weaknesses and vulnerabilities in the upper administrators of the LDS Church that he exploited through forged documents with negative implications for the church if disclosed publicly. The LDS Church apparently never made the connection between the information being leaked to the press and Hofmann as the seller of "confidential" documents deemed embarrassing to the church. In addition, the question of whether or not there were controls in place to prevent upper administrators from evaluating and purchasing these types of documents did not appear to exist. Without any type of controls, organizational funds could be vulnerable and could lead to a misappropriation of funds. In this case study, the upper administrators should never have judged a book by its cover, which in this example led to deceit, financial loss, and, when two individuals attempted to uncover Hoffman's criminal actions, to murder by Hoffman so that he could keep his criminal actions undiscovered.

Chapter 24

Gandhi Memorial International Foundation — Fraud — 1996

Phase I — Situation

You are the chairman of the Democratic National Committee (DNC). During the 1996 presidential campaign, you had to return a large contribution that was solicited by John Huang, a senior party finance official who was suspended after reports that he had been involved in questionable fundraising. The committee had said the contributions of $325,000 initially appeared to have come from Yogesh K. Gandhi, a great-grandnephew of Mohandas K. Gandhi. The donation was made during a fundraising event in May 1996 in a Washington hotel at which he and an associate, a Japanese spiritual leader named Hogen Fukunaga, gave President Clinton a peace award. A few months later, Gandhi told a court in California that he had no assets or bank accounts in the United States. Party officials admitted that his court testimony had raised questions in their minds about the true source of the contribution and prompted them to return the money to Gandhi. The refund was the largest of several that the Democratic Party had to make in its fundraising process for the 1996 presidential campaign in support of President Clinton's race (Labaton, 1996).

Questions that should be asked by the administrator at this phase:

1. Should there be a formal investigation of the allegations against Democratic Party, and, if so, what form should the investigation take (i.e., internal, external)?

2. What might be the impact on the organization if these allegations are found to be true?
3. Other than Huang, are there other members of your organization who should be held accountable in the event these allegations are true?
4. Should law enforcement be contacted at this time? Or should there be an internal investigation first, and by whom should it be conducted?
5. Should the DNC request the Federal Election Commission to investigate the contributions?
6. Had the DNC relaxed their procedures for reviewing sources of large donations?

Potential Public Relations Issues

Huang, a high-profile fundraiser for the DNC presidential campaign, could very well be embroiled in a public scandal that could impact the race for the presidency and President Clinton himself. Federal law prohibits any foreign citizens who are not legal residents of the United States from making contributions to political parties. Foreign corporations are also forbidden from making contributions (Weisberg, 1996).

Such a scandal, especially if it involves criminal activity, could result in significant negative publicity, considerable scrutiny of President Clinton and the DNC, and could have materially affected the 1996 presidential race. It undoubtedly could have had a negative impact on the president's chance to win a second term in office.

Phase II — First Issue

After the announcement of the return of Gandhi's money, the DNC announced its own inquiry into the contributor and requested the Federal Election Commission investigate the matter as well. At the same time, the Justice Department also announced that it was studying whether an independent council should be appointed to investigate a variety of questions about Democratic fundraising, including the contributions Huang solicited (Miler, 1996).

It was discovered that Gandhi, a distant relative of Mohandas K. Gandhi and president of the Gandhi Memorial International Foundation, made the large donation at a May 1996 dinner. At a separate room at the site, he presented President Clinton with a life-size bust of Mohandas K. Gandhi on behalf of the foundation. Officials of the DNC and the White House said there was no link between the campaign funds and the opportunity to meet the president (Miler, 1996).

Some additional issues arose after the presentation to the president, such as some contradictory assertions that Gandhi had made about whether he was a US citizen, the sources of funding for his foundation, and a claim by the foundation that a former New York governor once served on its board (Miler, 1996).

Questions that should be asked by the administrator at this phase:

1. How could the issue of these discrepancies with Gandhi and his foundation go unnoticed or unchecked by the organization?
2. What internal procedures, if any, were/are in place for the review of the reports provided by Huang regarding the donations made by Gandhi to the DNC, and who reviews those reports?
3. Does the DNC use an outside firm to conduct audits of financial reports and accounting practices that document their contributions and the donors? If not, should you consider using such a firm?
4. Does the DNC have a code of ethics? If not, should one be established?

Potential Issues for Public Relations

Public relations issues concerning where Gandhi came up with so much money would continue to plague the DNC and the White House until better information could be produced regarding Gandhi's donations, his citizenship status, and the legitimacy of his foundation.

Phase III — Second Issue

The DNC said it had no reason to question whether the $325,000 was his own money. They said that Gandhi was permitted to contribute to US campaigns because he had a green card certifying that he was a legal resident of the United States. Further complicating matters for the DNC and the White House was while the Gandhi Memorial Foundation had awarded the Mohandas K. Gandhi World Peace Award to such recipients as Mother Teresa, Ronald Reagan, and Mikhail S. Gorbachev, it had also given the award to two controversial Japanese figures: a billionaire who had alleged ties to organized crime, and a Japanese religious leader who some former adherents claimed had bilked them of large sums of money, according to published accounts (Miler, 1996).

Questions that should be asked by the chairman of the DNC at this phase:

1. Did Huang always ask his contributors if they were all legal residents of the United States and therefore eligible to make campaign contributions in the US?
2. Was the DNC knowingly accepting illegal contributions?
3. Was the DNC trading favors for contributions?
4. Was Huang, a former US Department of Commerce official, abusing his government position to raise campaign money?
5. How are you going to address the concerns of your political opponents of the legality of your campaign?

6. How is the organization going to repair its image and reputation during this time of negative publicity and public opinion?

Potential Issues for Public Relations

Why did the Democratic Party abandon its own procedure for vetting contributions for legality? There was pressure coming from the White House to raise extraordinary amounts of money for the upcoming 1996 presidential race. The culture of fundraising rewards quantity, and discourages close scrutiny and asking too many questions. The less you ask, more you get. And given that there has been no real enforcement of the rules in the past, fundraisers haven't lost sleep about contributions that turned out to be tainted. If the money goes bad, you simply return it with the appropriate regretful noises (Weisberg, 1996).

Phase IV — Third Issue

Did the efforts by the DNC to raise money for the 1996 presidential campaign make the US electoral system vulnerable to influence from foreign citizens, foreign governments, and foreign corporations? Did the contributions influence any of the president's decisions during his term in office? Why didn't the DNC employ any of the standard methods to check out the Gandhi Memorial International Foundation to see if it was a legitimate organization and could provide funding for a US presidential election?

Questions that should be asked by the administrator at this phase:

1. Did the DNC do a thorough check of the website for the Gandhi Memorial International Foundation?
2. Was Huang trained to ask if all his contributors were legal residents of the United States and eligible to make political contributions?
3. Did the DNC check to see if the foundation was on the federal government's charity drive website?
4. Did the DNC check to see if the foundation was on the Better Business Bureau's Wise Giving Alliance website?
5. Did Huang or anyone on the DNC staff employ the Guidestar.org website to get financial information about the foundation?
6. Did Huang or anyone on the DNC staff ask the charity itself for information about its work and finances?

Potential Issues for Public Relations

Questions concerning the lack of oversight by the DNC board add to the increased scrutiny of the party, the White House, and President Clinton. With the chairman and the board of directors under question, it is imperative for the DNC to use effective public relations to manage and improve its image.

Phase V — Resolution and Conclusion

After the revelations of Huang's fundraising efforts from questionable individuals in the 1996 presidential campaign, the DNC decided to terminate Huang's employment. It returned nearly half of the funds raised by Huang. In addition, a House investigation, headed by Republican Dan Burton, focused on allegations of campaign finance abuse, including the contributions channeled through Huang and others. The US Senate Committee also held public hearings on the campaign finance issues, but neither investigation discovered anything of substance (*Washington Times*, 1999).

With the 2010 US Supreme Court ruling in *Citizens United v. the Federal Elections Commission*, which eliminated barriers to corporate funding of US elections, one wonders if the issue of funding controls and funding from foreign individuals and foreign corporations that arose during the 1996 Huang scandal had any lasting effect on fundraising issues regarding foundations and foreigners, now that funding limits have been essentially removed.

Chapter 25

United Nations Oil-for-Food Scandal — 1996

Phase I — Situation

You are a high-level administrator with the United Nations. Your organization was established in 1945 after World War II (United Nations, 2012). The organization is responsible for assisting in maintaining world order and resolving issues that cut across international boundaries (United Nations, 2012). Iraq, which has had sanctions placed on it by the United Nations since 1990, has recently been the beneficiary of the United Nations Security Council Resolution 706, which allows Iraq to sell oil for food (Federation of American Scientists, 1991). The Oil-for-Food Program started in 1996 and was relied on by millions of Iraqis for food (United Nations — Office of the Iraq Programme Oil-for-Food, 2012). Out of $65 billion that the Iraqi government has paid into an escrow account for food, $46 billion was actually spent on approved items not under embargo, with the rest going to war reparations, United Nation's administrative costs, and weapons inspection programs (United Nations — Office of the Iraq Programme Oil-for-Food, 2012). It has recently come to your attention that money has been siphoned off to Iraqi government officials and, even worse, to United Nation officials (CNN, 2004). What action steps are you going to take?

Questions that should be asked by the administrator at this phase:

1. What are the current policies and procedures in place to run and administer this program?
2. What individuals are responsible for the implementation and oversight of this program?
3. What controls and audit procedures are in place to ensure that money is not being siphoned from the purpose of the program and put into something else that is not sanctioned by the United Nations?
4. How will you contend with United Nations officials who are using the funds for their own benefit?

Potential Issues for the Administrator to Consider

The first order of business is to determine who has access to the funds and where the funds are ultimately being deposited and expended. There should be a process and a set of procedures that can provide an audit trail to determine where the money is flowing through the program and where the money is ultimately being spent and deposited. There should be a set of policies and procedures that provide fiscal controls for the United Nations personnel that should be utilized by the upper administrators of the organization.

Phase II — First Issue

The head of the program, Benon Sevan, has been a defender of the program but will not allow Dileep Nair, the United Nation's corruption watchdog, to investigate and audit the program (Lynch, 2004). In response to the potential investigation, Iqbal Riza chief of staff of the United Nations has ordered the shredding of ten years' worth of documents regarding the Oil-for-Food Program (Rosett and Russell, 2005). In light of possible damaging evidence being destroyed, what will be your next step regarding the program as well as Sevan's actions?

Questions that should be asked by the administrator at this phase:

1. Does Sevan have the authority to prevent an internal audit by the United Nations?
2. Can you prevent Sevan from destroying documentation?
3. Can Sevan be put on administrative leave?
4. What other issues should you be concerned with at this time?

Potential Issues for the Administrator to Consider

When an administrator attempts to block an internal audit, it may serve as a warning to the upper administrators that something could be wrong with how the administrator is conducting himself professionally or managing the program. It should serve as an even bigger warning that the administrator who is head of the program is destroying documentation when an internal investigation is being initiated. In light of those actions, the organization should suspend the head of the program immediately and launch an investigation upon any type of financial aspects of the program. Those findings should be made public, and any discrepancies that are found should be investigated in further detail. If issues are found, the head of the program should be held accountable, and if fraud is apparent, a criminal investigation should be called for to investigate the program in even further detail, as well as others that work with the Oil-for-Food Program.

Phase III — Second Issue

You have now received an interim report that was filed by Paul Volcker's commission, which states that much of the food that was supplied as part of the aid "was unfit for human consumption," and that Sevan had received almost $150,000 in bribes for actions he took while managing the program (*BBC News*, 2005). The United Nations has now suspended Benon Sevan as head of the program (*BBC News*, 2005). What do you propose to do now?

Questions that should be asked by the administrator at this phase:

1. Who is responsible for checking the quality of the food product that was being delivered for the program?
2. What individuals are responsible for the implementation and oversight of this program?
3. What audits should be put in place to catch anyone taking bribes who oversee these types of programs?
4. How is your organization's credibility going to be impacted by this latest series of revelations?

Potential Issues for the Administrator to Consider

The credibility of your organization is at stake with the world's leaders and the general population when corruption and graft are apparently ongoing with a major United Nation's program that is supposed to help downtrodden people. The United Nation's upper administrators need to take harsh repercussions against anyone that is affiliated with their organization who is caught taking bribes or operating in a corrupt manner.

Phase IV — Third Issue

Al Mada, a newspaper in Iraq, has stated that several alleged individuals and organizations received oil contracts through the Oil-for-Food program (*The*

Washington Times, 2004). The allegations in the newspaper further stated that individuals or organizations that were sympathetic to the Iraqi regime were given oil contracts through the Oil-for-Food Program (Otterman, 2005). Allegedly, the companies that bought the oil could retain a "transaction fee" when the oil was resold through the open market, which would then in turn be "refunded" back to the Iraqi government essentially as a kickback (Otterman, 2005). An alleged similar arrangement was made to organizations that were providing food to Iraq where the organizations would essentially pay the Iraqi government a kickback for receiving the contract, since the organizations would overcharge for the food sold to Iraq (Otterman, 2005). As an administrator, how should you react to this type of information?

Questions that should be asked by the administrator at this phase:

1. How should the United Nations launch an investigation into this alleged fixing of contracts?
2. How should the United Nations' audit the charging of hidden fees as well as kickbacks to the Iraqi government?
3. What controls, policies, and procedures should you put in place to prevent contract fixing from occurring, as well as kickbacks?

Potential Issues for the Administrator to Consider

These are very serious allegations that again threaten to damage the reputation and credibility of not only the program but also the United Nations itself. If a program is found to be corrupt or circumventing the very resolutions your organization passed initially to prevent the Iraqi government from buying weapons or supplies for their military, then the program has failed, and the resolution that was passed earlier will cause the economic sanctions to be ineffective against the Iraqi government and military. The organization needs to put policies and procedures in place that will effectively track the money that is being contracted by the companies to ensure that kickbacks do not go to the Iraqi government or military.

Phase V — Fourth Issue

After an investigation has been launched, it is discovered that BNP Paribas did not have proper controls in place when goods were to be delivered and payment to third parties were issued, even though the parties in question were not authorized to receive such payments (Associated Press, 2004; Exptica.com, 2004). The United Nations had relied on BNP Paribas as the only bank to manage financial aspects of the Oil-for-Food Program (Associated Press, 2004). What actions can the United Nations take to recover funds from BNP Paribas that could have been paid to unauthorized individuals?

Questions that should be asked by the administrator at this phase:

1. Why did your organization use only one bank?
2. Who vetted the bank to ensure it had proper controls, policies, and procedures in place? Was the person qualified who vetted the bank?
3. How will you recover the funds that have been paid out for goods and services not rendered?

Potential Issues for the Administrator to Consider

If an organization is going to use only one bank for such an important program, it should vet the bank to ensure that proper controls, policies, and procedures will be used for administration of all financial contracts. Whoever the United Nations sends to vet the bank should have the proper training and experience to verify that the bank is indeed qualified to administer such financial transactions in a professional manner. If the project is too large for the bank to handle, then the United Nations should consider distributing the workload to other banks and vet those with professionals with good credentials and experience. The United Nations should also ensure that any bank that will be administering financial transactions for any United Nations program will be subject to third party auditors on a regular and unscheduled basis. The United Nations will need to apply pressure to the bank to recover any funds that were paid out without the proper authorization, since the bank is responsible for allowing those transactions to occur.

Phase VI — Fifth Issue

A report has just been released, the Duelfer Report, which indicates that the Oil-for-Food Program actually assisted the Iraqi regime in getting financial assets to buy arms for their military (Lynch, 2004). In addition, you are now beginning to receive complaints that the Kurdish segment of the population, which was supposed to receive a portion of the relief from the Oil-for-Food Program, has not received aid for a hospital for their region that was to be managed by the World Health Organization, which is under your auspices (United States Congress — Committee on International Relations House of Representatives, 2004). The program is becoming a failure full of initial good intentions. What should your organization do at this point in time?

Questions that should be asked by the administrator at this phase:

1. How is the United Nations' reputation in light of the information that has been uncovered on the Duelfer Report?
2. What will you do to rectify the situation of the Kurdish segment not receiving aid to build their hospital by the World Health Organization?

Potential Issues for the Administrator to Consider

The United Nations should audit the World Health Organization to understand why the Kurdish population has not been receiving the proper support for health resources. In addition, the United Nations should undertake a review of all of its programs, which should properly funnel aid to populations in need of food, medicine, or other resources to assist the population.

Phase VII — Resolution and Conclusion

In 2003, after the coalition had successfully invaded Iraq, the General Accounting Office (GAO) began an investigation on members of Saddam Hussein's regime to account for all of their assets as well as auditing the Oil-for-Food Program (United States Congress — Committee on International Relations House of Representatives, 2004). The investigation concluded that the Oil-for-Food Program was responsible for Saddam Hussein's regime receiving $10.1 billion illegally (United States Congress — Committee on International Relations House of Representatives, 2004). A Pentagon study also stated that out of 759 Oil-for-Food contracts, almost half were found to have overcharged for the goods and services rendered (Lynch, 2004). Essentially, the GAO reported that the United Nations secretary general and the Security Council were responsible for oversight of the program and failed to provide the controls and procedures necessary to ensure the program was implemented as it was intended (United States Congress — Committee on International Relations House of Representatives, 2004). The Oil-for-Food Program officially ended in 2010 (MacFarqhar, 2010).

Recommendations and Concluding Remarks

The United Nations will need to address shortfalls in auditing procedures, policies, financial controls, and leadership issues, as well as programs that do not deliver resources effectively or efficiently to populations in need. The Oil-for-Food Program appears to have the opposite intended effect on the Iraqi government and military by providing Iraq with a much needed infusion of cash that was used to apparently prop up the government and bolster its military at the expense of the civilian population.

The United Nations will need to establish an auditing unit that can act independently of upper administrators who can stonewall financial investigations into fraud, embezzlement, kickbacks, and bribes. The United Nations also needs to contemplate how administrators over such programs can be held not only financially liable, but also criminally liable if corruption knowingly occurs under their auspices. The reputation of the United Nations as an organization depends upon getting the appropriate controls, policies, and procedures in place in an attempt to prevent corruption and graft with programs that are intended to provide lifesaving resources to needy people around the world.

Chapter 26

Tampa Bay Lowry Park Zoo — Salisbury Scandal — 2008

Phase I — Situation

Tampa's first zoo was a small collection of exotic animals in the Plan Park on the grounds of the University of Tampa located across the Hillsborough River from downtown Tampa. In the 1950s, Mayor Nick Nuccio led the effort to move the zoo to a more spacious location. Land near the neighborhood of Seminole Heights was chosen. The zoo was named Lowry Park after General Sumter Loper Lowry, a local resident celebrated for civic contributions and his service in several wars. The new Lowry Park Zoo opened in 1957. The Tampa Lowry Park Zoological Gardens was situated on land owned by the city of Tampa, Florida. The zoo was operated by the Lowry Park Zoological Society under a lease and operation agreement with the city of Tampa. The society operates as a 501(c)(3) non-profit charitable organization and in furtherance of education and conservation purposes to benefit the general public (Lowry Park Zoo, Audit, 2009).

The lease and operation agreement with the city states that the real property shall remain the property of the city, and all future real or personal property donations shall become the sole property of the city. The agreement continues that the animals, as of the date of the agreement, will be leased to the society and "the progeny of these animals and any animals acquired shall become and remain assets for the City." In the agreement, the society agreed to abide by the standards of the American Association of Zoological Parks and Aquariums (AAZPA) on the management of transfers of animals between zoos and species survival plans for the animals entrusted to the Lowry Park Zoo by the AAZPA (Lowry Park Zoo, Audit, 2009).

Questions that should be asked by the board at this phase:

1. When the city of Tampa entered into the agreement with the Lowry Park Zoological Society under a lease agreement, should it have resulted in the city having control over the zoo's operations, hiring, or training?
2. Why were the city's representatives on the zoo board not engaged or informed?
3. When you have the mayor, a council member, the park and recreation director, and the neighborhoods coordinator as the city's representatives on the board, do you have an inherently weak structure to protect the city's interest?
4. Are the two city staff appointees to the board really free to exercise their influence, since they serve with two elected officials who are their ultimate supervisors?
5. Did the city have too much faith in the zoological society and the society's executive director and did not provide the close supervision any executive director of a non-profit should be subject to in the daily administration of their duties?

Phase II — First Issue

The issues at the Lowry Park Zoo began in April 2008 when 15 patas monkeys escaped from Safari Wild, a for-profit animal attraction under development east of Tampa in rural Polk County. This situation brought media attention to the venture, which was owned and operated by Lowry Park Zoo Director Lex Salisbury. These incidents led to several investigations into the relationship between Safari Wild and the Lowry Park Zoo (Zayas, 2008).

The relationship between Safari Wild and the Lowry Park Zoo began in 2007, when the executive director had presented the idea to solve the zoo's need for more space. Salisbury had offered 10 acres of his property in Polk County as home for the zoo animals needing a respite from being on exhibit. One executive board committee member raised an objection to the non-profit zoo partnering with Salisbury's for-profit business. Another executive board committee member voiced concerns about zoo animals that belong to the city of Tampa being housed in another county. However, an agreement was made to establish a relationship between the two operations. Assets were mingled, with the moving of bison and white-tailed deer that ultimately died on Salisbury's property. In the first half of 2008, the Lowry Park Zoo received invoices totaling more than $150,000 for capital projects at Safari Wild. The invoices were approved by Salisbury and the Lowry Park Zoo chairman, Fassil Gavremariam. When the Lowry Park Zoo board discovered the relationship, they dissolved the relationship. *The St. Petersburg Times* took a deeper look at the Salisbury ties with Wild Safari and the Lowry Park Zoo. The *Times* uncovered private transactions between the operations, such as loans, trades, sales, and outright gifts of animals and joint capital improvements (Helgeson, 2008).

Questions that should be asked by the board at this phase:

1. What are the current policies and procedures in place to address conflicts of interests?
2. What individuals are responsible for oversight of the executive director?
3. What controls and audit procedures are in place to ensure that money and resources are not being siphoned from the Lowry Park Zoo?
4. How will you contend with zoo employees, such as Salisbury and others that are using the funds for their own benefit?

Potential Issues for the Board to Consider

The first order of business was to determine how funds were being expended without the board's knowledge and why the financial and purchasing internal controls were not being followed. Also, how was it possible that the executive director and Lawry Park board chairman were able to have financial transactions approved with little or no documentation? Why was the executive director given the authority to authorize expenditures of more than $1,000 without supervision or as he deemed necessary? Why did the board operate so informally and give such great deference to Salisbury's executive decisions? (Lowry Park Zoo, Audit, 2009)

Phase III — Second Issue

The news stories, especially those from the *Times*, led to then-Tampa Mayor Pam Iorio to call for audit, which revealed that Salisbury made a handwritten change in his payroll paperwork that increased his quarterly bonus from $13,885 to $20,827 and that he charged the zoo for a three-day stay in Paris. Zoo benches and bamboo plants also wound up on Salisbury's property.

The audit also stated that the executive director took more than $200,000 in animals and supplies to help start his private exotic-animal park (Staff, 2008).

Questions that should be asked by the board and the city of Tampa at this phase:

1. Why were transactions between Safari Wild and Lawry Park Zoo not properly documented or recorded?
2. Why were transactions between Salisbury and the zoo not properly identified or ethics and conflicts of interest not disclosed?
3. Why did the organization not have adequate controls over the various financial processes or transactions of the zoo?
4. Why were in-kind donations not properly recorded or controlled?
5. Why were controls over purchases not adequate?

6. Why were employment processes in place that were not appropriate or adequately documented?

Potential Issues for the Administrator to Consider

Anytime an executive director does not comply with standard procedures and internal controls that apply to them, it should have raised red flags to the board and other staff members that things were not right. To many, the executive director's success with the Lowry Park Zoo operations contributed largely to the leadership of Salisbury, who received very little rigorous supervision from the board or the city of Tampa. Also the fact that two of the city appointments on the zoo's non-profit board were city staff members could result in meaningful weaknesses in the city's supervision of the zoo operation, as the two staff members might be too deferential to the mayor and the city council member appointed to the board to point out inappropriate behavior. In addition, the mayor, the city council member, and the high-ranking staff members are extremely busy and might not allocate sufficient time and energy while on the board to protect the city of Tampa's interest in all zoo operations, as the land on which the zoo sits is owned by the city.

Phase IV — Third Issue

The audit ordered by the city identified dozens of recommendations in a 60-plus-page report. The audit had many worthy and insightful recommendations for the zoo board to implement and was strong on the need for financial and human resource management controls; however, the report spent no time on the issues of conflicts of interest, board committee structure and reporting, and training for all board members on their roles as trustees of the zoo and the city (Lowry Park Zoo, Audit, 2009).

Questions that should be asked by the administrator at this phase:

1. Who should have checked for the quality of the product that was being bought and delivered for the program?
2. What individuals are responsible for the implementation and oversight of this program?
3. What audits should be put in place to catch anyone overseeing these types of programs from taking bribes?
4. How is your organization's credibility going to be impacted by this latest series of revelations?

Potential Issues for the Administrator to Consider

The credibility of your organization is at stake with the city's elected and appointed officials, the public, the employees, zoo visitors, and other zoo stakeholders. The public could lose confidence in the arrangement the city has with the zoological society to manage the zoo and the property owned by the city. As a public institution, it is imperative that the zoological society carry out its duties as required in the lease with the city. Failure to do so would jeopardize the relationship and the trust the city and the public have placed in the zoological society.

Phase V — Fourth Issue

After completion of the audit ordered by the zoological society, the former executive director Salisbury and the board entered into discussions to close out the matter through a settlement process. In the agreement, the former executive director agreed to a small payment, return of property that belonged to the city, and not to recruit any of the zoological society staff to his private wildlife park for two years. The zoological society determined that it was in the best interests of the society and city that the matter be settled, as they determined that litigation would be disruptive and the cost of litigation would prohibitive (Staff, 2008).

Questions that should be asked by the administrator at this phase:

1. Was the settlement fair and sufficiently strong enough to quiet the critics who felt that the former zoo executive director had made adequate reparations to the city and the society?
2. Should the city have gone along with the settlement, or should it have pushed for stronger action against the former executive director of the zoo?
3. What controls, policies, and procedures should you put in place to prevent this situation from occurring again at the Lowry Park Zoo?

Potential Issues for the Administrator to Consider

There was still the matter of whether the Florida Department of Law Enforcement was going to file charges against the former executive of the zoo. In addition, the zoological society and the city were going to have to prove to the public that new policies and procedures were in place or were going to be enacted to ensure that these types improper activities could not occur again at the zoo.

Phase VI — Resolution and Conclusion

After the Florida Department of Law Enforcement dismissed almost all of the 16 allegations of criminal misconduct as civil or noncriminal matters, the department found only conflicts of interest but no criminal intent. The Lowry Park Zoo moved forward with a new chairman of the board and a new executive director (Zayas and Vartan, 2010).

Some of the issues that came to light as a result of the investigation then came to the top of the agenda for the zoological board and the city. The audit found the need for additional land for the zoo, updating of the zoo's financial controls, and stronger conflict of interest rules. The board closed out the matter by requiring that all possible conflicts of interest had to be reported to the board. A new zoo hotline that will allow staffers to voice concerns without fear of retaliation was approved. Zoo officials were assigned to determine the new salary for the new executive director, and unbudgeted expenditures above a certain threshold had to be approved by the entire board (Zayas, 2009).

However, the weakest feature of the lease agreement between the zoological society and the city of Tampa was the fact that the city had two elected representatives and two staff representatives on the zoological society board. The pressure will still be on the two elected officials to stay engaged with the operations of the Lowry Park Zoo and to be regular attendees at board meetings and be fully engaged members of the board. This will need to occur on an ongoing basis to make sure a similar incident does recur at the Lowry Park Zoo.

Chapter 27

The Bernie Madoff Scandal — 2008

Phase I — Situation

You are one of the many senior-level administrators of some of the important Jewish non-profits in the country. Millions of dollars of your donors' funds were invested in the Bernie Madoff firm when the FBI arrested Madoff in December 2008 for one of the largest Ponzi schemes in the history of the United States. The year 2008 happened to be when Madoff's massive Ponzi scheme came to light. In the two years that followed, at least 13 Jewish organizations experienced financial losses. Several of the organizations provided explanations of the losses. Yeshiva University's 2008 financial returns noted that Madoff was a former university trustee and described how multiple investments wended their way into Madoff's portfolio, eventually adding up to $95 million loss. The return also described the steps taken by YU in response.

The university enhanced its conflict of interest policy, the university reported. Under the enhanced conflict of interest policy, members of the university board of trustees may not be engaged in business with the university. Other Madoff victims are terser in describing their relationships with the swindler, in some cases not even naming him. The American Israel Cultural Foundation's explanation of how it lost $14 million to Madoff amounted to this: "The custodian of the investment pool did not invest the funds and stole the remaining moneys under his custody."

Some organizations were hit indirectly by Madoff. The Jewish Federation of Greater Los Angeles and at least three California family foundations reported millions of dollars in losses through investments made by the Jewish Community

Foundation, which reported in its 2008 return an overall loss of more than $23 million to the Ponzi scheme. One of the filers, the American Jewish Congress, reported $18.2 million in losses due to Madoff in its 2008 return (Kampeas, 2013).

Questions that should be asked by the administrator at this phase:

1. Should there be a formal investigation of the allegations against Madoff, and, if so, what form should the investigation take (i.e., internal, external, criminal)?
2. What might be the impact on the organization if these allegations are found to be true?
3. Other than the executive directors, are there other members of your organizations who should be held accountable for the losses of donor funds?
4. What are the advantages and disadvantages to your making the allegations public at this time?
5. Can we recover some or all our losses from our insurance carrier, and how can our legal counsel assist us in the recovery of our funds?
6. Should law enforcement be contacted at this time? Or should there be an internal investigation, contact with legal counsel, and contact with the insurance carrier?
7. If an internal investigation is conducted, by whom should it be conducted?

Potential Public Relations Issues

The Madoff arrest placed many prominent Jewish non-profit organizations in a public relations nightmare, with the potential loss of millions of dollars in donor funds, fatal losses of capital, endangerment of hundreds of grant-funded organizations, and the unwanted glare of media coverage on how such prominent Jewish non-profit organizations could so carelessly invest their precious funds with such fraud (Kampeas, 2013). Such a scandal, especially if it involves criminal activity, could result in significant negative publicity, considerable scrutiny of the organization, and a long-term public relations recovery. It would undoubtedly have a negative impact on the involved Jewish non-profit organizations and their ability to successfully fundraise to continue the organizations' missions.

Initially, all these Jewish non-profit organizations could anticipate damage to the image of and trust in the organization, and if the allegations, including criminal activity, proved to be true, the damage could be devastating: withdrawal of corporate partners and sponsorships, substantial reduction in donations, and even closure of some these non-profits.

Once an issue such as discovered, such as the fraudulent investments being handled by the Madoff firm, every non-profit organization is faced with a difficult decision. Does the NPO retain sufficient credibility with its members, donors, the public, the media, governmental entities, and other related stakeholders to conduct an internal investigation, or does the matter require a credible external entity to conduct the investigation? Regardless of how the NPO decides to proceed, it needs to take the following steps:

1. An investigation should be initiated, perhaps first internally, focusing on an audit of the all the organizations' accounting practices and a full reconciliation of the organizations' collected revenues and expenditures. Depending on the depth of the initial findings, it may be necessary for an outside independent investigator to take over the process to avoid any appearance of a cover-up, as well as hiring or consulting with investment advisers.
2. A thorough review should be made of the investment policies, and a meeting of the investment committees should be called. In addition, if the non-profits employed any investments advisors, they also should be involved in the investment review process.
3. In the event of possible criminal improprieties, federal law enforcement agencies should be contacted to perform a thorough criminal investigation. Consideration should also be given to suspending or relieving all the executive directors and board members found to be involved in the decision to invest their organizations' funds with Madoff.

Phase II — First Issue

A bevy of foundations, their donors, and their financial advisors were fooled by Madoff's pyramid scheme. Many of these Jewish non-profits invested so much of their capital in Madoff's investment vehicles that when he was exposed, they went out of business overnight. The question for all these Jewish non-profits became this: Were the donor funds misappropriated simply by blindly investing with the Madoff fund?

Questions that should be asked by the administrator at this phase:

1. Had the boards, the executive directors, the investment committees, and the investment advisors of the various non-profits involved in this scandal done their due diligence prior to investing in their funds with Madoff's firm?
2. Did the non-profits have investment guidelines?
3. Did some of these non-profits ignore their own guidelines for audits and controls?
4. Why did the executives or board members at these non-profits not know the viability of these investments?
5. Did these non-profit executives and board members ignore their own investment policies and conflict of interest polices?
6. Why did none of the non-profit executives or board members question the box operations of the Madoff firm?
7. Why did none of the non-profit executives or board members question the Madoff audit done by a relatively unknown audit firm, and shouldn't the

small size of the audit firm employed by the Madoff firm have been a giant red flag for anyone investing large sums of funds with the Madoff firm?
8. Did these non-profits use outside firms to conduct audits of financial reports and accounting practices? If not, should you consider using such a firm?
9. Did all of the non-profits have codes of ethics? If not, should codes of ethics be established for all these organizations?

Potential Issues for Public Relations

Public relations issues concerning the investment policies of these Jewish non-profit organizations could potentially cripple the fundraising operations of these organizations, which would have a negative effect on the ability of the organizations to effectively work with their local corporate partners and individual donors to secure funds for continuing operation.

Phase III — Second Issue

When this scandal came to light, everyone was asking, "Where were the Securities and Exchange Commission (SEC), the IRS, and the foundations themselves in policing Madoff's operations?" Many people were also asking, "Why were the foundations and their donors so comfortable with Madoff?" Madoff's scheme was not caught by the SEC or the investment advisers of the foundations. During this period of time, there was an increasing deal of interest on the part of non-profit foundations to invest in nontraditional investment vehicles, such as hedge funds, and alternative investment vehicles in an attempt to boost returns (Kampeas, 2013).

Questions that should be asked by the administrator at this phase:

1. What is the process to review the stewardship of the executive directors and board members of the Jewish non-profits that invested with the Madoff firm?
2. How are all these Jewish non-profit firms going to address the concerns of corporate partners and individual donors regarding loss of millions of foundation funds by Madoff?
3. How are you going to address the concerns of donors in regard to the safety of their donations?
4. How are these organizations going to repair their reputations during this time of negative publicity and public opinion?

Potential issues for Public Relations

The conviction of Madoff only serves to increase the media scrutiny and negative publicity surrounding possible impropriety involving donations of all the Jewish non-profits involved with the Madoff firm. The increased scrutiny and negative publicity can only increase questions and decrease donations. These organizations must determine how to provide better accountability of funds invested by executive-level personnel and board members.

Phase IV — Third Issue

The board of directors of these Jewish non-profit organizations should look at their roles in this matter; what fault lies with the boards? Should the boards have expected some form of independent external reporting regarding executive investments of the organizations' funds? This growing scandal calls into question the oversight of executive staffs by the boards.

Questions that should be asked by the administrator at this phase:

1. Did the boards authorize all the investments with Madoff?
2. Did the organizations have insurance that might have covered all or some of their losses? What are the legal responsibilities of the boards in oversight of their organizations' investment policies, and have the boards, as a whole, lived up to their responsibilities?
3. Are any members of the boards complicit in the executives' actions?

Potential Issues for Public Relations

Questions concerning the lack of oversight by the boards add to the increased scrutiny of all these boards. With the top executives and the boards of directors under question, it is imperative for these Jewish non-profit organizations to use effective public relations to manage and improve their images.

Phase V — Resolution and Conclusion

The Madoff scandal has left a path of destruction through the Jewish non-profit community in this country. The Chais Family Foundation, a California-based charity that earned about $12.5 million annually, was forced to shut down after investing, and losing, all its money with Madoff. The Boston-based Robert I. Lappin Charitable Foundation, which paid to send Jewish youths to Israel, fired four staff members and shut down operations. Billionaire Mort Zuckerman, CEO of Boston Prosperities and owner of the *New York Daily News*, lost $30 million. And the list of other prominent Jewish leaders that lost funds they invested with Madoff is a very long one. The situation just brings into focus the continuing needs of non-profit executives and board members to remember that reputational references and trust are important, but they cannot be trumped by due diligence. Boards need to be of sufficient size and be comprised of individuals with diverse backgrounds to ensure proper governance and to recognize when they need to rely on professional expertise to assist with their policy and managerial decision making. Boards need to be of sufficient size and comprised of individuals with diverse backgrounds to ensure proper governance and to recognize when they need to rely on professional expertise to assist with shaping and making policy, examine managerial-decision making, and to understand when it is imperative that they need to follow the advice of their professional advisors. Lastly, non-profits must maintain policies and practices that constantly support ethical behavior and the disclosure of all organizational information (Cohen, 2009).

Chapter 28

Renewing American Leadership — Gingrich Non-Profit Organization Paying His For-Profit — 2011

Phase I — Situation

You are a board member of a non-profit dedicated to the goal of spurring conversation about restoring Christian principles in Washington. Through the media, you discover allegations that your charity organization, which is a 501(c)(3), is paying money to your founder's for-profit business. Your charity, founded by Newt Gingrich, is alleged to have paid Gingrich's for-profit company $200,000 over two years. Renewing American Leadership (ReAL) is a non-profit that has paid full price for Gingrich's books and DVDs. This non-profit is one of the ways that presidential hopeful Newt Gingrich has stayed in the public eye. While out of office, Gingrich has become rich. He has purchased a $1 million house in the suburbs of Washington, secured a $500,000 line of credit from Tiffany's, and, most recently, went on a two-week luxury cruise. ReAL paid Gingrich Communications $200,000 a year as compensation for Rick Tyler, the executive director of ReAL and Gingrich's spokesman. While Gingrich's name and face were splashed all over ReAL's materials, Gingrich did not have a seat on the board. That meant Gingrich did not have to disclose payments made to his consulting firm by the non-profit. Tyler, who spent 20 hours a week working for the non-profit, said he never asked Gingrich to join the board because he did not want to take up any more of Gingrich's time. Before Tyler quit the board, he said that ReAL did not pay for political activity and did nothing to promote anyone's political career (Reeve, 2011).

Questions that should be asked by the administrator at this phase:

1. Should there be a formal investigation of the allegations against Tyler, and, if so, what form should the investigation take (i.e., internal, external, criminal)?
2. What might be the impact on the organization if these allegations are found to be true?
3. Other than Tyler, are there other members of your organization who should be held accountable in the event these allegations are true?
4. Should there be an internal investigation first, and by whom should it be conducted?
5. Did the organization violate the spirit of operating a non-profit organization to work for the public good while it was involved in politics?

Potential Public Relations Issues

Gingrich, the high-profile corporate face of the organization, could very well be embroiled in a public scandal concerning the payment of the non-profit's funds to his for-profit business and engaging in political activity. It is clear that 501(c)(3) non-profit organizations are not allowed to intervene in political campaigns. In addition, there were allegations that the non-profit organization was generating, and then giving away, a list of donors who support and share the views of a particular political candidate, which is a misuse of tax-subsidized charitable resources (Reeve, 2011).

Phase II — First Issue

In presidential politics, some are saying winning is no longer everything. Some were wondering if Gingrich was using his presidential race and his non-profit as a kind of savvy marketing campaign built around his personality. There was a feeling in some quarters that some of the people running for the Republican presidential nomination were just as interested in the marketing of their brands and making money as they were in winning the prize of being the Republican standard bearer. Part of the Gingrich organization includes several for-profit businesses. Gingrich Communications oversees Gingrich's paid speaking engagements and his Fox News contract.

Gingrich Group also provides consulting services. Gingrich Productions makes his feel-good documentaries with themes grounded in religion and American tradition. During the campaign, Gingrich released his 24th book, with many of his upcoming campaign stops doubling as marketing events for his book and movies, raising more questions about the true intentions of the campaign. Questions were raised about the non-profit ReAL, which was founded by Gingrich, when its website contained advertisements for Gingrich's books. The ads selling such items as the Gingrich books were taken down from the website when complaints were raised about the matter. It is not clear that it is a charity, said Ellen Miller, the executive director of the nonpartisan group The Sunlight Foundation; it is an organization that looks like it is mixing public purpose and Gingrich's private political purpose. The charity also paid for charter jets used by Gingrich to promote movies that his private businesses produced. The Sunlight Foundation report notes that the exempt organization paid retail price for the Gingrich books and DVDs.

The report suggested that the exempt organization is violating what experts call the "private benefit doctrine." As stated by Darryll K. Jones, the Associate Dean for Academic Affairs and Professor of Law at Florida A&M University College of Law.

> In another contest, though, I have suggested that when a charity is operated in such a manner that it necessarily benefits an insider's private business, the charity violates the private inurement prohibition even if the charity can be to receive quid pro quo from the profit making entity. I call this sort of relationship "joint venture private inurement." It is the Charity's grant of the franchise to an insider, I think, that make such cases a private inurement/excess benefit violation as too much wiggle room. In other words, the private benefit issue tolerates a certain degree of private profit. Charities must benefit someone in order to achieve a charitable purpose. But when that "someone" is an insider, the benefit seems less coincidental and more purposeful, as is the case when an insider "skims" profit for his own benefit.
>
> Conventional wisdom holds that if the charity gets what it paid for no private inurement/excess benefit violation occurs. The only objection is whether the charity should be engaging in the particular transaction and that requires an illegitimate second insider who is the intended, not just coincidental collateral beneficiary of the charity's pursuit of its charitable goal, the rest of us are justified in questioning even a quid pro quo transaction. In other words, the presence of the insider in a fair market value transaction makes the transaction more like a skimming than an incidental private benefit. I don't mean to foist the private foundation rules on public charities lock stock and barrel, but cases like this — which are also rampant amongst the mega-churches where the churches typically grant what amounts to a lucrative, fair market value franchise to an insider's private benefit — demonstrates that the deference inherent in simply asking whether the transaction was had at fair market value is wholly insufficient (Jones, 2011).

Questions that should be asked by the administrator at this phase:

1. How do these payments further the organization's exempt purpose?
2. What internal procedures, if any, were/are in place for the review of expense reports submitted by Tyler, and who approves these payments to Gingrich?
3. Does ReAL use an outside firm to conduct audits of financial reports and accounting practices? If not, should you consider using such a firm?
4. Does ReAL have a code of ethics? If not, should one be established?

Potential Issues for Public Relations

Public relations issues concerning potential conflicts of interest between Tyler and Gingrich and Gingrich's non-profit and for-profit businesses could grow, which would have a negative effect on the ability of the non-profit to raise funds for the organization's purpose of bringing Christian principles to Washington.

Phase III — Second Issue

ABC news found evidence of payments in a May 2011 audit commissioned by the West Virginia secretary of state's office from the non-profit ReAL to Gingrich's for-profit businesses. The report alleged that Gingrich founded and operated charities in a manner that benefited his private for-profit making entities and, to a lesser extent, his political ambitions (Alavrez, 2011).

Questions that should be asked by the administrator at this phase:

1. What is the process in place to fill the position left by Tyler?
2. How are you going to address the concerns of corporate partners and individual donors regarding possible misuse of ReAL money by Tyler?
3. How are you going to address the concerns of donors in regard to the safety of their donations?
4. How is the organization going to repair its image and reputation during this time of negative publicity and public opinion?

Potential Issues for Public Relations

The resignation of Tyler only serves to increase the media scrutiny and negative publicity surrounding possible impropriety involving the use of donations for political purposes. The increased scrutiny and negative publicity can only increase questions and decrease donations.

You must determine how to provide better accountability of funds used by executive-level personnel; however, the most pressing matter at this time is to identify and secure a replacement for Tyler as ReAL's executive director (Alavrez, 2011).

Phase IV — Third Issue

The board of directors should look at its role in this matter; what fault lies with the board? Should the board have expected some form of reporting regarding these noncore expenses, such as for private jets? This growing scandal calls into question the oversight of Tyler by the board.

Questions that should be asked by the administrator at this phase:

1. Did the board authorize Gingrich's travel and expenditures?
2. What are the legal responsibilities of the board in oversight of the position of executive director, and has the board, as a whole, lived up to its responsibilities?
3. Are any members of the board complicit in Tyler's actions?

Potential Issues for Public Relations

Questions concerning the lack of oversight by the board add to the increased scrutiny of ReAL. With the top executive and the board of directors under question, it is imperative for ReAL to use effective public relations to manage and improve its image.

Phase V — Resolution and Conclusion

After being found guilty of ethics violations during his time as speaker of the House of Representatives due to the misuse of funds from a non-profit organization, one would expect that Gingrich would not use his ReAL non-profit to funnel funds to his for-profit businesses while he was running for Republican presidential candidate in the 2012 race against President Barack Obama. It would seem that anyone running for public office would steer clear of any activity that would blur the lines between politics and the non-profit world, especially since non-profits are not supposed to engage in any type of political activity that might jeopardize their non-profit status.

BRIBERY IN NON-PROFIT ORGANIZATIONS

VI

Chapter 29

International Olympic Committee — Bribe for Location — 1998

Phase I — Situation

You are the head of the International Olympic Committee (IOC). Your organization is charged with hosting the Olympic Games and has a role in picking the host city for the upcoming Olympics (IOC, 2012). The IOC has been managing the Olympics since 1894 and has its headquarters located in Switzerland (IOC, 2012). You have just been notified that one of your former member's daughters has been receiving money to attend American University from the Salt Lake Olympic Organizing Committee (SLOC) (Mallon, 2000). These payments began when Salt Lake City was in the running to host the winter Olympic Games for 2002 (Mallon, 2000). This could lead to more of your committee members being implicated for bribery. What actions do you propose to take?

Questions that should be asked by the administrator at this phase:

1. How do you determine how widespread and deep is the issue of bribery in the organization?
2. How should an investigation be conducted? How many years should the investigation review information from to determine if bribery is a pattern at the IOC?
3. What policies are in place to prevent this type of activity from occurring?
4. What action should be taken with committee members that are implicated?

Potential Issues for the Administrator to Consider

A scandal of this nature could severely damage the reputation and credibility of the IOC. If there is proof that bribery did occur with awarding the Winter 2002 Olympic Games to Salt Lake City, then the next question should be how many host cities took a similar approach in the past to obtain the award, and how many committee members have been involved in bribery throughout the years. Before anything can be fixed, an administrator should have an idea on the extent of the problem as well as an indication on the level that the bribery has hit the organization's committee members. How can an organization that is supposed to be administering the games with integrity be seen as credible when the potential for bribery could exist on such a wide scale?

Phase II — First Issue

As a top administrator, you are obviously concerned with these types of allegations that are now being brought forth against not only a former committee member, but also against the IOC itself. As more information is coming out, it has now been revealed that five more individuals that received "scholarships" were in fact close to IOC members (Mallon, 2000). The IOC President Juan Antonio Samaranch has now asked for a Juridical Commission investigation into the allegations regarding the scholarships that had been given to the individuals (Mallon, 2000). As an administrator, what are your concerns at this point?

Questions that should be asked by the administrator at this phase:

1. How widespread is the potential for corruption among the members in the IOC?
2. What other mechanisms might be used to influence IOC members to vote for host cities?
3. What are the civil litigation and criminal charges that could be brought forth in light of these allegations?
4. What controls, policies, and procedures are in place currently, and which controls, policies, and procedures should be created to prevent these types of alleged activities from occurring?
5. How should the administrators contend with the press and government agencies?

Potential Issues for the Administrator to Consider

The organization now has a potential publicity nightmare to contend with in addition to any civil litigation or criminal charges that may be pending. Furthermore, the upper administration will need to determine who in the organization has allegedly accepted bribes and then will need to take action on members that are found to have accepted bribes for votes. To determine what other mechanisms may have been used to gain votes, the IOC will need to consider investigating its members' credit history and their financial records to see if the members have accepted any financial payout that is out of the ordinary.

The IOC should be very concerned with backlash from countries' governments that did not receive an award to host the Olympics, in light of the allegations, as well as the potential for criminal investigations to occur from multiple countries against certain members. The IOC should cooperate fully with government officials and criminal investigators in an effort to uncover what transactions may have occurred between the IOC and various national organizations that were attempting to gain the bid for the Olympics.

Phase III — Second Issue

You have now been informed that three people who have connections to an IOC member have received free medical treatment from Intermountian Health Care in Salt Lake City (Mallon, 2000). More news has come out that the mayor of Salt Lake City has hired the son of an IOC member as an intern, and another member involved with the bidding process at the 2000 Sydney Olympic Games was proposed a deal to deliver the votes from African Nations for a price so that Sydney could host the games (Mallon, 2000). It has also come to light that the president of your organization received guns from Salt Lake City, which in turn the president donated to the Olympic Museum (Mallon, 2000). Your organization now has two additional headaches with the US Olympic Committee (USOC) and the Federal Bureau of Investigation (FBI) starting investigations on the SLOC's activities (Mallon, 2000).

Questions that should be asked by the administrator at this phase:

1. What actions should the organization take against the IOC members that allegedly were offered free medical treatment?
2. What should the IOC do about lobbyists who are attempting to broker "deals" for IOC member votes?
3. Should the president of the IOC resign even though he donated the guns to the Olympic Museum?
4. How should your organization contend with the investigations by the FBI and the USOC?

Potential Issues for the Administrator to Consider

The IOC will need to provide real consequences to its members for taking compensation for votes. Regardless of whether the compensation is a football ticket or medical care, it is still an effort by the bidding committees to buy votes. Unless the action of a lobbyist attempting to broker deals is reported to the IOC leadership, there is very little the organization can do to prevent individuals from bartering for votes except to penalize members who participate in activities that are banned by the organization. Even though the president of the IOC ultimately donated the guns to the Olympic Museum, it shows an incredible lack of judgment for a leader of an organization that preaches ethics to athletes. The president should resign from the organization, and the organization should cooperate fully with the investigations that are being conducted by the USOC and the FBI.

Phase IV — Third Issue

The president of the IOC has now admitted wrongdoing in the bid scandal. Prior to this, two members of the IOC handed in their resignations (Mallon, 2000). One of the members in your organization also appeared to have received a real estate deal that netted more than $70,000 (Mallon, 2000). As a result of the multiple investigations, the IOC has created two new committees, and Ethics Commission and the IOC 2000 Commission (Mallon, 2000). The Ethics Commission, in particular, was responsible for adding mandates on how the IOC members must conduct themselves both internally and externally to the organization (Mallon, 2000). What other aspects of the IOC should be addressed?

Questions that should be asked by the administrator at this phase:

1. Will expelling the members from the IOC set the proper example for members taking part in activities that are unbecoming of IOC members?
2. Will the creation of the two commissions resolve the issue of "buying" votes for hosting the Olympic Games?
3. How will you monitor the IOC members' financial assets to see if any of them are indeed receiving money for votes?

Potential Issues for the Administrator to Consider

The IOC had very little choice but to take action against the IOC members, or the organization would fail to retain any credibility internationally when discussing ethics among athletes, as well as the governments that sponsor those athletes. With the level of corruption that was uncovered, the only way that the IOC could attempt to get back on the right path was to expel or suspend members that had been found conducting unethical actions. The formation of the two commissions may not stop vote buying, but it may make it much more difficult for IOC members that are guilty of this infraction to do so without being caught and expelled by the organization. In addition, the IOC should investigate any IOC member that has a financial transaction that contends with a potential host country. This policy would at least give the IOC a means to root out corruption if vote buying was ever alleged against an IOC member.

Phase V — Resolution and Conclusion

Criminal investigations would continue, which would lead to David Simmons former chairman of Keystone Communications pleading guilty to a federal misdemeanor tax charge, and John Kim being indicted on the felony charge of fraudulently obtaining a US visa (Mallon, 2000) by accepting a phony job from Simmons in order to secure residency. A US congressional investigation would disclose that improper monetary incentives had been utilized by the Atlanta Olympic Committee, as well the Atlanta Olympic Committee keeping personal information on the IOC members in an attempt to win their votes (Mallon, 2000). The IOC, in response to the various committees' recommendations, made 50 changes, from how long members serve to the process of bidding for the games (Mallon, 2000).

Recommendations and Concluding Remarks

Lack of oversight and internal controls led to the IOC members being able to buy votes in exchange for not only financial gain, but also for their relatives to gain in the form of free scholarships, free medical benefits, and free traveling. Without the proper mechanisms in place, the IOC members that were alleged to have sold their votes for goods and services were allowed to operate at will without fear of reprisals. For an organization that is supposed to hold athletes and sponsoring countries to a high level of ethical and moral conduct, this scandal reflected poorly on the IOC, and the organization's reputation and credibility have suffered in light of the allegations. An organization such as the IOC needs to maintain the ability to investigate its members as well as the how the process of bidding for the host city is being implemented by the organization. Having the bidding process and voting process open to the public is the right direction to take, as well as revising the manner in how the members for the IOC are now chosen and how long they serve in their positions. It will take several more years for the IOC to fully recover its reputation and credibility from the scandal. However, the IOC appears to be taking investigative reports external to their organization seriously and is attempting to make modifications to its business practices.

Chapter 30

Fiesta Bowl Scandal — 2010

Phase I — Situation

You are a member of the Fiesta Bowl non-profit board that is tasked with the job of operating the Fiesta Bowl, an American college football bowl game held every year in the University of Phoenix Stadium in Glendale, Arizona. The bowl game brings billions of dollars to the Arizona economy. Currently, John Junker is the CEO for your non-profit organization. You read in December 18, 2009, in *The Arizona Republic* that past and current Fiesta Bowl employees are encouraged to write checks to specific political candidates and that the bowl reimbursed them, which is illegal. The employees tell the paper that the effort was coordinated by the bowl and that the money was delivered by lobbyists whom the bowl employed. Fiesta Bowl Chief Executive John Junker and bowl board members deny the allegations. *The Arizona Republic* reports that large fees were paid to lobbyists, and that free tickets and trips were provided to politicians in possible violation of state law. In December 22, 2009, you and the rest of the Fiesta Bowl board hired former Arizona Attorney General Grant Woods to examine the misconduct allegations. Shortly after *The Arizona Republic* began its inquiries, Woods tells the bowl's executive committee that his independent review of less than a week found "no credible evidence that the bowl's management engaged in any type of illegal conduct." Alan Young, chairman of the bowl at the time, declares bowl administrators exonerated (Harris, 2011).

On December 28, 2009, the Playoff PAC, a federal political committee dedicated to discarding the Bowl Championship Series and establishing a college-football playoff, asks the Arizona Secretary of State's Office to investigate the Fiesta Bowl based on *The Arizona Republic* findings (Harris, 2011).

On December 30, 2009, the Secretary of State's Office notifies the Fiesta Bowl that is investigating the bowl. State Elections Director Amy Bjelland asks the bowl for a copy of the Woods' investigation. The bowl refuses to provide the records. The bowl subsequently confirms that the investigation at that point had no report and few records (Harris, 2011). On January 25, 2010, Bjelland says the bowl is not cooperating with the state's investigation (Harris, 2011).

On May 16, 2010, Secretary of State Ken Bennett asks the Arizona Attorney General's Office to investigate, saying questions remain about allegations that one of the bowl's non-profit organizations reimbursed employees for political contributions (Harris, 2011). In late August 2010, the Attorney General's Office issues formal subpoenas for witnesses to appear before a grand jury (Harris, 2011). On September 23, 2010, Playoff PAC files a complaint with the Internal Revenue Service, claiming that the Fiesta Bowl and two of the nation's other premier bowls violated their tax-exempt status by paying excessive salaries and engaging in undisclosed lobbying (Harris, 2011).

Questions that should be asked by the administrator at this phase:

1. Should there be a formal investigation of the allegations against John Junker the CEO of the Fiesta Bowl non-profit organization, and, if so, what form should the investigation take (i.e., internal, external, criminal)?
2. What might be the impact on the organization if these allegations are found to be true?
3. Other than Junker, are there other members of your organization who should be held accountable in the event these allegations are true?
4. Should law enforcement be contacted at this time? Or should there be an internal investigation first, and by whom should it be conducted?

Potential Public Relations Issues

Junker, the high-profile corporate face of the organization, could very well be embroiled in a public scandal concerning his expenses being paid from the Fiesta Bowl non-profit proceeds, as well as improper or criminal activities involving organizational funds due to the improper reimbursement of political contributions to political officials made by Fiesta Bowl employees from Fiesta Bowl funds.

Initially, the Fiesta Bowl can anticipate damage to the image of and trust in the organization, and if the allegations, including criminal activity, prove to be true, the damage could be devastating: withdrawal of corporate partners and sponsorships and substantial reduction in funds.

An investigation should be initiated, perhaps first internally, focusing on an audit of the organization's accounting practices and a full reconciliation of the organization's collected revenues and expenditures. Depending on the depth of the initial findings, it may be necessary for an outside independent investigator to take over the process to avoid any appearance of a cover-up. In the event of possible criminal improprieties, federal law enforcement agencies should be contacted to perform a thorough criminal investigation. Consideration should also be given to suspending or relieving Junker of his duties, pending the outcome of the investigation(s).

Phase II — First Issue

On October 8, 2010, the Fiesta Bowl, reporting that it had new information, appoints a special independent committee to investigate whether employees were reimbursed for making political contributions. The new information came from Junker's assistant.

On October 27, 2010, the bowl hires Minneapolis-based Robins, Kaplan, Miller, and Ciresi as counsel for its internal investigation. A special committee and the special legal counsel determined that the Woods investigation was not very thorough and was done too quickly to be of any value. Neither the Fiesta Bowl executive committee nor the full board made extensive inquiries about the scope of the Woods investigation or otherwise reviewed in detail the work done by Woods.

The new investigation was exceedingly thorough. The investigation conducted 87 different interviews with 52 different people, reviewed 55 gigabytes of electronic data and approximately 10,000 documents that had been scanned and coded, and additional paper documents gathered from various locations and people. On March 29, 2011, the bowl made public the special committee's 276-page report. The special committee's investigation uncovered evidence of inappropriate conduct in four areas (Report of the Task Force Reviewing the Fiesta Bowl, 2011):

1. Reimbursement of campaign contributions and improper involvement in politics is prohibited since the Fiesta Bowl is a NPO with a 501(c)(3) status. The 501(c)(3) status by federal law, prohibits the NPO from making political contributions to any political entity.
2. The initial investigation by Woods
3. Expenses and reimbursements
4. Gifts

Questions that should be asked by the administrator at this phase:

1. How could the issue of improper use of funds, poor recordkeeping, and accounting discrepancies go unnoticed or unchecked by the organization?
2. What internal procedures, if any, were/are in place for the review of expense reports submitted by Junker, and who approves those reports?

3. Does the Fiesta Bowl use an outside firm to conduct audits of financial reports and accounting practices? If not, should you consider using such a firm?
4. Does the Fiesta Bowl have a code of ethics? If not, should one be established?

Potential Issues for Public Relations

Public relations issues concerning allegations involved the Fiesta Bowl losing its non-profit status and being eliminated from the Bowl Championship Series, which could mean billions of dollars lost to the Phoenix and Arizona economy. It would also be a tremendous loss to the reputation of the Arizona tourism industry (Report of the Task Force Reviewing the Fiesta Bowl, 2011).

Phase III — Second Issue

The investigation determined that the political contributions and other activities were meant to curry the favor of high-level elected and corporate leaders who could provide helpful legislation, secure a new stadium, and to ensure television network contracts for televising of the bowl game. The investigation uncovered a wide range of findings that support inappropriate conduct in at least three major areas:

1. Reimbursement of campaign contributions
2. Inappropriate bowl expenses
3. Personal benefit from Fiesta Bowl-provided gifts to the Fiesta Bowl CEO John Junker

The report also looked at the reforms ushered in by the bowl after the scandal to evaluate their sufficiency:

1. Reorganized the board to ensure proper oversight of its executive staff
2. Implemented changes in the way that expense reimbursements are handled for the senior executive staff
3. Established criteria for service on the board
4. Revised bylaws
5. Revamped the ethics policy and other standard operating procedures and policies
6. Required the establishment of a whistleblower policy, which implements an independent hotline that will allow staff to report inappropriate conduct in a way which will reach the board without fear of reprisal, including loss of employment
7. Undertook a comprehensive review of the scope and procedures used in its financial audit

8. Replaced senior staff and disassociated itself from some former board members, including the former chairman (Report of the Task Force Reviewing the Fiesta Bowl, 2011)

Questions that should be asked by the administrator at this phase:

1. What is the process in place to fill the position left by Junker?
2. How are you going to address the concerns of corporate partners regarding possible misuse of Fiesta Bowl money by Junker?
3. How are you going to address the concerns of donors and corporate partners in regard to the safety of their donations?
4. How is the organization going to repair its image and reputation during this time of negative publicity and public opinion?

Potential Issues for Public Relations

Junker's firing only serves to increase the media scrutiny and negative publicity surrounding possible impropriety involving misuse of bowl funds. The increased scrutiny and negative publicity can only increase questions and decrease donations from individuals and corporate partners. You must determine how to provide better accountability of funds used by executive-level personnel; however, the most pressing matter at this time is to identify and secure a replacement for Junker as the Fiesta Bowl's executive director.

Phase IV — Third Issue

The board of directors should look at its role in this matter. First, the investigation found that board oversight had been lacking and that far too much authority, often unquestioned, had been invested in the executive staff of the organization. The senior staff had established a culture in which certain business practices were not questioned, and staff members did not believe that they could question practices of management. Second, there were no mechanisms in place to allow staff to raise issues with the board members without jeopardizing their employment status. Third, the audits were not as comprehensive as they should have been. Fourth, the Fiesta Bowl board failed in its oversight responsibilities. Fifth, the cursory nature of the of the December 2009 investigation by Woods hindered the uncovering of evidence found by the new special committee.

Questions that should be asked by the administrator at this phase:

1. Did the board authorize Junker's expenditures?
2. What are the legal responsibilities of the board in oversight of the position of president, and has the board, as a whole, lived up to its responsibilities?

3. Are any members of the board complicit in Junker's actions?

Potential Issues for Public Relations

Questions concerning the lack of oversight by the board add to the increased scrutiny of the Fiesta Bowl. With the top executive and the board of directors under question, it is imperative for the Fiesta Bowl to use effective public relations to manage and improve its image.

Phase V — Resolution and Conclusion

After Junker's termination, the bowl's board of governors took the following actions:

1. The Fiesta Bowl would pay a monetary sanction in the form of a mandatory distribution of a minimum of $1 million to charities that benefit youths in Arizona recommended by the BCS Group.
2. The board removed members of the board implicated in any inappropriate conduct or wrongdoing as a result of the investigation by government agencies.
3. New criteria for serving on the board would be developed.
4. The Fiesta Bowl would require an independent internal control audit be conducted annually, and deficiencies that are found must be corrected within 90 days and a clean report presented from the auditor to the BCS executive committee.
5. The audit firm of the Fiesta Bowl was replaced.
6. The Fiesta Bowl must meet annually with the representatives of the BCS Group to review that reforms implemented by the bowl, as well as the bowl's governance, operation, and management.
7. A new executive director with the highest ethical standards was hired (Report of the Task Force Reviewing the Fiesta Bowl, 2011).

VII

ELECTION FRAUD IN NON-PROFIT ORGANIZATIONS

Chapter 31

LULAC — Alleged Election Scandal/Public Funds — 2011

Phase I — Situation

You are the newly elected president of the League of United Latin American Citizens (LULAC) in July 2011. LULAC is the oldest and largest Hispanic civil rights organization in the United States. The organization is embroiled in a controversy over the election of its new president, Margaret Moran. Jamie Martinez, a former national treasurer for LULAC, was defeated by Moran in his bid for the LULAC presidency. Martinez filed a suit to overturn the results of the election that was conducted at the national conference in Albuquerque, New Mexico, in July 2011.

Martinez's lawsuit in Bexar County, Texas, argues that since LULAC was involuntarily dissolved by the state of Texas for failure to file a periodic report for a non-profit corporation as required by law, the organization had no authority to conduct any business or official actions, such as the election of the organization's president. Martinez also stated that Moran had won the election in large part due to the fact that LULAC had received a training contract from the federal Office of Personnel Management (OPM). This training contract was to provide training to Hispanic and other individuals to enhance their leadership skills and thereby increase the number of Hispanic professionals in leadership positions in the federal government. Martinez alleges that the Puerto Ricans involved in the Federal Training Institute (FTI) run by LULAC were recruited to attend the national LULAC convention and were induced to vote for Moran in the election held at the

Albuquerque LULAC national conference. The allegation essentially stated that Puerto Ricans had been used to give Moran a sufficient voting block to swing the election in her favor (Alvarez, 2011).

Questions that should be asked by the administrator at this phase:

1. Should there be a formal investigation of the allegations against LULAC, and, if so, what form should the investigation take (i.e., internal, external, criminal)?
2. What might be the impact on the organization if these allegations are found to be true?
3. What are the advantages and disadvantages to your making the allegations public at this time?
4. Should federal law enforcement be contacted at this time? Or should there be an internal investigation first, and by whom should it be conducted?

Potential Public Relations Issues

The possible misuse of federal training funds for electioneering in the LULAC presidential campaign could result in the loss of the training grant from the OPM. The possible misuse of these funds could also require repayment of federal funds if it was proven that federal funds were used to entice FTI students to travel to New Mexico and vote for Moran as president of LULAC. Such a scandal, especially if it involves criminal activity, could result in significant negative publicity, considerable scrutiny of the organization, and a long-term public relations recovery. It would undoubtedly have a negative impact on LULAC and its ability to successfully fundraise from its members, individual donors, and corporate partners to continue the organization's mission.

Initially, LULAC can anticipate damage to the image of and trust in the organization, and, if the allegations, including criminal activity, prove to be true, the damage could be devastating: withdrawal of a federal grant, criminal charges, and the loss of corporate partners and sponsorships.

An investigation should be initiated, perhaps first internally, focusing on an audit of the organization's financial practices and a full management review of the FTI grant. Depending on the depth of the initial findings, it may be necessary for an outside independent investigator to take over the process to avoid any appearance of a cover-up. In the event of possible criminal improprieties, federal law enforcement agencies should be contacted to perform a thorough criminal investigation.

Phase II — First Issue

The newly elected Moran responded to all the allegations brought forward by Martinez. Moran did say that LULAC had a 25-year partnership with the OPM, and it has operated the FTI, which is open to all government and public sector employees. FTI is nonpartisan, and the training sessions meet the requirements of Title 5, US Code Chapter 41 (Independent Film, 2012).

Since 1986, the FTI has enabled government employees to enhance their leadership skills and helped the federal government increase Latino representation in leadership positions. Puerto Ricans, in particular, have received many job offers in the federal government as a result of LULAC's efforts. A total of 24 Puerto Rican government employees participated in the FTI at the 2011 LULAC National Convention in Albuquerque, New Mexico, contrary to the Martinez's claims that all 270 members of the LULAC Puerto Rico delegation who attended the convention also attended the FTI (Independent Film, 2012).

Moran pointed out that she had an overwhelming victory for national president in 2010, winning 68.7 percent of the vote and picking up 17 of the 19 state delegations that were counted before Martinez conceded victory to Moran. Moran said Martinez's claim that he would have won the election but for the Puerto Rican vote was completely false (Independent Film, 2012).

Questions that should be asked by the administrator at this phase:

1. Was the electoral process for the presidency well understood by all the LULAC members?
2. Was the election process and the selection of the delegates to vote for president done in a transparent manner?
3. Were all the LULAC nominations for officers and the election process held in conformance with the LULAC's bylaws?
4. Did LULAC need to use an outside firm to conduct audits of the election process for president?

Potential Issues for Public Relations

Public relations issues concerning potential strife between the two presidential candidates for the presidency of LULAC have a negative effect on the LULAC's ability to operate as a non-profit and to effectively work with its members and corporate partners and to secure funding for its operation.

Phase III — Second Issue

Early in 2011, after his grievances were ignored by the Federal Bureau of Investigation (FBI), Martinez filed a lawsuit in the District Court of Bexar County, Texas. On December 15, 2010, the court dismissed most of Martinez's claims. Thereafter, in July 2011, after oral arguments, the court dismissed the balance of Martinez's case for lack of evidentiary support (Alvarez, 2011).

Questions that should be asked by the administrator at this phase:

1. Why did Martinez not use LULAC's internal grievance procedure to have election issues addressed by the organization?
2. How are you going to address the concerns of Martinez's supporters in regard to his claims that Moran stole the election?
3. How is the organization going to repair its image and reputation during this time of negative publicity and public opinion regarding Martinez's allegations?

Potential Issues for Public Relations

The claims of a stolen election by Martinez only serve to increase the media scrutiny and negative publicity surrounding possible impropriety involving the electoral process of LULAC. The increased scrutiny and negative publicity can only cause more questions and could bring an audit from the OPM of the grant for LULAC's FTI grant.

Phase IV — Third Issue

The FBI found his complaints to be uncorroborated, and a file was never opened on the alleged election fraud regarding the election for president of LULAC.

Questions that should be asked by the administrator at this phase:

1. Did the board need to review its election bylaws?
2. Did the board need to have LULAC executive staff review the compliance of federal regulations in regard to its OPM FTI grant to assure the LULAC members that FTI students were not being involved in the LULAC presidential election processes?

Potential Issues for Public Relations

After the courts dismissed Martinez's claims and the FBI chose not to pursue the LULAC matter, were there any other obligations for the board in regard to Martinez's mishandling of the election for LULAC president?

Phase V — Resolution and Conclusion

Moran is currently serving her fourth term as president of LULAC after her first election in 2010, which was disputed by Martinez. Allegations of improper elections did not go anywhere, nor resulted in charges against Moran, nor required a new election to be held. Every non-profit organization must have a transparent selection processes for all its corporate officers. The membership of any non-profit organization must have confidence in its leadership and the validity of the process to select its organization's officers.

Chapter 32

North Carolina Democratic Party — Election Scandal — 2012

Phase I — Situation

You are a member of the North Carolina Democratic Party (NCDP). You find out that the NCDP executive director, David Parmley, has been accused of sexual harassment by one of the party employees. The NCDP chairman, David Parker, accuses you of knowing about the sexual harassment and attempting to cover it up. North Carolina is one of the swing states that is in play for the 2012 presidential election. The Democratic and Republican parties are both committing funds and resources to winning the state's very valuable 15 electoral votes.

This scandal occurred during the 2012 presidential campaign in Charlotte, North Carolina, where the Democratic National Convention is being held. One of the reasons that the convention is being held in Charlotte, North Carolina, is the hope that it will provide a kick start in winning the state for President Barack Obama. The controversy became public when a young male employee accused Parmley of misconduct. Parker disputed the implications of the claim at first. Parmley fired the employee after the sexual harassment complaint was filed (Leslie, 2012).

The employee claimed that he had been fired in retaliation for his complaints of sexual harassment. A separation agreement was prepared and submitted to the employee in return for a confidentiality agreement and release on the condition that he would get a financial settlement package as part of his termination. The package he requested to stay quiet was a provision of severance equal to one year's pay and that the NCDP would pay for his health coverage for a year or until he found employment, whichever came first (Frank, 2012). The separation might have been a good organizational decision in relation to a lawsuit, but the agreement was not well received by all members of the state Democratic Party. In the corporate world, payment to an employee prior to his or her release can often be seen a prudent financial transaction which limits future liability. However, in a non-profit with such a political charter, the use of funds to limit risk can be viewed as unsavory and lacking in transparency.

Parmley resigned after the story of the alleged sexual harassment and the settlement package broke. After the resignation, several high-ranking state Democratic Party officials demanded Parker's immediate resignation (Frank, 2012).

Questions that should be asked by the board at this phase:

1. Should there be a formal investigation of the allegations against Parmley and Parker, and, if so, what form should the investigation take (i.e., internal, external, criminal)?
2. What might be the impact on the organization if these allegations are found to be true?
3. Other than Parmley and Parker, are there other members of your organization who should be held accountable in the event these allegations are true?
4. Should law enforcement be contacted at this time? Or should there be an internal investigation first, and by whom should it be conducted?

Potential Public Relations Issues

Parmley and Parker, the high-profile corporate faces of the organization, were embroiled in a public scandal concerning Parmley's alleged sexual harassment of a state Democratic Party employee, and Parker's alleged involvement in a cover-up of the sexual harassment accusations by granting a settlement package to the fired employee (Munro, 2012). Such a scandal could result in significant negative publicity, damage President Obama's presidential campaign in the state of North Carolina and in the country, bring considerable scrutiny of the organization, and result in a long-term public relations recovery. It would undoubtedly have a negative impact on the national Democratic Party and the NCDP, and their ability to successfully fundraise to continue the organization's mission to reelect the president and democratic candidates throughout the state (Munro, 2012).

Initially, national and state Democratic parties can anticipate damage to the image of and trust in the organizations. If the allegations, sexual harassment, and a cover-up prove to be true, the damage could be devastating: withdrawal of corporate partners and sponsorships, substantial reduction in donations, and loss of the state electoral votes for President Obama and the other Democratic candidates running for congressional and state positions (Munro, 2012).

An investigation should be initiated, perhaps first internally, focusing on an audit of the organization's accounting practices and a full reconciliation of the organization's collected revenues and expenditures. Depending on the depth of the initial findings, it may be necessary for an outside independent investigator to take over the process to avoid any appearance of a cover-up. In the event of possible sexual harassment improprieties and possible election violations, federal law enforcement agencies should be contacted to perform a thorough investigation. Consideration should also be given to relieving Parker of his duties as state party chairman, pending the outcome of the investigation(s) (Munro, 2012).

Phase II — First Issue

At a press conference on April 10, 2012, Parker refused to immediately relinquish his post, despite intense national pressure. He announced that he would step aside only after a special election by the party's executive committee tentatively scheduled at the time for May 12, 2012. Parker defended his decisions during the scandal and condemned what he said was the "bubble, rush to judgment world where political decisions are made instead of deciding what is right." He said that most of his fellow Democrats are asking him to stay and fight and continue to lead the party. He declined to name his supporters. Parker's decision at the time left the state Democratic Party in disarray with no clear successor as it was poised to play a major role in the presidential election and to serve as host to the Democratic National Convention. President Obama, who was pinning his hopes on a victory in North Carolina, was scheduled to be in North Carolina on the Tuesday after Parker's news conference (Morrissey, 2012).

More than a dozen top North Carolina Democrats, including then-Governor Bev Perdue, had called for Parker to resign his post. A national Democratic Party official called Parker a man without a party (Morrissey, 2012). Following the press conference, the conservative Civitas Institute filed a complaint with the state elections board asking for an investigation into the money used for the settlement of sexual harassment allegations and termination (Morrissey, 2012),

Questions that should be asked by the NCDP board members at this phase:

1. Why did the state Democratic Party attorney advise Parker that the charges made by the employee were not sufficient to fire Parmley?
2. How was the settlement money paid to the employee, and where did the money come from to pay for the settlement?
3. Why did the NCDP bylaws not allow the board to immediately replace Parker?

Potential Issues for Public Relations

Public relations issues concerning potential strife between the Democratic National Party and the NCDP could continue to grow, which would have a negative effect on the ability of the national party and the NCDP to effectively work with their national and state supporters to secure donations.

Phase III — Second Issue

As Parker stayed in his position as chairman, the Parmley issue continued to raise its head. A lawyer for Adrian Ortega, the fired employee, asked the NCDP to preserve information related to his client's claim of sexual harassment because Ortega was weighing a lawsuit. After the news conference, the North Carolina Republican Party repeatedly pressured elected officials, including Governor Perdue, to disclose more about the way the Parmley affair unfolded internally at the NCDP (Morrissey, 2012).

Questions that should be asked by the administrator at this phase:

1. What is the process in place to fill Parmley's position?
2. How are you going to address the concerns of donors regarding possible misuse of NCDP money by Parker?
3. How are you going to address the concerns of donors in regard to the safety of their donations?
4. Would this impede people giving money to Democratic candidates and the Democratic Party?
5. How could the Obama presidential team route money around the NCDP without Parker getting his hands on it?
6. How are the national and state organizations going to repair their images and reputation during this time of negative publicity and public opinion?

Potential Issues for Public Relations

The resignation of Parmley and continuance of Parker to serve as the NCDP chairman only served to increase the media scrutiny and negative publicity surrounding possible sexual harassment of a state party employee and the use of donor funds to settle the employee's complaints. The increased scrutiny and negative publicity can only increase questions and decrease donations. You must determine how to provide better accountability of funds used by executive- and party-level personnel and the proper supervision of state party employees; however, the most pressing matters at this time are to identify and secure a replacement for Parmley and the ouster of Parker.

Phase IV — Third Issue

At the NCDP state convention, Parker offered to resign, but the convention voted not to accept his resignation. After this vote by the NCDP members, the host committee of President Barack Obama's 2012 convention in Charlotte temporarily suspended Parker as chairman of the North Carolina Democratic Party (NCDP). They also suspended his participation in the 2012 National Democratic Party convention being held in Charlotte, North Carolina. The move excised an embarrassment for the Obama reelection campaign, which saw the Tarheel State as a must-win in November 2012 (Morrissey, 2012).

Questions that should be asked by the NCDP board members at this phase:

1. After the election, should the NCDP use a lengthier and more formal vetting process for the new NCDP chairman and NCDP executive director?
2. What are the legal responsibilities of the board in its oversight of the position of chairman and the executive director, and has the board, as a whole, lived up to its responsibilities?
3. Are any members of the board complicit in Parmley and Parker's actions?

Potential Issues for Public Relations

Questions concerning the lack of oversight by the board add to the increased scrutiny of the NCDP and the national Democratic Party. With the top executive and the chairman under question, it is imperative for the NCDP to use effective public relations to manage and improve its image.

Phase V — Resolution and Conclusion

After Parmley and Parker's resignations, the NCDP replaced Parker with Randy Voller and Parmley with Robert Dempsey. However, the NCDP has appeared to learn much from its adventures with Parker and Parmley. Voller had revealed that he had unpaid state and federal taxes. One of Voller's first actions was to fire Dempsey and propose replacing him with Ben Chavis, the former executive director of the NAACP who had been removed from his job for improper behavior with an employee and misuse of NAACP funds. However, Dempsey was replaced instead by Casey M. Mann after the NCDP board rejected Voller's proposed selection of Chavis (Carlson, 2014). The NCDP is now out of power and embroiled in turmoil again about spending and strategy. All state parties are facing questions about their roles in an era of big-dollar, independent organizations. The NCDP lost the governor's mansion and the statehouse for the first time in more than a century.

VIII

GOVERNMENT ACTIONS AGAINST NON-PROFIT ORGANIZATIONS

Chapter 33

Greenpeace — Sinking of the *Rainbow Warrior* by French Government — 1985

Phase I — Situation

Established in 1971, Greenpeace is an international non-profit organization headquartered in Canada that claims to be "the leading independent campaigning organization to use peaceful protests and creative communication" (Radford, 2011). Your non-profit organization is primarily focused on environmental concerns with the protection and well-being of the planet's natural resources, as well as fostering peace (Greenpeace, 2012). Historically, Greenpeace has been extremely concerned about the effects of nuclear testing and nuclear power plants (Radford, 2011). It is 1985, and your organization has been protesting for years about the danger of nuclear power. Your organization currently has two ships at their disposal and has received funds from donors for operating costs (Radford, 2011). Your organization has learned that the French government is about to perform a nuclear test at Mururoa Atoll in the Pacific (NZ History, 2012).

Questions that should be asked by the administrator at this phase:

1. What can the organization do to protest the French nuclear tests at Mururoa Atoll?

2. What type of public relations tactics should be taken by the organization to promote the organization and put pressure on the French government to stop their nuclear tests?
3. What resources can and should your organization deploy to protest the nuclear tests at Mururoa Atoll?

Potential Issues for the Director to Consider

The director has several things to consider in terms of drawing media attention to the French government's nuclear test. The first issue is that the French government can take political and military action against your non-profit organization protests, because the French government is performing those tests in the interests of their country's national security. When the specter of national security is raised by a government, one should always be cautious about how one's organization will interact with that government. The government can feel justified in taking several actions against your organization, which could include military action on your assets and personnel and endangering your members' lives. If lives or assets are lost due to decisions that you are making as a leader of the non-profit organization, how will that justify the actions that your organization has been directed to take?

Second, how will the organization publicize the fact that the French government is conducting a test that could cause damage to the environment (i.e., Bikini Atoll)? The effort to publicize such an event will be costly. If the French government does test a nuclear weapon, your organization will have difficulty getting near the test site to get any video or photographs due to the security around the test site as well as the dangerous levels of radioactivity that are bound to be near the blast zone. These factors could create serious problems on obtaining support for your publicity campaign.

Third, what country would serve as a host from which the organization can launch its protest from, and how will the organization support the protest logistically? Some governments may be very reluctant to have a non-profit group protesting a government test site from their soil, since this could create international tension for the host country.

Fourth, how will you ensure the safety of your personnel while protesting near the nuclear test site? Not only does the organization need to worry about members being exposed to dangerous levels of radioactivity, but it will also need to provide set guidelines to their members on how to interact with any law enforcement or military personnel that they might come in contact with to give members the best chance of not being harmed during a confrontation.

Phase II — First Issue

As the administrator for the organization, you decide to send one of your ships, the *Rainbow Warrior*, to Auckland, New Zealand (NZ History, 2012). The ship was once a rusted-out research vessel that your organization had refitted and converted to be the flagship of its protest navy (Radford, 2011). New Zealand is in close proximity to the nuclear test site and is perfect for launching a protest against the nuclear testing that the French government is planning. This ship represents half of your organization's fleet and is an important asset to drawing media attention to your environmental causes around the world. Once the *Rainbow Warrior* has arrived at Auckland, it docks at Marsden Wharf in an effort to disrupt the French nuclear testing program (Brown, 2005). You are well aware of the history of the French government using violence against your organization, such as tear gas, boarding your vessels, and beating your crew members. There is cause for concern that violence could occur during this operation as well (Brown, 2005).

Questions that should be asked by the administrator at this phase:

1. How will the director ensure the protection of their members and assets in a foreign port?
2. What happens if something goes wrong and there is an issue created that causes harm to the crew of the *Rainbow Warrior* or the ship itself? How will the director interact with the New Zealand government to gain assistance?
3. How will you logistically supply your ship and crew with the necessary items they will need during the protest?

Potential Issues for the Director to Consider

Now that you have deployed half of your assets to a foreign country, you have an additional burden to ensure that logistics are taken care of and that you can interface successfully with the New Zealand government if trouble does arise. You will need to find a mechanism that will allow you to act quickly and in a flexible manner if an incident does occur. After all, this is a very dangerous situation that your organization's ship and crew will be sailing into to protest the nuclear weapons test.

Phase III — Second Issue

On July 10, 1985, just before midnight, two explosions rock the *Rainbow Warrior* while docked alongside the wharf (NZ History, 2012). One individual was killed in the explosion after going back for a camera from below decks (NZ History, 2012). The explosion sinks the *Rainbow Warrior*, effectively destroying the ship (NZ History, 2012). As the director, you want to know how an explosion occurred and, if the explosions were nonaccidental, who was responsible for the attack on the ship. The organization will be in disarray after a key resource has been destroyed and a person killed. As the director, what is your next management action that needs to be taken?

Questions that should be asked by the administrator at this phase:

1. How many other members of my organization are potentially hurt or killed besides the one confirmed death that is currently known?
2. Are the rest of the members in the organization currently in danger? Should they be evacuated from New Zealand as quickly as possible? If so, does the organization have the resources to evacuate them to another country?
3. Was the cause of the explosion accidental or deliberate?
4. Is the ship salvageable?
5. Whom should you interface with in regard to the host country's law enforcement and government officials?

Potential Issues for the Director to Consider

At this point in time, the most important item to resolve is that your members are all accounted for and uninjured. With one member already confirmed to have been killed, you need to make sure that everyone else is healthy and safe. Secondly, the director should consider the fact that leaving the members in a foreign country could be dangerous, since they are more vulnerable there than at headquarters or at some other friendly nation. The director should consider evacuating the remaining members to another country where contacts have been established and can provide safety. The director should work closely with the New Zealand government and police in discovering how the explosions occurred and, if the explosions were caused intentionally, bring those individuals to justice. The state of the ship will also have to be addressed. Is the ship salvageable, or is it a total loss that will require it to be disposed of properly? How much of the organization's money will be required to resolve this incident must be addressed with the organization's fiscal officer and the insurance companies. The most difficult thing the director will need to do is to notify the deceased member's family of the death.

Phase IV — Third Issue

The New Zealand government launches an investigation into the cause of the explosions that sank the *Rainbow Warrior*. It is discovered that three French Secret Service agents are responsible for planting the bombs in the ship to prevent its participation in protesting the nuclear tests (NZ History, 2012). The type of explosives used on the ship were Limpet mines, which caused the explosions to rip from the outside of the hull in toward the engine room (Brown, 2005). The ship is a total loss, and the organization has now lost half of its fleet, which restricts the type of operations that it can conduct.

Questions that should be asked by the administrator at this phase:

1. How will you deal with the political ramifications of being an international organization operating in a foreign country and having the government of another foreign country take a violent and secretive approach to stopping your organization from interfering with its national security aims?
2. Now that you know how your ship has been sunk and your member killed, what do you want to occur in the form of reparations from the offending government entity and justice for those responsible for the harm and damage inflicted upon your assets and personnel?
3. What lessons were learned on how the organization could secure their assets better while operating in a foreign country?
4. How will you, as a director of the organization, deal with the media on this incident?

Potential Issues for the Director to Consider

It has now been determined that illegal activity has taken place against your organization in a foreign country by another foreign government. The stakes are quite high for your organization, since you have just lost a member to the explosion, and you have lost a significant amount of your organization's assets. With the loss of the member, you will need to be especially concerned that the morale of your organization is not negatively impacted and that other members do not take reprisal actions on their own accord against France, as this would not benefit your organization in any aspect. Therefore, the director will need to keep track of the morale of the members as well as make statements that the organization will not tolerate any reprisals by members against France. The ship itself will need to be removed from the harbor for either salvage or scrapping purposes, which will be expensive.

Phase V — Fourth Issue

Two French Secret Service agents have now been apprehended in New Zealand (a third has escaped) and have been charged with murder and arson (Brown, 2005; NZ History, 2012). President François Mitterrand of France has officially denied all involvement with the sinking of the *Rainbow Warrior* (Paul Brown, 2005). In addition, the request from New Zealand to extradite the crew of a yacht suspected of supporting the operation was denied by the French government (Brown, 2005).

Questions that should be asked by the administrator at this phase:

1. How will you work with the New Zealand police and government to bring the people responsible to justice?
2. What type of strategy will you utilize to bring the incident to the media and public?

3. How will you contend with replacing your ship?
4. Will you proceed with the operation against the French nuclear testing program, given the state of your organization?

Potential Issues for the Director to Consider

The director should be channeling resources into apprehension and conviction of the individuals responsible for the bombing, as well as getting the international community involved with the situation. Since the organization is international and the attack happened in another country's territory, the United Nations should be contacted and brought into the situation in an attempt not only to resolve the issue, but to put sanctions upon France for carrying out this type of special operation against a civilian non-profit organization.

Phase VI — Resolution and Conclusion

It would be revealed years later that the former head of the French Secret Service confessed that President Mitterrand had in fact ordered the sinking of the *Rainbow Warrior* (Brown, 2005). Both French agents that were arrested were convicted of manslaughter and sentenced to 10 years in prison but were freed after a couple of years (Brown, 2005; NZ History, 2012). The French government was also required to pay New Zealand $13 million in compensation, apologize for the attack on the *Rainbow Warrior*, stop interfering with the trade agreement between New Zealand and the European Union, and compensate Greenpeace $8 million for damages (Brown, 2005; NZ History, 2012). The *Rainbow Warrior* was considered a complete loss, and as a result, was towed out of the harbor and sunk as an artificial reef (Brown, 2005). A new *Rainbow Warrior* was purchased with the compensation money and was redeployed to disrupt nuclear testing in 1996, where the French government used nonlethal force against the crew (Brown, 2005).

Recommendations and Concluding Remarks

The director of the non-profit organization had to contend with a high level of danger and risk, since it was essentially transgressing into a country's national security assets (nuclear weaponry). When these types of assets are valuable to an entity, there is always the potential for harm to occur to the non-profit organization. The director will need to consider that he or she will be facing forces that can be used against the organization, including military-type action. To plant Limpet mines requires specialized personnel to deploy the device against the hull of a ship and to obtain it presumably from military stockpiles. In short, the director will need to face a new set of challenges in securing his or her major assets and taking additional steps to safeguard members. To do this, a director may have to take proactive measures with government and law enforcement officials of the host country and inform them that the organization may antagonize a very powerful government entity.

CONCLUSION IX

Chapter 34

What Do We Take Away from These Case Studies?

With these case studies, the reader has seen what has actually occurred in the real world, which serves as good examples of what (and what not) to do when administering non-profit organizations. Why do these types of scandals and ethical lapses continue to happen in the non-profit world? These case study examples illustrate what can and will go wrong when a board or executive staff loses its way or stops watching. Non-profit organizations appear to repeat the same mistakes, which fall into familiar categories of unethical behavior, illegal activities, or public relations errors. Perhaps what can be a takeaway from this case study book is that every new board member, non-profit employee, and non-profit watchdog should be given the same checklist of things to look for to keep his or her organization from losing its way. It should also be noted that non-profit organizations should conduct board member orientation, as well as regular training sessions for the executive board to be effective in their supervision over organizational activities.

What would that checklist include to keep our non-profits on the correct path? Let us look at the common issues that faced the non-profits the authors have written about in this textbook. There are some common pitfalls and behavioral patterns that need to be especially flagged as a list of non-profits acting badly. There are the non-profits like the Boy Scouts of America that have gotten into trouble by becoming involved in the culture wars of the country, such as sexual orientation or church and state issues. Then there are the non-profits that had weak or absent controls over the actions of their chapters operating within their administrative and organizational umbrellas, as was the case with Alcoholics Anonymous and the American Cancer Society.

There are those non-profit organizations that fall prey to the allure of money or influence, such as the United Nations, the Democratic National Committee, the Republican National Committee, and the International Olympic Committee. Several organizations became too comfortable with the paid staff and leadership and relaxed their oversight, like in the American Red Cross, the Tampa Bay Zoo, the Fiesta Bowl Committee, and Penn State University. Other large non-profits ran into trouble because of their lack of financial and management controls, such as the NAACP, the American Cancer Society, and Oral Roberts University. Some of the more interesting troubles were those brought on by not carefully responding to the glare of media coverage, such as the Komen Foundation, ACORN, and the Catholic Church. Then there is the unique case of Greenpeace that involved poor risk management decisions by the non-profit. While its cause was important, non-profit organizations must not only press their cases, but they also need to manage the risks taken on by the organizations and risks that their employees and volunteers are exposed to when carrying on the missions of the organizations.

Many of our non-profits ran afoul of several of these issues and were also impacted by board members that were not fully engaged to make sure that the boards they sat on were being carefully supervised, that their internal controls were in good order, and that the executives and the staffs were accountable to the board. With thousands of boards in existence in the United States alone, it requires constant vigilance, training, and engagement to keep these organizations operating properly and serving the missions they were established to carry out for the donors, clients, staff, and the public. To insure good stewardship, you need dedicated board members and staff who are trained and committed to their goals and objectives. Before anyone even thinks about joining a board, they must know that it will require energy, commitment, and hard work to be a good board member. Staffs of non-profits will need to understand that they are not likely to be highly paid, and they can look forward to long hours and being short on staff and scarce on resources in most instances. The board needs not only people that believe in the mission of the non-profit, but also people from diverse professions, backgrounds, and skill sets to provide the range of skills to adequately manage a complex endeavor, as most non-profits are designated to serve. The non-profits must have well-selected and trained staffs governed by written rules for ethics, financial management, and board responsibilities. Everyone involved with a non-profit has an obligation to insure the safekeeping of the mission of the non-profit and how it goes about fulfilling it. In most instances, non-profit participants receive little or no pay but have substantial obligations to conduct themselves in a professional and ethical manner with small rewards or recognition.

The authors have cited several examples of when the president of the board and the executive director were both acting improperly, and it was the obligation of a board member or staff member to bring it to everyone's attention and to correct the situation, even if it means making his or her own life difficult. All participants involved with non-profits must take their responsibilities seriously. Upper administrators in non-profit organizations have to see the big picture. Additionally, these individuals need to be patient enough to read through boring monthly budget reports from the executive director, plan the activities of the non-profit well, be engaged, always be on the lookout for self-dealing, be careful when fundraising, manage how travel expenses are reimbursed, and prevent involvement in politics or controversial cultural issues outside the scope of the organization. Being involved in a non-profit at any level brings to mind the current homeland security catch phrase, "If you see something, say something!" Most importantly, if a member of a non-profit organization does see and say something, it is just as important to do something as well. The organization will not be corrected without intervention. It is the responsibility of the members and the elected board to ensure that proper corrections are applied in a timely manner.

References

Agence France Presse. 2013. *The Huffington Post.* "Cardinal George Pell admits abuse cover-up to protect Australian Catholic Church." Retrieved from www.huffingtonpost.com/2013/05/27/cardinal-george-pell-abuse-cover-up_n_3341302.html.

AJCU. 2003. Connections. A Conference on the Crisis. Retrieved from office.ajcunet.edu/connections/display.asp?issue = 12&article = 8&backissue = open.

Alcoholics Anonymous. 2012. "Origins," Alcoholics Anonymous. Retrieved on July 24, 2012, from http://www.aa.org/aatimeline/

Alcoholics Anonymous. 2002. "A.A. Preamble," Service Materials from the General Service Office. The AA Grapevine Inc. Retrieved on July 24, 2012, from http://www.aa.org/en_pdfs/smf-92_en.pdf.

Alvarez, Alex. June 14, 2011. "ABC News questions ties between Newt Gingrich's charity and for profit business." Retrieved on February 8, 2014, from http://www.mediaite.com/online/abc-news-questions-ties-between-newt-gingrichs-charity-and-for-profit-business/.

American Psychological Association. 2013. "Understanding child sexual abuse: What is child sexual abuse." Retrieved December 5, 2013, from www.apa.org/pubs/info/brochures/sex-abuse.aspx.

American Red Cross. 2012. "American Red Cross." Retrieved on August 3, 2012, from http://www.redcross.org/portal/site/en/menuitem.d8aaecf214c576bf971e4cfe43181aa0/?vgnextoid=477859f392ce8110VgnVCM10000030f3870aRCRD&vgnextfmt=default.

Ammon, John. December 13, 1999. "Waiting for John Huang." Retrieved on February 8, 2014, from http://www.washingtontimes.com/news/1999/dec/13/19991213-123426-7255r/.

Arenson, K. June 23, 1995). "Ex-United Way leader gets 7 years for embezzlement." *The New York Times.* Retrieved July 10, 2013, from http://www.nytimes.com/1995/06/23/us/ex-united-way-leader-gets-7-years-for-embezzlement.html.

Arnold, Matthew. March 1, 2012. "Komen Foundation nurses damaged brand." Medical Marketing & Media. Retrieved November 12, 2013, from http://www.mmm-online.com/komen-foundation-nurses-damaged-brand/article/228781/.

Associated Press. 2011. "Penn State scandal timeline: Key dates in the Jerry Sandusky sex abuse case." Huffington Post. Retrieved from http://www.huffingtonpost.com/2011/11/09/penn-state-scandal-timeline-jerry-sandusky_n_104204.html.

Associated Press. 2011. "Report: Armstrong paid banned doctor's front company," *Fox News.* September 21, 2011. Retrieved on March 21, 2012, from http://www.foxnews.com/sports/2011/09/21/report-armstrong-paid-banned-doctors-front-company/.

Associated Press. 2010. "Pedophile ex-priest Gilbert Gauthe out of Texas jail." Retrieved from www.nola.com/crime/index.ssf/2010/04/pedophile_ex_priest_gilbert_ga.html.

Associated Press. 2010. "Parents: All Haitian 'orphans' had relatives," Associated Press. February 21, 2010. Retrieved on August 15, 2012, from http://www.msnbc.msn.com/id/35507224/ns/world_news-haiti_earthquake/.

Associated Press. 2007. "Scandal brewing at Oral Roberts University," USAToday.com. October 5, 2007. Retrieved on August 6, 2012, from http://www.usatoday.com/news/nation/2007-10-05-oral-roberts-univ_N.htm.

Associated Press. 2005. "Despite huge Katrina relief, Red Cross criticized," MSN.com. September 28, 2005. Retrieved on August 3, 2012, from http://www.msnbc.msn.com/id/9518677/ns/us_news-katrina_the_long_road_back/t/despite-huge-katrina-relief-red-cross-criticized/.

Associated Press. 2004. "French bank targeted in Oil-for-Food scam." *Fox News*. September 27, 2004. Retrieved on September 18, 2012, from http://www.foxnews.com/story/0,2933,133696,00.html.

Babington, Charles. March 30, 2010. "Republicans say Steele will survive nightclub flap." Retrieved on February 12, 2014, from http://www.bigbigforums.com/news-information/636896-republicans-say-steele-will-survive-nightclub-flap.html, http://www.bigbigforums.com/news-information/636896-republicans-say-steele-will-survive-nightclub-flap.html .

Baklinski, Thaddeus. July 18, 2012. "Boy Scouts of America uphold ban on homosexual leaders." LifeSiteNews.com. Retrieved August 14, 2013, from http://www.lifesitenews.com/news/boy-scouts-of-america-uphold-ban-on-homosexual-leaders.

Barr, Andy. March 29, 2010. "'Bondage club' expense irks insiders." Retrieved on February 9, 2014, from http://www.politico.com/news/stories/0310/35148.html.

Bassett, L. September 27, 2011. "An abuse of government resources, Democrats charge." *The Huffington Post*. Retrieved November 14, 2013, from http://www.huffingtonpost.com/2011/09/27/planned-parenthood-investigation-government-resources_n_984002.html.

BBC News. 2005. "Oil-for-Food chief 'took bribes'," *BBC*. August 8, 2005. Retrieved on September 17, 2012, from http://news.bbc.co.uk/2/hi/middle_east/4131602.stm.

Berg, Manfred. 2012. National Association for the Advancement of Colored People. Retrieved on May 27, 2014, from http://www.oxfordaasc.com/oa/article/opr/t0005/e0862?p=oamonthAgVXHpkc7Wr1I&d=/opr/t0005/e0862, http://www.oxfordaasc.com/oa/article/opr/t0005/e0862?p=oamonthAgVXHpkc7Wr1I&d=/opr/t0005/e0862.

Bird, David. December 19, 1985. "Ex-fund raiser at Cancer Society indicted in $4 million tax fraud." Retrieved October 20, 2013, from http://www.nytimes.com/1985/12/19/business/ex-fund-raiser-at-cancer-society-indicted-in-4-million-tax-fraud.html.

Bock, James. July 17, 1995. "Audit finds NACCP exercised little control over officers' expense accounts." Retrieved on October 25, 2013, from http://articles.baltimoresun.com/1995-07-17/news/1995198091_1_naacp-convention-audit-cash-advances.

Bock, James. July 13, 1995. "NAACP audit reportedly shows over $111,000 in disputed expenses by ex-chief." Retrieved on October 25, 2013, from http://articles.baltimoresun.com/1995-07-13/news/1995194025_1_gibson-naacp-board-board-members.

Boys and Girls Club of America. 2005. Mission statement. Boys and Girls Club of America. Retrieved August 7, 2013, from http://bgca.org/whoweare/Pages/Mission.aspx.

Boy Scouts of America. 2013. About the BSA. Boy Scouts of America. Retrieved September 13, 2013, from www.scouting.org/About.aspx.

Boy Scouts of America. 2014. About the BSA. Boy Scouts of America. Retrieved January 5, 2014, from www.scouting.org/About.aspx.

Boy Scouts of America. 2013. Mission & vision. Boy Scouts of America. Retrieved September 13, 2013, from www.scouting.org/scoutingsource/Media/mission.aspx.

Boy Scouts of America. February 6, 2002. National executive board resolution on gays & atheists. Scoutingforall. Retrieved August 14, 2013, from http://www.scoutingforall.org/data/layer02/aaic/boyscoutsbsa.pdf.

Boy Scouts of America. n.d. Religious partnerships. Boy Scouts of America. Retrieved August 14, 2013, from www.scouting.org/scoutsource/membership/charter_partners/religious.aspx.

Boy Scouts of America. May 23, 2013. Statement. Boy Scouts of America. Retrieved July 21, 2013, from www.scouting.org.sitecore/content/membershipstandards/resolution/results.aspx.

Boy Scouts of America v. Dale. (n.d.). Lambda Legal. Retrieved August 14, 2013, from http://www.lambdalegal.org/in.

Branstetter, Ziva. 2007. "Richard Roberts resigns as Oral Roberts University president." *Tulsa World*. November 24, 2007. Retrieved on August 6, 2012, from http://www.tulsaworld.com/news/article.aspx?articleID=071124_1__Embat80818.

Brown, Paul. 2005. "Felling of a warrior." *The Guardian*. July 14, 2005. Retrieved on June 20, 2012, from http://www.guardian.co.uk/environment/2005/jul/15/activists.g2.

Bruno, Anthony. 2012. "The disappearance of Jimmy Hoffa." Crime Library. Retrieved on August 9, 2012, from http://www.trutv.com/library/crime/notorious_murders/famous/jimmy_hoffa/1.html.

BSA National Executive Board. 2012. Affirms Membership Standards. Retrieved from www.documentscloud.org/documents/400600-boy-scouts-of-america-statement-reaffirms-ban-on.html.

BSA National Executive Board. February 6, 2002. Resolution on gays & atheists. Scouting for all. Retrieved August 15, 2013, from www.scoutingforall.org/data/layer02/aaic/BoyscoutsBSA.pdf.

BSA Position Statement. 1991. Reaffirmation of Position on Duty to God. Retrieved from www.bsa-discrimination.org/html/bsa-god_policy.html.

BSA traditional membership survey. 2013. Scouting.org. Retrieved August 15, 2013, from www.scouting.org/About/AnnualReports/BSATraditionalMembershipSurvey.aspx.

Carbone, N. November 8, 2011. "Jerry Sandusky scandal: Seven key players in the Penn State abuse case." *Time* NewsFeed. Retrieved January 12, 2013, from http://newsfeed.time.com/2011/11/09/jerry-sandusky-scandal-seven-key-players-in-the-penn-state-abuse-case/.

Carlson, Jonathan. February 9, 2014. "NC Dems to name new executive director after firing." Retrieved, April 6, 2014, from http://www.wate.com/story/24676694/exec-director-of-nc-democratic-party-fired, http://www.wate.com/story/24676694/exec-director-of-nc-democratic-party-fired .

Catholic Church. n.d. Wikipedia. Retrieved from http://en.wikipedia.org/wiki/Catholic_Church.

Catholic sex abuse cases. n.d. Retrieved from http://community.compuserve.com/n/docs/docDownload.aspx?webtag=ws-politics&guid=51ccfafa-b530-48b3-a22a-7d9395e4b07f.

Center for Constitutional Rights. February 2013. "Fighting for the future: Adults survivors work to protect children and end the culture of clergy sexual abuse — an NGO report." New York, NY: Gallagher, K. & Spees, P. Retrieved from https://www.ccrjustice.org/files/SNAP%20Shadow%20Report%20to%20UN%20CRC.pdf.

Center for Military Readiness. 2002. "The Tailhook scandals." January 14, 2002. Retrieved on August 10, 2012, from http://cmrlink.org/social.asp?docID=106.

Chao, Elaine L. 2013. United Way of America 1996–2001. Elainelchao.com. Retrieved July 10, 2013, from http://www.elainelchao.com/united-way/.

Chappell, B. June 21, 2012. "Penn State abuse scandal: A guide & timeline." *NPR.* Retrieved August 12, 2012, from http://www.npr.org/2011/11/08/142111804/penn-state-abuse-scandal-a-guide-and-timeline.

Church of Jesus Christ of Latter-day Saints, 2012. "The Church Jesus Christ of Latter-Day Saints." Retrieved on August 23, 2012, from http://www.lds.org/?lang=eng.

Cohen, Rick. January 3, 2009. Lessons for Charities and Foundations from Bernie Madoff. Retrieved on October 30, 2013, from https://nonprofitquarterly.org/policysocial-context/23908-5-lessons-from-bernie-madoff-for-the-nonprofit-sector-and-all-of-us.html.

CNN. 2004. "U.N. defends oil-for-food letter." CNN International. May 3, 2004. Retrieved on September 17, 2012, from http://edition.cnn.com/2004/US/05/03/un.oil.for.food.letter/.

CNN. 2010. "Dominican official: I warned U.S. church leader about Haitian kids." CNN World. February 4, 2010. Retrieved on August 15, 2010, from http://articles.cnn.com/2010-02-04/world/haiti.border.arrests_1_haitian-children-laura-silsby-interpreters?_s=PM:WORLD.

CNN. 2005. "Dozens indicted in alleged Katrina scam." CNN Justice. December 29, 2005. Retrieved on August 3, 2012, from http://articles.cnn.com/2005-12-28/justice/katrina.fraud_1_contract-workers-mcgregor-scott-false-claims?_s=PM:LAW.

Cohrs, Brent. 2012. "Lance Armstrong enlists GOP congressman to investigate anti-doping agency." Chicago Now. July 13, 2012. Retrieved on August 24, 2012, from http://www.chicagonow.com/easy-as-riding-a-bike/2012/07/lance-armstrong-enlists-gop-congressman-to-investigate-anti-doping-agency/.

Cox, C. April 8, 2003. "Abuse in the Catholic Church." Dart Center for Journalism & Trauma. Retrieved October 14, 2013, from dartcenter.org/content/abuse-in-catholic-church#UmAv13B9vVo.

Curry, C. December 7, 2011. "Jerry Sandusky arrested on new sex abuse charges." ABCNews. Retrieved February 19, 2013, from http://abcnews.go.com/US/jerry-sandusky-arrested-sex-abuse-charges/story?id = 15104944.

Duant, Tina. February 2, 2012. "Hollywood ditching Susan G. Komen Foundation in wake of scandal." *The Hollywood Reporter.* Retrieved October 8, 2013, from http://www.hollywoodreporter.com/news/susan-komen-planned-parenthood-breast-cancer-286892.

Eckholm, E. July 17, 2012. "Boy Scouts to continue excluding gay people." *The New York Times.* Retrieved August 21, 2012, from http://www.nytimes.com/2012/07/18/us/boy-scouts-reaffirm-ban-on-gay-members.html?_r=2&.

Editorial. October 10, 2008. "What is ACORN?" *Washington Times.* Retrieved March 8, 2013, from http://www.washingtontimes.com/news/2008/oct/10/what-is-acorn/.

Epstein, Samuel. 2010. "Financially bloated American Cancer Society fails to prevent cancer." Project Censored: The News That Didn't Make the News. April 30, 2010. Retrieved on September 1, 2014, from http://www.projectcensored.org/3-financially-bloated-american-cancer-society-fails-to-prevent-cancer/.

Expatica.com. 2004. "BNP Paribas 'ignored abuses' in Iraq Oil-for-Food scheme: US report." Expatica.com. November 18, 2004. Retrieved on September 18, 2012, from http://www.expatica.com/fr/news/local_news/bnp-paribas-ignored-abuses-in-iraqbr-oil-for-food-scheme-us-report-14070.html.

Federation of American Scientists. 1991. "Pickering says oil sale meant to help Iraqi civilians." Retrieved on September 17, 2012, from http://www.fas.org/news/iraq/1991/910919-197740.htm.

Fessler, P. September 16, 2009. "ACORN grapples with fallout of damaging videos." *NPR*. Retrieved March 8, 2013, from www.npr.org/templates/story/story.php?storyId=112904370.

Fish, Mike. 2010. "Woods' foundation carries on mission." ESPN. March 24, 2010. Retrieved on May 8, 2012, from http://sports.espn.go.com/golf/news/story?id=4999660.

Fisher, Marc. 2007. "AA renegade dies — Whither Midtown?" *The Washington Post* — Raw Fischer. August 22, 2007. Retrieved on July 24, 2012, from http://voices.washingtonpost.com/rawfisher/2007/08/aa_renegade_dieswhither_midtow.html.

Fox News. 2009. "Lance Armstrong: Sheryl Crow's 'biological clock' led to our split." *Fox News*. May 8, 2009. Retrieved on March 27, 2012, from http://www.foxnews.com/entertainment/2009/05/08/lance-armstrong-sheryl-crows-biological-clock-led-split/.

Frank, John. April 20, 2012. "Democratic chairman disputes claims, refuses to resign." Retrieved on April 6, 2014, from http://www.newsobserver.com/2012/04/20/2012335/with-political-theater-democratic.html.

Frank, John. April 20, 2012. "North Democratic party chair ousted from Charlotte DNC Convention Committee." Retrieved on April 6, 2014, from http://dailycaller.com/2012/04/20/north-carolina-democratic-party-chair-ousted-from-charlotte-dnc-convention-committee/.

Fredrix, Emily, and Liedtke, Michael. 2010. "Doping scandal may hurt Lance Armstrong Foundation." MSNBC. August 3, 2010, Associated Press. Retrieved on March 20, 2012, from http://www.msnbc.msn.com/id/38540813/ns/us_news-giving/t/doping-scandal-may-hurt-lance-armstrong-foundation/.

Friess, S. May 5, 2009. "Acorn charged in voter registration fraud case in Nevada." *The New York Times*. Retrieved March 9, 2013, from www.nytimes.com/2009/05/05us/05acorn.html?_r+1&pagewanted=print.

Gifford, Bill. 2012. "It's not about the lab rats." *Outside Magazine*. February 2012, January 5, 2012. Retrieved on March 20, 2012, from http://www.outsideonline.com/outdoor-adventure/athletes/lance-armstrong/Its-Not-About-the-Lab-Rats.html?page=1

Gilgoff, D. March 19, 2010. "Catholic Church's sex abuse scandal goes global." CNNWorld. Retrieved November 27, 2013, from www.cnn.com/2010/WORLD/europe/03/19/catholic.church.abuse/.

Glaser, J. 1994. *The United Way Scandal: An Insider's Account of What Went Wrong and Why*. New York, New York: John Wiley & Sons Inc.

Grad, Shelby. May 8, 2010. "RNC officials ousted in scandal over L.A. bondage themed nightclub spending." Retrieved on February 9, 2014, from http://latimesblogs.latimes.com/lanow/2010/05/rnc-officials-ousted-in-scandal-over-la-bondagethemed-nightclub-spending.html.

Gray, Mark M., & Perl, P. M. April 2006. "Catholic reaction to the news of sexual abuse vases involving Catholic clergy" (Working Paper 8). Washington, DC: CARA Georgetown University. Retrieved February 22, 2013, from http://cara.georgetown.edu/caraservices/frstats/cara%20workingpaper8.pdf.

Greenpeace. 2012. "Greenpeace." Retrieved on May 5, 2012, from http://www.greenpeace.org/usa/en.

Harris, Craig. March 29, 2011. "Fiesta Bowl report: Long road to bowl crisis." Retrieved on February 23, 2014, from http://www.azcentral.com/news/politics/articles/20130524fiesta-bowl-timeline-report.html.

Harris Interactive. 2012. "Scandal rocks America's support for Susan G. Komen for the Cure." Retrieved from www.harrisinteractive.com/NewsRoom/PressReleases/tabid/446/mid/1506/articleId/994/ctl/ReadCustom%20Default/Default.aspx.

Harshbarger, S., & Crafts, A. September 7, 2009. "An independent governance assessment of ACORN. The path to meaningful reform." Proskauer. Retrieved March 16, 2013, from www.proskauer.com/files/uploads/report2.pdf.

Hearn, R. G. 2006. "The New York City Department of Investigation's findings regarding fraud and financial mismanagement at the Gloria Wise Boys and Girls Club." Retrieved August 8, 2013, from http://www.nyc.gov/html/doi/downloads/pdf/gw_report_v2.pdf.

Helgeson, Baird. August 21, 2009. "Lowry Park Zoo, Salisbury reach settlement." Retrieved on October 29, 2013, from http://tbo.com/news/lowry-park-zoo-salisbury-reach-settlement-83327.

Helgeson, Baird. August 29, 2008. "Lowry Park Zoo call for audit to ferret out conflicts." Retrieved on 29, 2013, from http://tbo.com/news/central-tampa/2008/aug/29/me-zoo-calls-for-audit-to-ferret-out-conflicts-ar-133039/.

Holmes, Steven A. 1995. "Gibson is ousted as NAACP head." *The New York Times*. February 19, 1995. Retrieved on October 25, 2013, from http://www.nytimes.com/1995/02/19/us/gibson-is-ousted-as-naacp-head.html.

Honan, Edith. January 23, 2012. "Penn State hit with unprecedented penalties for Sandusky scandal." Reuters. Retrieved January 12, 2013, from http://www.reuters.com/article/2012/07/23/us-usa-pennstate-idUSBRE86L07F20120723.

HROT. 2014. "Top outsourced screening services provider." HR Today. Retrieved on September 1, 2014, from http://www.hrotoday.com/content/2222/top-outsourced-screening-services-provider.

Hrywra, M. March 23, 2012. "Komen chair steps aside, former board member returns." *The Non Profit Times*. Retrieved October 15, 2013, from http://www.thenonprofittimes.com/news-articles/komen-chair-steps-aside-former-board-member-returns/.

Indra Irmawan. 2013. "American cancer." Retrieved on October 30, 2013, from http://zodiacxs.blogspot.com/2013/05/american-cancer-sign-ribbon-cells.html, http://zodiacxs.blogspot.com/2013/05/american-cancer-sign-ribbon-cells.html.

Internal Revenue Service. 2012. "Publications 557 (10/2011), Tax-exempt status for your organization." Retrieved on August 9, 2012, from http://www.irs.gov/publications/p557/ch04.html#en_US_2011_publink1000200303.

IOC. 2012. "The organisation." International Olympic Committee. Retrieved on September 21, 2012, from http://www.olympic.org/about-ioc-institution?tab=Organisation.

James, S. June 7, 2012. "Boy Scouts consider opening organization to gays." ABCNews.com. Retrieved May 12, 2013, from http://abcnews.go.com/Health/boy-scouts-allowing-gays-join-local-troops/story?id=16513417.

John Jay College of Criminal Justice. 2004. "The nature and scope of sexual abuse of minors by Catholic priests and deacons in the United States 1950–2002." Retrieved from www.usccb.org/issues-and-action/child-and-youth-protection/upload/The-Nature-and-Scope-of-Sexual-Abuse-of-Minors-by-Catholic-Priests-and-Deacons-in-the-United-States-1950-2002_pdf.

Jones, Darryl, K. 2011. "Newt's nonprofits under scrutiny." Law Professor Blogs, Nonprofit Blogger, Associate Dean for Academic Affairs & Professor of Law, Florida A&M University College of Law. Retrieved June 14, 2011, from http://lawprofessors.typepad.com/nonprofit/2011/06/newts-nonprofits-under-scrutiny.html

Jones, Melanie. 2012. "Richard Roberts: Oral Roberts' son, ORU president arrested for DUI." *International Business Times*. January 24, 2012. Retrieved on August 6, 2012, from http://www.ibtimes.com/articles/286943/20120124/richard-roberts-oral-oru-president-arrested-dui.htm.

Kampeas, Ron. October 29, 2013. "Bernie Madoff scam, fires and fraud cost Jewish nonprofits dearly." Retrieved on October 30, 2013, from http://www.jewishexponent.com/madoff-fire-and-theft-how-jewish-nonprofits-lost-money.

Kingkade, T. July 12, 2012. "Penn State administration, Joe Paterno covered up Jerry Sandusky's child abuse." *The Huffington Post*. Retrieved January 15, 2013, from http://www.huffingtonpost.com/2012/07/12/freeh-report-penn-state-coverup-joe-paterno-jerry-sandusky_n_1667727.html.

Kinkead, Lucinda Dillon. 2005. "Hofmann shuns spotlight, keeps mostly to himself." *The Deseret News*. July 20, 2005. Retrieved on August 23, 2012, from http://www.deseretnews.com/article/600149762/Hofmann-shuns-spotlight-keeps-mostly-to-himself.html?pg=all.

Knowles, David. 2011. "Exclusive: Tailhook victim speaks out on Capt. Owen Honors scandal." AOL News. January 4, 2011. Retrieved on August 10, 2012, from http://www.aolnews.com/2011/01/04/exclusive-tailhook-victim-speaks-out-on-capt-owen-honors-scand/.

Labaton, Stephen. November 11, 1996. "Democrats Question, and Return, Donation." *The New York Times*. Retrieved on February 8, 2014, from http://www.nytimes.com/1996/11/08/us/democrats-question-and-return-donation.html.

Lacy, Marc, and Urbina, Ian. 2010. "Trafficking charges for adviser to jailed Americans in Haiti." *The New York Times*. February 15, 2010. Retrieved on August 15, 2012, from http://www.nytimes.com/2010/02/16/world/americas/16haiti.html

Langlois, E. and Pfohman, R. 2007. Catholic News Service. "Portland Archdiocese ends bankruptcy with $75 million settlement." Associated Press. July 14, 2007.

Law Professor Blogs. June 14, 2011. "Newt's nonprofits under scrutiny." Retrieved on February 8, 2014, from http://lawprofessors.typepad.com/nonprofit/2011/06/newts-nonprofits-under-scrutiny.html.

Lawrence, C. October 20, 2008. "Ex-ACORN worker: I paid the price for voter registration fraud." CNNPolitics.com. Retrieved March 12, 2013, from www.cnn.com/2008/POLITICS/10/22/voter.fraud/.

Leslie, Laura. May 12, 2012. "NC Democratic Party Chairman resigns but gets vote to stay." Retrieved on April 6, 2014, from http://www.wral.com/news/state/nccapitol/story/11096546/.

Levinson, Mason, and Novy-Williams, Eben. 2011. "Armstrong doping case seen costing cancer charity $10 million." Bloomberg. June 6, 2011. Retrieved on March 20, 2012, from http://www.bloomberg.com/news/2011-06-07/lance-armstrong-doping-case-seen-costing-his-cancer-foundation-10-million.html.

Lindsey, Robert. 1987. "Dealer in mormon fraud called a master forger." *The New York Times*. February 11, 1987. Retrieved on August 22, 2012, from http://www.nytimes.com/1987/02/11/us/dealer-in-mormon-fraud-called-a-master-forger.html.

Livestrong. 2012. "Livestrong." Retrieved on March 20, 2012, from http://www.livestrong.org/.

Lombino, D. September 28, 2006. "Air America funds return to a Bronx Boys and Girls Club." *New York Sun*. Retrieved July 7, 2013, from http://www.nysun.com/new-york/air-america-funds-returned-to-a-bronx-boys/40533/.

Lowry Park Zoo Audit. March 20, 2009. Retrieved on May 27, 2014, from http://www.tampabay.com/specials/2009/PDFs/Zoo_Audit.pdf.

Lynch, Colum. 2004. "Oil-for-Food official may have blocked inquiries." *The Washington Post*. November 14, 2004, Page A26. Retrieved on September 17, 2012, from http://www.washingtonpost.com/ac2/wp-dyn/A48225-2004Nov13?language=printer.

Lynch, R. February 3, 2012. "Komen learns power of social media: Facebook, Twitter fueled fury." *Los Angeles Times*. Retrieved November 12, 2013, from http://latimesblogs.latimes.com/nationnow/2012/02/facebook-twitter-fueled-fury-against-in-susan-g-komen-for-the-cure-.html.

MacFarquhar, Neil. 2010. "Security council removes restrictions on Iraq." NYTimes.com. December 15, 2010. Retrieved on September 18, 2010, from http://www.nytimes.com/2010/12/16/world/middleeast/16nations.html?_r=0.

Madden, M. March 1, 2010. "Brooklyn prosecutors clear local ACORN office." *SALON*. Retrieved March 8, 2013, from www.salon.com/2010/03/01/acorn_cleared/.

Mallon, Bill. 2000. "The Olympic bribery scandal." International Society of Olympic History. *Journal of Olympic History*, May 2000. Retrieved on September 18, 2012, from http://www.la84foundation.org/SportsLibrary/JOH/JOHv8n2/johv8n2f.pdf.

Maloney, B. March 14, 2007. "Air America radio, Gloria Wise Boys & Girls Club scandal: Still no justice." The Radio Equalizer. Retrieved May 15, 2013, from radioequalizer.blogspot.com/2007/03/air-america-radio-wise-boys.html.

Marks, E., and Richards, C. n.d. "A message from our chair and president." Planned Parenthood Federation of America Annual Report 2006–2007. Retrieved from http://www.plannedparenthood.org/files/AR_2007_vFinal.pdf.

Marshall, M. April 13, 1993. "Update: United Way tries to portray united front: A year after scandal racked the nation's largest philanthropic group, it is still grappling with local defections and a marked drop in fund raising." *Los Angeles Times*. Retrieved June 3, 2013, from http://articles.latimes.com/1993-04-13/news/mn-22399_1_alternative-fund-raising.

Martinez, A., and Kucher, K. September 7, 2007. "San Diego priest abuse claims settled." *San Diego Union-Tribune*. Retrieved November 22, 2013, from legacy.utsandiego.com/news/metro/20070907-1449- bn07diocese3.html.

McCrostie, James. February, 2010. "The TOEIC in Japan: Scandal made in heaven." Retrieved on October 20, 2013, from http://jalt.org/test/mcc_1.htm.

Mechling, J. 2001. *On My Honor: Boy Scouts and the Making of American Youth*. Chicago: University of Chicago Press.

Mehegan, D. November 9, 1993. "Gospel of shame: Facing fact about abusive priests." *The Boston Globe*. Retrieved February 15, 2013, from www.boston.com/globe/spotlight/abuse/extras/book_reviews/110933_burkett.htm.

Memmott, M. January 31, 2012. "Furor erupts over Susan G. Komen halt of grants to Planned Parenthood." *NPR*. Retrieved October 18, 2013, from http://www.npr.org/blogs/thetwo-way/2012/01/31/146177902/furor-erupts-over-susan-g-komen-halt-of-grants-to-planned-parenthood.

Memoli, M.A. November 2, 2010. "ACORN filing for Chapter 7 bankruptcy." *Los Angeles Times*. Retrieved March 7, 2013, from http://articles.latimes.com/2010/nov/02/news/la-pn-acorn-bankruptcy-20101103.

Miller, Alan C. October 24, 1996. "Controversy swirling around Gandhi donation grows." Retrieved on February 8, 2014, from http://articles.latimes.com/1996-10-24/news/mn-57235_1_mahatma-gandhi/2.

Morgan, D. 2012. "Catholic bishops pressured Komen over Planned Parenthood." Reuters. Retrieved April 8, 2013, from www.reuters.com/articles/2012/03/15/us-komen-catholic-idUSBRE82E12Q20120315.

Morrissey, Ed. April 19, 2012. "NC Democrat Party chair refuses to step down after scandal." Retrieved on April 6, 2012, from http://hotair.com/archives/2012/04/19/nc-democrat-party-chair-refuses-to-step-down-after-scandal/.

MyHealthNewsDaily. 2012. "Swine flu outbreak 15 times Deadlier than thought, study finds." Retrieved on August 2, 2012, from http://bullwatch.com/news/marketandbusiness-5/20120725#.

Murphy, Austin. 2012. "Is Lance Armstrong's doping investigation really closed?" Murphy's Law. February 14, 2012. Retrieved on May 23, 2012, from http://sportsillustrated.cnn.com/2012/writers/austin_murphy/02/14/Is-Armstrong-investigation-really-over/index.html.

Murphy, D. 2014, January 1, 2014. "Boy Scouts of America open door to gay scouts with new policy." *New York Daily News*. Retrieved January 5, 2014, from http://www.nydailynews.com/news/national/boy-scouts-america-open-door-gay-scouts-new-policy-article-1.1563595.

NBC4.com. 2007. "Midtown AA accused of sexual exploitation." NBC4.com. May 11, 2007. Retrieved on July 24, 2012, from http://www.religionnewsblog.com/18262/midtown-aa.

Nbcnews.com. July 14, 2007. "L.A. archdiocese to settle suits for $660 million." Retrieved November 25, 2013, from http://www.nbcnews.com/id/19762878/ns/us_news-life/t/la-archdiocese-settle-suits-million/.

Nebehay, Stephanie. 2010. "WHO admits shortcomings in handling flu pandemic." Reuters. April 12, 2010. Retrieved on August 2, 2010, from http://www.reuters.com/article/2010/04/12/us-who-idUSTRE63B2TL20100412.

New Life Children's Refuge, 2010. "Haitian orphan rescue mission." Retrieved on August 15, 2012. http://www.esbctwinfalls.com/clientimages/24453/pdffiles/haiti/nlcrhaitianorphanrescuemission.pdf

Newsweek. 1992. "Tailhook: Scandal time." *The Daily Beast*. July 5, 1992. Retrieved on August 10, 2010, from http://www.thedailybeast.com/newsweek/1992/07/05/tailhook-scandal-time.html.

Nola.com. April 26, 2010. "Pedophile ex-priest Gilbert Gauthe out of Texas jail." Retrieved October 23, 2013, from www.nola.com/crime/index.ssf/2010/04/pedophile_ex_priest_gilbert_ga.html.

NZ History. 2012. "Sinking of the Rainbow Warrior — nuclear-free New Zealand." New Zealand History Online. Retrieved on May 22, 2012, from http://www.nzhistory.net.nz/politics/nuclear-free-new-zealand/rainbow-warrior.

O'Leary, N. March 7, 2013. "Sex abuse: The scandal the Catholic Church cannot shake." Reuters. Retrieved November 15, 2013, from http://www.reuters.com/article/2013/03/07/us-pope-succession-abuse-idUSBRE92611A20130307.

Office of the Attorney General. 2010. Report of the Attorney General on the Activity of ACORN. Retrieved from ag.ca.gov/cms_attachments/press/pdfs/n1888_acorn_report_pdf.

Oral Roberts University. 2012. "About ORU." Retrieved on August 6, 2012, from http://www.oru.edu/the_new_oru/.

Ornstein, C. September 27, 2005. "Hospital halts organ program. *Los Angeles Times*. Retrieved from http://articles.latimes.com/2005/sep/27/local/me-organ27.

Ornstein, C. April 27, 2006. "Medical Center faces new woes." *Los Angeles Times*. Retrieved September 19, 2013, from http://articles.latimes.com/2006/apr/27/local/me-stvincent27.

Otterman, Sharon. 2005. "Iraq: Oil for Food scandal." Council on Foreign Relations. October 28, 2005. Retrieved on September 17, 2012, from http://www.cfr.org/un/iraq-oil-food-scandal/p7631.

Oyez project. Oyez.com. Retrieved August 18, 2013, from www.oyez.com.

Pederson, J.P. 2001. *International Directory of Company Histories: United Way of America*, vol. 36. Detroit, Michigan: St. James Press. Retrieved June 5, 2013, from http://www.fundinguniverse.com/company-histories/united-way-of-america-history/.

Penn State. n.d. Penn State. Retrieved August 15, 2012, from http://www.psu.edu/.

Peoples, S. April 4, 2011. "GOP presidential candidates oppose Planned Parenthood funding." *Roll Call*. Retrieved December 21, 2013, from www.rollcall.com/news/gop_presidential_candiates_oppose_planned_parenthood_funding-204565-1.html.

Planned Parenthood of America annual report. 2006–2007. Planned Parenthood. Retrieved December 7, 2013, from http://www.plannedparenthood.org/files/AR_2007_vFinal.pdf.

Position statement. June 12, 1991. Reaffirmation of the position of the Boy Scouts of America on "Duty to God." BSA-Discrimination.org. Retrieved August 14, 2013, from http://www.bsa-discrimination.org/html/bsa-god_policy.html.

Radford, Philip D. 2011. "Greenpeace 2010/2011 annual report." Retrieved on May 21, 2012, from http://www.greenpeace.org/usa/Global/usa/planet3/PDFs/ANNUAL_REPORT2010-11.pdf.

Ramsland, Katherine. 2012. "The genius bomber." Crime Library. Retrieved on August 23, 2012, from http://www.trutv.com/library/crime/criminal_mind/forensics/mormon_forgeries/index.html.

Reeve, Elspeth. June 14, 2011. "Gingrich's charity paid money to Gingrich's business." Retrieved on February 8, 2014, from http://www.thewire.com/politics/2011/06/gingrich-charity-paid-cash-gingrich-business/38810/.

Report of the Attorney General on the activity of ACORN. April 1, 2010. Office of the Attorney General. Retrieved March 15, 2013, from ag.ca.gov/cms_attachments/press/pdfs/n1888_acorn_report_pdf.

Reuters. April 5, 2013. "Pope Francis on sex abuse: Catholic church must 'act decisively'." *The Huffington Post*. Retrieved from www.huffingtonpost.com/2013/04/05/pope-francis-sex-abuse_n_3019405.html.

Rivera, Manuel E. February 23, 2012. "LULAC scandal reaches FBI." Retrieved on February 9, 2014, from https://groups.yahoo.com/neo/groups/lulac-mn/conversations/messages/9938.

Romero, Simon, and Urbina, Ian. 2010. "Judge releases eight Americans jailed in Haiti." *The New York Times*. February 17, 2010. Retrieved on August 15, 2012, from http://www.nytimes.com/2010/02/18/world/americas/18haiti.html?_r=1.

Roberts, Kate. June 10, 2000. "Cancer Society rechecks safeguards." Retrieved on October 30, 2013, from http://enquirer.com/editions/2000/06/10/loc_cancer_society.html.

Rossett, Claudia, and Russell, George. 2005. "New U.N. scheme: Alliance of civilizations." *Fox News*. November 22, 2005. Retrieved on September 17, 2012, from http://www.foxnews.com/story/0,2933,176362,00.html.

Rossouw, Mandy. 2010. "SA gives aid after Haiti quake." Mail and Guardian: Africa's Best Read. January 15, 2010. Retrieved on August 15, 2012, from http://www.mg.co.za/article/2010-01-15-sa-gives-aid-after-haiti-quake.

Rovell, Darren. 2012. "Lance Armstrong won't fight charges." ESPN.com. August 24, 2012. Retrieved on August 24, 2012, from http://espn.go.com/olympics/cycling/story/_/id/8298135/usada-ban-lance-armstrong-life-seven-tour-de-france-titles-risk-charges-used-performance-enhancing-drugs-cycling-career.

Sager, Jeanne. 2011. "Drug scandal makes Lance Armstrong a bully." The Stir. January 19, 2011. Retrieved on May 23, 2012, from http://thestir.cafemom.com/in_the_news/115140/drug_scandal_makes_lance_armstrong.

Salter, Chuck. 2010. "Can Livestrong survive Lance Armstrong and a doping scandal?"Fast Company.com. October 18, 2010. Retrieved on May 23, 2012, from http://www.fastcompany.com/magazine/150/can-livestrong-survive-lance.html.

Schaffer, M. June 25, 2012. "Sex-abuse crisis is a watershed in the Roman Catholic Church's history in America." *The Inquirer* Philly.com. Retrieved October 22, 2013, from http://articles.philly.com/2012-06-25/news/32394491_1_canon-lawyer-catholic-priests-catholic-bishops.

SCU conference on the crisis. December 2003. AJCU Connections. Retrieved February 10, 2013, from office.ajcunet.edu/connections/display.asp?issue = 12&article = 8&backissue = open.

Selthoffer, Steven. 2012. "WADA and corrupt anti-doping labs threaten swimming and other sports: How does inside information get to the media." *Swimming World*. May 15, 2007. Retrieved on March 27, 2012, from http://www.swimmingworldmagazine.com/lane9/news/14730.asp.

Shepard, C.E. February 28, 1992. "United Way head resigns over spending habits." *The Washington Post*. Retrieved June 5, 2013, from tech.mit.edu/V112/N9/united-way.09w.html.

Sherman. J. September 12, 2009. "Census bureau cuts its ties with ACORN." *The Wall Street Journal*. Retrieved May 15, 2013, from online.wsj.com/news/articles/SB125271412822705239.

Siegal, Jack. 2007. "Oral Roberts University $70million is quite a lever: Richard Roberts is history, but ORU will survive." Charity Governance Consulting LLC. November 28, 2007. Retrieved on August 7, 2012, from http://www.charitygovernance.com/charity_governance/oral_roberts_university/.

Sieminski, P. December 21, 2006. "Gloria Wise Boys and Girls Club: Mistakes you need not make." *NPO*. Retrieved May 15, 2013, from https://nonprofitquarterly.org/management/587-gloria-wise-boys-and-girls-club-mistakes-you-need-not-make.html.

Silverman, Stephen M. 2006. "Lance's ex felt smothered by marriage." *People*. May 9, 2006. Retrieved on March 27, 2012, from http://www.people.com/people/article/0,,1192564,00.html.

Smith, C. July 25, 2012. "Penn State fallout: Loss of sponsorships, possible credit downgrade." *Forbes*. Retrieved January 18, 2013, from http://www.forbes.com/sites/chrissmith/2012/07/25/penn-state-fallout-loss-of-sponsorships-possible-credit-down grade/.

Smith, P. June 11, 2003. "Archdiocese to pay victims $25.7 million for sex abuse." *The Courier-Journal*. Retrieved March 12, 2013, from www.courtroomlaw.com/news_arch.shtml.

Somasheklar, S. October 20, 2012. "Planned Parenthood's funding is targeted in partisan debates." *The Washington Post*. Retrieved November 15, 2012, from http://www.washingtonpost.com/politics/decision2012/in-abortion-battle-funding-of-planned-parenthood-is-political-fodder/2012/10/20/bfa08254-13cc-11e2-be82-c3411b7680a9_story.html.

Sontag, D. April 22, 1992. "Affiliates feeling pinch of United Way scandal." *The New York Times*. Retrieved July 7, 2013, from http://www.nytimes.com/1992/04/22/nyregion/affiliates-feeling-pinch-of-united-way-scandal.html.

SOS Children's Villages. 2010. "Haiti orphans: Urgent breaking news baby and child traffickers caught." January 31, 2010. Retrieved on August 15, 2012, from http://www.emergency-appeal.org/haiti-earthquake/haiti-orphans-urgent-breaking-news-baby-and-child-traffickers-caught.

Stevenson, G.E. May 23, 2013. Boy Scouts of America national annual meeting keynote speech. Retrieved September 7, 2013, from http://www.mormonnewsroom.org/article/bishop-gary-e-stevenson-boy-scouts-of-america-national-annual-meeting-keynote-speech.

Stokes, Shane. 2011. "Lance Armstrong investigation: Former federal prosecutor speaks about possible witness tampering charges." Velonation. June 22, 2011. Retrieved on May 22, 2012, from http://www.velonation.com/News/ID/8826/Lance-Armstrong-investigation-Former-federal-prosecutor-speaks-about-possible-witness-tampering-charges.aspx.

Strobbe, Mike. 2010. "Expired swine flu shots amount to $260 million loss." NBCNews.com. July 1, 2010. Retrieved on August 2, 2012, from http://bullwatch.com/news/marketandbusiness-5/20120725#.

Strom, S. October 10, 2008. "On Obama, ACORN and voter registration." *The New York Times*. Retrieved February 20, 2013, from http://www.nytimes.com/2008/10/11/us/politics/11acorn.html?_r = 0.

Strom, Stephanie. 2006. "Red Cross sifting internal charges over Katrina aid." *The New York Times*. March 24, 2006. Retrieved on August 3, 2012, from http://www.nytimes.com/2006/03/24/national/nationalspecial/24cross.html.

Strom, Stephanie. 2005. "President of Red Cross resigns; board woes, not Katrina cited." *The New York Times*. December 14, 2005. Retrieved on August 3, 2012, from http://www.nytimes.com/2005/12/14/politics/14redcross.html.

Suddath, C. October 14, 2008. "A brief history of ACORN." *Time*. Retrieved April 25, 2013, from http://www.time.com/time/printout/0,8816,1849867,00.html.

Summers, Nick. 2007. "A struggle inside AA." *Newsweek: The Daily Beast*. May 6, 2007. Retrieved on June 20, 2012, from http://www.thedailybeast.com/newsweek/2007/05/06/a-struggle-inside-aa.html.

Susan G. Komen. 2013. "Susan G. Komen: About us." Retrieved February 9, 2013, from http://ww5.komen.org/AboutUs/AboutUs.html.

Tailhook. 2012. "Tailhook Association." Retrieved on August 10, 2012, from http://tailhook.org/.

Tanner, Jerald. 1987. "Tracking the White Salamander." Retrieved on August 22, 2012, from http://www.utlm.org/onlinebooks/trackingcontents.htm.

Taubenberger, Jeffery, and Morens, David. 2006. "1918 influenza: The mother of all pandemics." Emerging Infectious Diseases, Centers for Disease Control and Prevention. Volume 12, Number 1 — January 2006. Retrieved on August 2, 2012, from http://wwwnc.cdc.gov/eid/article/12/1/05-0979_article.htm.

Taylor, A. September 14, 2009. "Senate votes to deny funds to ACORN." *Seattle Times*. Retrieved April 19, 2013, from seattletimes.com/html/politics/2009865345_apuscongressacorn.html?syndication = rss.

Teamsters. 2012. "Teamster history." Retrieved on August 9, 2012, from http://www.teamster.org/history/teamster-history/overview.

Teamsters Local 177. 2012. "Teamster history timeline." Retrieved on August 9, 2012, from http://www.teamsterslocal177.org/index.cfm?zone=/unionactive/teamster_content/teamster_timeline.htm.

Telegraph. 2012. "International Cycle Union president Pat McQuaid 'shocked' at evidence in Lance Armstrong report." Retrieved on October 16, 2012, from http://www.telegraph.co.uk/sport/othersports/cycling/9607197/International-Cycling-Union-president-Pat-McQuaid-shocked-at-evidence-in-Lance-Armstrong-report.html.

Terkel, A. February 8, 2012. "Susan G. Komen fallout: Corporate partners stick with charity despite lingering concern." *The Huffington Post*. Retrieved Febraury 9, 2013, from http://www.huffingtonpost.com/2012/02/08/susan-g-komen-corporate-partners_n_1260625.html.

Terry, Don. July 14, 1995. "Audit faults NACCP on accounting." Retrieved on October 25, 2013, from http://www.nytimes.com/1995/07/14/us/audit-faults-naacp-on-accounting.html.

The Huffington Post. November 9, 2011. "Penn State scandal timeline: Key dates in the Jerry Sandusky sex abuse case." *The Huffington Post*. Retrieved January 9, 2013, from http://www.huffingtonpost.com/2011/11/09/penn-state-scandal-timeline-jerry-sandusky_n_1084204.html.

The Huffington Post. April 5, 2013. "Pope Francis on sex abuse: Catholic Church must 'act decisively'." *The Huffington Post*. Retrieved November 15, 2013, from http://www.huffingtonpost.com/2013/05/05/pope-francis-act-decisive_n_3218983.html.

The Huffington Post. May 27, 2013. "Cardinal George Pell admits abuse cover-up to protect Australian Catholic Church." *The Huffington Post*. Retrieved October 22, 2013, from http://www.huffingtonpost.com/2013/05/27/cardinal-george-pell-abuse-cover-up_n_3341302.html.

The Oklahoma State Court Networks. 2008. "No. CJ-2007-6543 — Civil Relief more than $10,000: Cause #1 — Breach of Contract/Wrongful Discharge." October 23, 2008. Retrieved on August 7, 2012, from http://www.oscn.net/applications/oscn/GetCaseInformation.asp?submitted=true&viewtype=caseGeneral&casemasterID=2032027&db=Tulsa.

The Venture Online. December 2011. "Election scandal rocks LULAC, president responds." Retrieved on February 9, 2014, from http://www.lulacdistrict12.com/election-scandal-rocks-lulac-president-responds/.

The Washington Post. February 7, 2012. "Timeline of key events in Komen controversy." *The Washington Post*. Retrieved August 10, 2013, from http://www.washingtonpost.com/national/health-science/timeline-of-key-events-in-komen-controversy/2012/02/07/gIQAX4EWxQ_story.html.

The Washington Times. 2004. "World leaders on list of oil recipients." *The Washington Times*. April 22, 2004. Retrieved on September 17, 2012, from http://www.washingtontimes.com/news/2004/apr/22/20040422-114353-8420r/.

Thompson, Ginger. 2010. "Case stokes Haiti's fear for children, and itself." *The New York Times*. February 1, 2010. Retrieved on August 15, 2010, from http://www.nytimes.com/2010/02/02/world/americas/02orphans.html.

Title VII of the Civil Rights Act of 1964. 1964. Statutes. U.S. Equal Employment Opportunity Commission. Retrieved August 23, 2013, from http://www.eeoc.gov/laws/statutes/titlevii.cfm.

Turner, Wallace. 1981. "Mormon document raises doubts on succession of church's leaders." *The New York Times*. March 19, 1981. Retrieved on August 22, 2012, from http://www.nytimes.com/1981/03/19/us/mormon-document-raises-doubts-on-succession-of-church-s-leaders.html.

Unheard No More! June 2010. Retrieved on February 12, 2014, from http://unheardnomore.blogspot.com/2010/06/richard-steele.html.

USA Today. 2010. "U.S. missionary convicted in Haiti, but free." *USA Today*. May 17, 2010. Retrieved on August 15, 2012, from http://www.usatoday.com/news/world/2010-05-17-Haiti_N.htm.

USCCB. 2013. United States Conference of Catholic Bishops' Charter for the Protection of Children and Young People. Retrieved from www.usccb.org/issues-and-action/child-and-youth-protection/charter.cfm.

United Nations. 2012. "Charter of the United Nations." Retrieved on September 17, 2012, from http://www.un.org/en/documents/charter/intro.shtml.

United Nations — Office of the Iraq Programme Oil-for-Food. 2012. "About the Programme." Retrieved on September 17, 2012, from http://www.un.org/Depts/oip/background/index.html.

United Network for Organ Sharing. 2013. United Network for Organ Sharing: Data. Retrieved November 12, 2013, from www.unos.org/about/index.php.

United States Congress — Committee on International Relations House of Representatives. 2004. "The United Nations Oil-for-Food Program: Issues of accountability and transparency." April 28, 2004. Retrieved on September 18, 2012, from http://commdocs.house.gov/committees/intlrel/hfa93391.000/hfa93391_0f.htm.

United States, 2014. Department of Internal Revenue Service. Retrieved on December 22, 2014. http://www.irs.gov/Charities-&-Non-Profits/Charitable-Organizations/Exemption-Requirements-Section-501%28c%29%283%29-Organizations.

United States Department of Health and Human Services. 2006. "OPTN/UNOS levies member sanction against St. Vincent Medical Center." Retrieved September 19, 2013, from http://optn.transplant.hrsa.gov/news/newsDetail.asp?id = 559.

United States Equal Opportunity Commission. n.d. Title VII of the Civil Rights Act of 1964. Retrieved from http://www.eeoc.gov/laws/statutes/titlevii.cfm.

The United Way. n.d. Vision, Mission, and Goals. Retrieved from http://www.unitedway.org/pages/mission-and-goals/.

Vinton, Nathaniel. 2014. "Texas court denies Lance Armstrong appeal as disgraced cyclist was trying to avoid paying back bonus money." *New York Daily News*. May 31, 2014. Retrieved on June 6, 2014, from http://www.nydailynews.com/sports/more-sports/texas-court-denies-lance-armstrong-appeal-article-1.1811589.

Vu, Michelle. 2010. "Haitian officer: U.S. Baptist team made earlier attempt to take children." *ChristianPost*. February9,2010. RetrievedonAugust15,2012, fromhttp://www.christian-post.com/news/haiti-police-u-s-baptist-team-tried-to-take-children-before-43688/.

Wallis, D. November 8, 2012. "Komen Foundation struggles to regain wide support." *The New York Times*. Retrieved August 10, 2013, from http://www.nytimes.com/2012/11/09/giving/komen-foundation-works-to-regain-support-after-planned-parenthood-controversy.html?_r = 0,

Wan, W. July 16, 2010. "Vatican issues new rules on abuse by priest; Activists call them inadequate." *The Washington Post*. Retrieved November 7, 2013, from http://www.washingtonpost.com/wp-dyn/content/article/2010/07/15/AR2010071501453.html.

The Washington Post Staff. 2012. "Timeline of key events in Komen controversy." *The Washington Post.* Retrieved from articles.washingtonpost.com/2012-02-07/national/35444734_1_karen-handel-mollie-williams-founder-nancy-brinker.

Weisberg, Jacob. December 7, 1996. "Does everybody do it?" Retrieved on February 2, 2014, from http://www.unz.org/Pub/Slate-1996dec-00020.

Welsh v. Boy Scouts of America, 742 F. Supp., 1990. August 9, 1990. Leagle. Retrieved August 28, 2013, from www.leagle.com/decision/19902155742FSupp1413_11947.

Welsh v. Boy Scouts of America, U.S. Court of Appeals, Seventh Circuit, 993 F. 2nd 1267. May 17, 1993. Retrieved August 18, 2013, from www.bsa-discrimination.org/Welsh_Appeal_Decision.PDF.

Wheaton, S. September 23, 2009. "Acorn sues over video as I.R.S. severs ties." *The New York Times.* Retrieved May 9, 2013, from www.nytimes.com/2009/09/24/us/politics/24acorn.html?_r=0.

Willard, Adam. 2007-1. "The Oral Roberts University scandal from students' perspectives." Yahoo! Voices. October 10, 2007. Retrieved on August 6, 2012, from http://voices.yahoo.com/the-oral-roberts-university-scandal-students-595575.html.

Willard, Adam. 2007-2. "Oral Roberts' Richard Roberts fights back against lawsuit." Yahoo! Voices. November 5, 2007. Retrieved on August 6, 2012, from http://voices.yahoo.com/oral-roberts-richard-roberts-fights-back-against-lawsuit-640208.html?cat=17

Wingert, P. April 7, 2010. "Mean men: The priesthood is being cast as the refuge of pederast. In fact, priests seem to abuse children at the same rate as everyone else." *Newsweek.* Retrieved December 9, 2013, from mag.newsweek.com/2010/04/07/mean-men.html.

Wooden, C., and Hidalgo, E. 2007. "L.A. archdiocese reached agreement with more than 500 abuse claimants." Catholic News Service/US Conference of Catholic Bishops. Retrieved December 7, 2013, from www.americancatholic.org/News/ClergySexAbuse/.

World Health Organization. 2014. "Cumulative number of confirmed human cases for avian influenza A(H5N1) reported to WHO, 2003-2014." Retrieved on September 1, 2014, from http://www.who.int/influenza/human_animal_interface/EN_GIP_20140124CumulativeNumberH5N1cases.pdf?ua=1.

World Health Organization. 2012. "About WHO." World Health Organization. Retrieved on August 2, 2012, from http://www.who.int/about/en/

Zayas, Alexandria. December 30, 2008. "Lowry Park Zoo audit dictates course of director." Retrieved on October 29, 2013, from http://www.tampabay.com/news/business/lowry-park-zoo-audit-dictates-course-of-director/953656.

Zayas, Alexandria, and Varlan, Bill. March 31, 2010. "Former Tampa Zoo president cleared of criminal misconduct." Retrieved on October 29, 2013, from http://www.tampabay.com/news/localgovernment/former-tampa-zoo-president-cleared-of-criminal-misconduct/1084224.

Zayas, Alexandrea. January 16, 2009. "Lowry Park Zoo board approves new policies; its chairman resigns." Retrieved on October 29, 2013, from http://www.tampabay.com/news/politics/local/lowry-park-zoo-board-approves-new-policies-its-chairman-resigns/968406.

Zorn, E. 2013. "The Boy Scouts and the Atheists." *Chicago Tribune.* Retrieved from http://blogs.chicagotribune.com/news_columnists_ezorn/2013/02/the-boy-scouts-and-the-atheists.html.

Index